INSTRUCTOR'S MANUAL
PRINCIPLES AND PRACTICE OF MARKETING

INSTRUCTOR'S MANUAL TO ACCOMPANY

PRINCIPLES AND PRACTICE OF MARKETING

David Jobber

Reader in Marketing
Management Centre
University of Bradford
United Kingdom

McGraw-Hill Book Company

London · New York · St Louis · San Francisco · Auckland · Bogotá · Caracas
Lisbon · Madrid · Mexico · Milan · Montreal · New Delhi · Panama · Paris
San Juan · São Paulo · Singapore · Sydney · Tokyo · Toronto

Published by
McGraw-Hill Book Company Europe
Shoppenhangers Road, Maidenhead, Berkshire, SL6 2QL, England
Telephone 01628 23432
Facsimile 01628 770224

ISBN 0–07–709168–X

McGraw-Hill

A Division of The McGraw-Hill Companies

Printed and bound in Great Britain

**Principles and Practice
of Marketing**

Contents

On Using the Instructor's Manual

The purpose of this *Instructor's Manual* is to help busy marketing academics in their job of teaching the subject. It is not intended to suggest that there is 'one way' of using the textbook, 'one way' of analysing the case studies and study questions, and 'one way' of teaching marketing. In short, it is intended to supplement not supplant your creative skills in teaching marketing. Together with the textbook and the two-colour acetates which are provided free of charge if you have adopted the textbook, the *Instructor's Manual* forms a package of materials designed to facilitate course development and execution.

The *Instructor's Manual* is divided into two sections:

Part 1 provides teaching notes for the 25 cases that appear in the textbook, and Part 2 supplies brief guides to answering (and in some instances using) the study questions that appear at the end of each chapter.

Using the Case Notes

Case summaries are provided on pages xi and xii. They are designed to give you an easy guide to case selection. The information indicates the marketing topic covered and whether the case focuses on a business-to-business, consumer goods or services issue.

The case summaries are followed by the teaching notes for the specific cases. Each teaching note follows a common structure:

- **Synopsis:** this provides a short resumé of the case to give you a greater insight into the nature of the case than that provided in the case summaries.
- **Teaching Objectives:** these illustrate the educational aims of the case and you may find it useful when selecting cases to check the degree to which their objectives match your needs.
- **Suggested Teaching Approach:** all case contributors have outlined a way of handling the case in a teaching situation. I asked all contributors to provide detailed notes on case analysis to facilitate this process. But this does not imply that these are the only ways of teaching the cases. The analyses are provided because you may find it useful to know how the case writer views the case. Of course, you are encouraged to provide your own analysis for teaching purposes.

Most of the cases are short because my research prior to writing the textbook indicated that this was what most marketing academics wanted. Each end of chapter case is designed to illustrate aspects of marketing developed in the chapter. At the end of each module are longer cases which typically cover aspects of marketing from more than one chapter. The breadth of the 25 cases, both in terms of geography and subject matter, is a substantial contribution to the textbook. Their inclusion within the textbook, rather than as a separate case book, is convenient for both yourself and your students who will also benefit from not having the extra expense of buying two books for their introductory marketing course.

Some of you may be new to teaching marketing through case study. As an experienced case study teacher I can recommend them as a means of not only offering vicarious experience but more importantly of providing vehicles for developing analytical marketing skills, and creating and defending recommendations for marketing action. The actual organization of the case study session itself will be based on personal experience: I certainly do not intend to suggest a 'best' method. From my experience of talking to fellow academics three methods appear to be in common use. First, students are formed into groups with each group (or a selected number of groups) being asked to make a presentation of no more than ten minutes. A maximum of three presentations is recommended. The rest of the teaching period is used by the tutor to analyse the case with the students as a whole. Tutors need to develop their questioning skills so that the session is marked by a high level of student participation. Assuming a teaching period of one and a half hours, this allows the tutor ample time to provide a structured analysis of the case with the students, and to illustrate the key marketing lessons arising from it. Even within a one-hour period this structure can work, perhaps by asking for only five-minute presentations.

A second means of organizing a case study session is again to ask for ten-minute presentations but for the tutor and students to make more interjections during them. Most of the discussion, then, actually takes place during the presentations themselves, with the tutor perhaps allocating only ten minutes at the end to summarize the discussion and present the key learning points.

The third approach is to ask for individual or group analysis but not for student presentations. The tutor leads the discussion from the beginning of the teaching session perhaps starting by asking one student to give his/her views on a key issue of the case. If the students know beforehand that this will happen it may give an added spur for them to prepare the case adequately.

I should like to emphasize that these are not the only approaches to organizing a case study session nor are they necessarily the best: each person should experiment to find out which method works for them in which situation. They are presented to you as methods that have been used successfully by my colleagues and myself and so may be worthy of consideration.

Study Questions

Some of you may feel it presumptuous of me to prepare answers for study questions in an introductory marketing textbook. Surely marketing academics are capable of preparing their own without any help? This is indeed true. However, given the busy lives we lead I thought it helpful to provide at least an inkling of what was in mind when I set the questions. Hence, the answers I provide are brief. They certainly are not as full as you may expect from your students, but they do give the essence of what might be expected from them.

I have tried not to repeat paragraphs from the textbook when part of the answer can be found there. For convenience I have indicated the page numbers in the textbook where the relevant issues are discussed.

The study questions can be used in a variety of ways. They can be used as essay questions to test students' knowledge and understanding of the subject matter. Some of them may form the focus of a tutorial discussion. Also, you may wish to encourage students to use them as self-administered tests of knowledge and understanding of each chapter as they read the textbook.

Finally, I hope *Principles and Practice of Marketing* and the *Instructor's Manual* help you in your quest for a lively, stimulating, and imaginative course in marketing.

**Principles and Practice
of Marketing**

Case Summaries

Page numbers refer to the main text.

CASE STUDIES

Case 1

Goode Sure Components

Synopsis

A small, innovative and successful distributor of engineered re-buy products has achieved market dominance but also encountered market saturation. Having profited from some chance sales of industrial machines, the growth-oriented owner is now contemplating whether to expand proactively into machinery distribution. An opportunity to enlarge his premises has created a key decision situation.

Teaching Objectives

1. To introduce participants to the kinds of issues that need to be examined prior to expanding a company outside its core business.
2. To examine the implications for market segmentation and competitive capability of differences in buyer behaviour between re-buy and new task markets.
3. To introduce a range of market choice criteria to be analysed prior to a market entry decision.
4. To underline how an absence of sustainable differential advantage must inevitably result in failure when entering an existing market.
5. To encourage participants to consider a range of alternative growth strategies rather than going for the first apparently attractive opportunity.

Suggested Teaching Approach

This short case can be usefully read and discussed in a single session. However, it does provide opportunities to discuss a wide range of central issues in marketing and competitive strategy. It has also been used to introduce the three fundamental principles of marketing: customer value, differential advantage, and target marketing. The case provides a useful base for discussing these principles in more depth later in an introductory marketing course. It also provides a vehicle for introducing the concept of the decision-making unit (DMU) and growth options.

Participants are usually divided about equally as to whether GSC should venture into machinery, and this typically results in a lively discussion. Some participants claim that more information is needed but there is ample scope to reach a definite negative judgement concerning the proposed expansion. The instructor is thus able to make the valuable point that decisions can often be made in the absence of extensive information. The primary teaching points, however, are that an understanding of buyer behaviour, analysis of valid market choice criteria, and the capability for sustainable differential advantage must precede successful market entry. Towards the end of the session the instructor can ask the group to consider what alternative growth approaches could have been considered. The following set of questions has been used to structure the group discussion.

This teaching note was prepared by David Shipley, Professor of Marketing, Trinity College, University of Dublin, Ireland.

1. What have been the bases of GSC's success to date?

This opener usually loosens-up undergraduates, MBAs, and 'first day' delegates on post-experience courses. They usually list GSC's wide product range, competitive prices, good delivery, and customer service focus as key assets. The tutor may need to point out, however, that these strengths are founded on and/or supported by strong empathy with customer needs, probable tight customer relationships, and an innovation orientation.

2. What issues should be examined before making a drop or go decision?

Participants typically discuss the need for information on potential sales values, the types of services the company would need to provide, and possible margins. These are valid points but a more complete range of issues includes:

* Buying behaviour
* Market selection criteria
* Selling and service capabilities
* Investment and operating costs
* Potential sales volume
* Differential advantage

3. What differences in buying behaviour can be expected in the market for the existing range and the market for machinery?

Most participants are unable to offer many comments on this question. A few recognize that the current range consists of re-buys while machines are much more akin to new task purchases. A few also say that customers for the two product ranges are in the same segment. This is entirely erroneous. Potential machinery buyers do currently purchase re-buys from GSC. However, relative to re-buys, machinery buying involves different DMU compositions, different needs, different buying experiences, vastly different price levels, differences in perceived risk, and consequently different search patterns. The different DMU compositions could pose a serious problem for an unwary newcomer to the machinery market. For re-buy purchases the DMU probably involves no more than the production manager, the buying manager, and perhaps the factory storekeeper. For machinery buying, however, the DMU extends to other key influencers and deciders including purchasing, production, quality control, maintenance, safety and finance personnel and probably the managing director and his/her board. When the instructor points out that all of these players have different needs, participants recognize that the machinery segment is different and that the marketing task is different and greatly more complex. Moreover, the re-buy situation probably involves little or no search behaviour, whereas machinery customers will examine and perform value analyses on the offerings of multiple manufacturers and distributors. In the purchase of a machine costing say £250,000, the relative reputations of competing machinery suppliers may stand for much more than that of a local dealer, irrespective of how well known or well liked it is. This can be expected to take the machinery buyer well beyond a local distributor's showroom during the search process, even if that dealer stocks a wide and costly range of alternative manufacturer-brands.

4. What market selection criteria should GSC review prior to a decision?

At this stage participants typically refer again to market potential, margin potential, and service requirements. The instructor often has to explain that market choice requires an understanding of the fit between key success factors, risk and profits on the one hand, and the company's marketing/competitive capabilities on the other. Participants can then be pressed to consider the determinants of this necessary strategic fit such as market size and growth, the competitive situation, market structural forces, entry and exit difficulty and costs and the company's organizational competencies. The session leader can also emphasize the need to assess the full range of opportunity costs involved in a market entry decision.

5. What investment and operating costs may be involved in entering the machinery business?

This question usually evokes a discussion about whether to buy or try to lease the available premises. Attention also focuses on the costs of obtaining an able machinery sales and demonstration force, adequate after-sales capability, and credit-provision which is much greater for machinery than the existing range. However, many participants overlook the costs of holding machine stocks which could be awesome for a small company. Suppose GSC only stocks one each of, say, ten different types of machines. At an average ex-works price of around £200,000 per unit, total investment and operating costs would exceed £2.5 million. But this assumes that there would be no customer choice on offer. If GSC stocked the brands of only two manufacturers, the total rises to over £4.5 million, and a much larger choice may be required to limit customer search only to GCS's showroom. Participants now begin to realize that to be successful GSC needs a high sales volume.

6. What sales volume can GSC expect to achieve in the machinery market?

This is the crucial question and participants' estimates are almost always wildly over-optimistic. The types of machinery that GSC has received enquiries about are engineering machines. The company has around 500 customers but these are spread across a range of industries. Threading machines are used almost exclusively in the engineering sector. The enquiries about other engineering machinery received by GSC have been made by customers who thread their own fasteners. Hence, the bulk of any possible future machinery sales can be expected to be in the engineering sector. However, less than one-third of Goode's current customers are engineering firms and GSC has a virtual monopoly of the market. Hence, only about 150 firms in GSC's area are users of engineering machines. But how many of these are large enough to be able to buy new machines at about £250,000 each? Small engineering firms typically buy second-hand machines. Suppose 20 per cent of the available market (i.e. 30 firms) buy new machines. How many do they buy annually? An estimate abased on a 15-firm telephone survey by the case writer suggests less than one machine every three years. Hence, market volume in GSC's target area is confined to about 10 units per year. Even if GSC won all of these, the contribution on direct costs would probably not sustain the high fixed costs involved. However, it is highly unlikely that GSC could win 100 per cent of target market purchases or anything like that percentage.

7. What would GSC's competitive position be in the machinery market?

By this stage of the analysis most participants doubt GSC's competitive capability. Nevertheless, some still agree with Goode's expectation that his close customer proximity provides demonstration, delivery, and after-sales service advantages. Some also maintain that Goode's customer understanding and image are major competitive assets. However, how relevant are these in the machinery supplier selection decision? Well-received studies report that the major buying criteria for industrial machines are technical specifications, other product quality dimensions, after-sales service, price, and delivery. GSC does not have clear superiority on any of these variables. Technical specifications and quality are unaffected by whether a machine is sold directly or through a dealer. Rapid delivery is irrelevant since machinery purchases are normally planned well ahead of usage. Reliable delivery is an issue but GSC does not have a demonstrable advantage on this in machinery. On the provision of after-sales services, GSC can be faster. But by how much? Other dealers would require, say, only one extra hour to reach the customer, while manufacturers could possibly do so within three or four hours. Further, GSC's minor speed advantage could be overturned by producers' greater maintenance experience and the full range of spares for their own machines which GSC would find costly to stock. On price GSC would be hopelessly disadvantaged. With a low expected volume the company would need high prices to cover the high investment and operating costs referred to. Distributor-competitors typically operate in larger geographical markets that provide economies to support lower prices, while direct manufacturers have no need to pay dealers' margins.

8.   Could GSC succeed on an agency basis?

Some participants suggest that GSC should proceed on an agency basis. That is, to arrange purchases and perhaps deliver machinery on request so as to avoid purchasing premises for stocks. There could be some merit in this. It would honour the pledge over GSC's counter and it would provide extra margins. However, Goode might still need to provide after-sales service which could prove costly in terms of stockholding and personnel. The main argument against this approach, however, is that it is barely worthwhile given the small potential market and the expectation that many customers would prefer to deal direct with producers. Moreover, GSC would still have to compete against imported machines offered by other distributors.

9.   What alternative growth option could Goode consider?

By entering into machinery distribution GSC would be involved with both new products and new markets/segments. It would be straying into the diversification cell of Ansoff's growth direction matrix without a sustainable differential advantage. Failure seems certain. What of Ansoff's other three options? GSC already dominates its existing saturated market, so there is little scope for further market penetration. It may be possible, however, to expand the existing product range with related re-buy items not already offered. The most appealing option, however, would be for the company to extend its existing range into new geographical markets. GSC has already demonstrated its ability to beat direct competitors. Expansion into adjacent market areas would provide further scale and experience economies and therefore margins growth. In the event, this was the strategy eventually embarked on by Goode. Initial results showed GSC to be repeating its earlier dramatic success in the re-buys business.

Note: Question 9 is optional. It provides an opportunity to introduce Ansoff's growth direction matrix if the tutor so wishes. Alternatively, growth options could be discussed without specific reference to the matrix.

Case 2

The Empire Theatre

Synopsis

The case describes the current marketing practices of a medium-scale arts venue in a small town in the East Midlands of the UK. The theatre is partially funded by the public sector and faces the problem of whether to opt for a purely 'commercial' programme of activities or to include a more artistic input. Current marketing activity is constrained by a limited information base. The theatre is at a cross roads; by using a formalized planning approach it is possible to draw out the options available to them and also possible strategies.

Teaching Objectives

1. To introduce participants to the complexity of marketing planning.
2. To give candidates the opportunity to use a formalized marketing planning process.
3. To highlight the need for market information and the problems that arise with information gaps.
4. To allow participants to identify information needs and develop a strategy for gaining information.
5. To highlight the difficulty of marketing planning when the objectives of the organization are not clarified.

Suggested Teaching Approach

The case can be read and discussed in a single session. Most participants read the case and feel that they can comfortably produce a plan to take the theatre forward. By forcing participants to follow a formal planning process, problems emerge that were previously unrecognized by superficial reading. It is suggested that the framework found in Figure 2.1 of the text be used as a framework for this case. The following set of questions have been used to structure discussion.

1. What is the theatre's mission?

This is often quite literally a show stopper! Participants often debate this issue for some time. By comparison to purely commercial organizations, the theatre has a number of funders who will obviously be stakeholders.

What business is this theatre in? Is it simply there to provide entertainment for the local community by attracting touring artists? What balance should there be between purely commercial events that fill the theatre and those with more artistic content which play to empty seats? Is the theatre a local resource for the community, allowing regional drama groups, etc., to perform?

This teaching note was prepared by Jim Saker, Gareth Smith and Alison Cooley of Loughborough University Business School, UK.

The issues can become quite emotional with participants often falling into two groups: the 'bottoms on seats' view and the mixed portfolio offerers. In reality the former group can put a strong case, but this is often tempered when the group is reminded of the funding agencies and their expectations.

Although no satisfactory answer is readily available, most groups end up with the view that the theatre is in business to provide a mixed portfolio of activity which attempts to meet both the artistic and commercial priorities of the stakeholders, but also the preferences of the local community.

2. What position is the theatre in?

The marketing audit and SWOT analysis are very powerful tools on this particular case. Students become aware of the precarious nature of the venue. As it does not produce its own product, the theatre books performances from artists who are passing through the area on tour. They are further constrained by the size of the theatre. Some artists would consider the venue uneconomic and would look for a larger auditorium to perform. Smaller companies may be unable to attract audiences large enough to justify hiring the theatre. The size of the local catchment area coupled with strong competition from nearby cities also restricts the desire of performers to come to the town. The lack of a developed marketing information system is also a critical weakness. It is interesting to see participants' evaluation of the marketing department and its spend. Some are often very critical of the lack of resources, whereas others recognize this as merely being a fact of life and focus more on whether what is done is effective.

3. What options are available to them?

By using the Strategic Options diagram in Figure 2.4 participants are able to see the number of different directions in which the theatre could in fact opt to go. Linking the SWOT analysis to this section, most people find it logical for the theatre to go for market penetration or expansion with some possible product development. The financial constraints severely limit the marketing activity which would limit market development.

A big issue that is often debated is what is in fact being marketed? Is it the theatre, is it the product, or is it both? Most participants opt for the fact that it is a combination of both. Shows at the theatre run for a very short period and in marketing terms have a very short lifecycle. Should the theatre market itself or a series of individual products? How can this be combined? Where should the emphasis lie? It is usually argued that the theatre is trying to position itself away from being a variety hall as if it went this route it would lack credibility when it came to offer drama, ballet, or opera.

4. What are the marketing objectives?

At this stage participants should be encouraged to draw up realistic objectives bearing in mind the starting position of the organization. Encouragement should be given to make these quantifiable, time based, and achievable. The overall strategic objective is to build, while the strategic thrust decision is aided by the strategic options analysis previously discussed.

5. What marketing mix strategies should be adopted?

The groups usually believe that the theatre should promote itself as an easy access local arts venue that serves the local community by bringing highly rated performers to the area.

Product: Unless some of the participants come from the arts, this discussion will inevitably be something of a brainstorm. In practice groups usually enjoy trying to construct a 6-month programme that fits with the constraints and also the positioning policy previously agreed by the group.

Often other discussions cover whether the theatre could increase its usage by offering daytime facilities for conference presentations or opening up the café/bar during the day.

Price: Pricing policy again can be developed that looks consistent with the type of product being offered.

Promotion: The existing promotional activity is fairly limited and participants are usually keen to improve this. The need for a computerized database and more sophisticated direct mail activity is often suggested. The advertising policy is worth examination.

Place: The location of the theatre is restrictive and it would appear difficult to attract people out of the neighbouring cities in numbers large enough to justify any major expenditure. It is useful for participants to consider the additional 'Ps' of marketing a service. The case can be used as an introduction to the three additional 'Ps'. Alternatively, the issues can be discussed using the traditional 4-P framework.

People: With large numbers of volunteers involved it is suggested that service quality is difficult to maintain and a professional image hard to sustain. Others argue that the volunteers give the place a local friendly appeal.

Process: The case does not give detailed information as to the processes involved but participants should be encouraged to discuss the type of processes needed to offer a quality service to customers.

Physical Evidence: Perhaps one of the most fascinating parts of the case is the reference in the first section to the refurbishment that took place. From a marketing point of view this was problematic in that the interior was redecorated but the exterior left untouched. The impression given to potential customers is therefore of a run-down establishment. The interior, which for the bulk of the performance is in the dark, is well appointed.

6. How is the strategy to be implemented?

Although the case does give much information about local advertising rates, etc., it is still possible for participants to draw up an implementation plan. Consideration can be given to possible internal resistance to a marketing-oriented approach and how this might be dealt with.

7. How is the process to be controlled?

One of the major weaknesses of the theatre's marketing is its lack of information systems. Participants should be encouraged to draw up an outline plan of the information required to monitor the success or otherwise of the strategy.

Case 3

Morris Services

Synopsis

The case examines a sales encounter between two inexperienced potential purchasers of a personal computer and a salesperson. Claire Morris, Managing Director of a cleaning company, requires a computer for cash flow monitoring. She visits a local retailer with her secretary in the vain hope of solving her problem.

Teaching Objectives

1. To illustrate the importance of understanding the customer's choice criteria in order to conclude a sale.
2. To understand customer requirements in a high involvement purchasing situation.
3. To illustrate the need for salespeople to adapt their selling strategy to fit the customer's decision-making process.

Suggested Teaching Approach

Although the buy situation illustrated in the case is technically a purchase for an organization, the situation does resemble that of many customer durable purchasers and can successfully illuminate a range of consumer behaviour issues. These will be discussed with reference to each of the questions set at the end of the case.

1. What choice criteria were important to Claire and Helen?

Claire was the initiator, decider, and buyer, and Helen the influencer and user in the *decision-making unit*. Their *choice criteria* appears to be as follows:

Claire Morris	Technical	– ability to conduct cash flow monitoring: ease of use
	Economic	– price/value for money
	Personal	– risk and hassle reduction
Helen Berry	Technical	– ease of use

Beyond the choice criteria that they used to evaluate the suitability of a personal computer, we can assume a key need from the purchasing encounter is to be treated sympathetically by the salesperson and not to be confused by jargon or shown up as lacking computer knowledge or expertise. Such fears can act as *need inhibitors*. A salesperson who fails to recognize these essential psychological needs of customers is likely to be rejected by them.

This teaching note was prepared by David Jobber.

2. Did the salesperson understand what was important to the customers? If not, why not? Did the salesperson make any other mistakes? Why do you think the salesperson chose that particular computer model?

The salesperson failed to understand the choice criteria being applied to the purchase and the psychological needs of Claire and Helen during the sales encounter. The reason was that the salesperson was focused on making statements (e.g. 'this machine is based on the Intel 486DX-33 processor...') rather than asking questions to discover what was important to the customers. Often making statements is much easier than having to think of intelligent questions to discover customers' needs. By displaying his/her knowledge of personal computing technology, the salesperson may have been massaging his/her ego in the mistaken belief that the customers would be impressed. The reality was that Claire and Helen's worst fears were realized as they were subjected to a meaningless barrage of computer jargon.

The salesperson made the classic mistake of presenting product features (e.g. 32 bit local bus graphics, 4 megabytes of RAM) without explaining the *customer benefits* that they confer to Claire and Helen. Without knowing their needs, it was impossible to choose those features that conferred those benefits (e.g. ease of use) that were important to Claire and Helen.

Although the salesperson opened positively by stating that 'we have a wide range of computers' it was inexcusable to leave Claire and Helen for five minutes without at least explaining why he/she had to go to the storeroom and asking if it was acceptable to do so. There may have been a compelling reason to leave (e.g. a delivery truck may have been about to leave without an important parcel); otherwise the salesperson should have delayed the visit or delegated it to someone else.

Finally the salesperson inadequately dealt with customer *objections*. Claire objected to the price by claiming that she had seen computers advertised in newspapers for a lot less. The salesperson's response was to counter with product features (graphic facilities and upgradable to Pentium technology) that were as unconvincing as they were incomprehensible to Claire and Helen. Helen complained about the computer looking complicated to use, which brought the reply that the salesperson's 10-year-old daughter could use it (reinforcing Helen's feeling of computer ignorance) and the statement that there was a special offer (which may have been relevant to Claire but certainly did not at all allay Helen's concerns about ease of use).

The salesperson may have chosen that particular computer model for any of a number of reasons.

- It was the one he/she would have chosen if he/she had wanted a new computer (self-reference criteria).
- It gave the highest commission.
- It was the model he/she knew most about.
- It was the most sophisticated, allowing the salesperson to display his/her extensive knowledge of computers

This illustrates the point that there can be many other forces acting on salespeople that distract them from understanding customers' needs and selling the most appropriate product that matches those needs.

3. You are the salesperson in the second shop they are about to visit. Based on your knowledge of buyer behaviour, plan how you would conduct the sales interview.

The sales interview should begin by attempting to understand why Claire and Helen have a need for a personal computer. This involves *questioning* them to discover the reason for purchase, what the computer is to be used for (applications), and how experienced the customers are in computer use. This conversation will undoubtedly reveal that Claire is the Managing Director of a small cleaning company and Helen is her secretary. Furthermore, by understanding their needs, their choice criteria became apparent. They should also be questioned about future computing needs.

Once a clear understanding of needs (choice criteria) has been achieved, the salesperson can select that computer model which best matches those requirements and relate:

$$\text{Product Features} \rightarrow \text{Benefits} \leftrightarrow \text{Customer Needs}$$

In doing so the salesperson is acting as a problem solver and thus providing added value to his/her customers who are clearly in a *high involvement* purchase situation since high expenditure and personal risk are involved. When a purchase is highly involving, customers are likely to carry out extensive evaluation, providing salespeople with an opportunity to aid that process. Even if extensive evaluation means that more than one store is visited, salespeople can build up goodwill (and hence improve their chances of the customer returning) by providing helpful advice.

Reference selling (citing other satisfied customers) can be used to build positive beliefs and attitudes towards the product. By raising purchase intentions in this way (see the Fishbein and Azjen model) a sale is more likely to be made.

Finally, the salesperson should remember that customers may suffer from *buyer remorse* and so he/she should follow-up the sale to check that Claire and Helen are having no problems with their recent purchase.

**Principles and Practice
of Marketing**

Case 4

Winters Company

Synopsis

A young salesperson observed that a sale was lost by the Gillis Company despite their work with the R&D department. The purchasing officer asked for quotes from three other companies and chose to place the order with one of them rather than Gillis.

Teaching Objectives

1. To show the dynamics of the decision-making unit in action.
2. To illustrate the importance of understanding the choice criteria of the decision-making unit members.
3. To appreciate that choice criteria are often related to the performance criteria relevant to each decision-making unit member.

Suggested Teaching Approach

The case can be used as part of a lecture on organizational buying behaviour after the 'who', 'how', and 'what' elements have been discussed. Used in this way it brings immediate realism to the ideas raised in the lecture. As part of a separate tutorial or seminar, the cases raise issues that can usually be discussed within 30 minutes and so might form part of a broader discussion/exercise.

1. The decision-making unit

The major problem of selling to an organization (a firm, a public body, etc.) is that frequently several individuals will be, or will feel that they should be, involved in the decision to make a purchase. Part of the marketing problem is to decide who these people are and to understand the role and authority of each of them. The situation is complicated by the fact that a person involved in the purchase of one product may not be involved in the purchase of that product at a later date. Thus for each purchase, the constitution of the decision-making group (those persons involved in a purchase decision) may be different.

The decision-making unit involves six roles:

1. Users—This group includes all those in the organization who use or are going to use the product being purchased. It may include people at all levels in the organization. Thus the decision to

This teaching note was prepared by Keith Blois, Fellow of Templeton College, Oxford, Donald Cowell, Professor of Marketing and Dean of the Department of Business and Management, University of Central England at Birmingham, and David Jobber, Reader in Marketing, University of Bradford Management Centre, UK.

purchase a particular type of powered hand-tool may well be influenced by the shop-floor workers who use the product.

2. Buyers—In most organizations there is a Purchasing or Buying Department. Certain members of this department will have formal responsibility and authority for signing contracts for purchases on behalf of the organizations. These are, in this context, the purchasing agents, together with any other persons with such authority.

3. Influencers—This is usually a large, ill-defined group as it includes all those who influence the decision process directly or indirectly by providing information and criteria for evaluating alternative buying actions. Thus a person may, as Scott does in this case, influence a decision by passing a comment on a quite different matter and perhaps without knowing that a buying decision was thus being affected.

4. Initiators—These are the people who begin the decision-making process. In this case Smith appears to be the initiator although we do not know the history of the situation: someone else not mentioned in the case may have acted as the initiator.

5. Deciders—This is the group with authority to choose amongst alternative buying actions. A buyer is not always a decider and vice versa. Thus when purchasing a very complex product of an advanced technological nature, a group of engineers and scientists may decide upon a particular supplier. Their decision might then be passed to a purchasing agent to be implemented purely in the sense of a drawing up of the necessary formal documents to complete the commercial aspects of the transaction.

6. Gatekeepers—These people control the flow of information into the decision-making unit. For example, secretaries may block access to managers.

Several individuals may occupy the same role and one individual may occupy more than one role. Thus Mr Jones is a buyer and a decider; Mr Smith is an influencer and initiator; Mr Scott is an influencer and a user. A call by Gillis on Jones (and possibly Scott) as well as Smith would have helped their case.

2. Choice criteria

A problem which arises from the variety of persons making up the decision-making group is that each will view the purchase from different points of view, and therefore use different choice criteria. Mr Smith is mainly interested in the technical capabilities of the chosen supplier, and will be much less concerned with other aspects of a supplier's offering such as regular deliveries or low price. Mr Scott, however, has indicated that the supplier's ability to deliver as promised, is to him a very important matter. The Purchase Agent, Mr Jones, appears to be particularly interested in price, but he is also concerned to maintain his authority in any buying situation. The convenience of not having to seek approval from his boss is also an important consideration.

3. The relationship between choice and performance criteria

The question arises as to the reason why different DMU members use different choice criteria. Table 1 illustrates the discussion so far, and introduces the notion of performance criteria as an explanation. Students should be asked for their opinion as to what purchase officers, production managers, and heads of R&D are evaluated on. The result is the final column of Table 1 which clearly shows the relationship between choice and performance criteria.

Table 1

Name	Title	Role in DMU	Choice Criteria	Performance Criteria
JONES	Purchasing Officer	DECIDER BUYER	Low cost Convenience Maintenance of authority	Cost saving
SMITH	Head of R&D	INFLUENCER INITIATOR	Technical assistance	Technical competence
SCOTT	Production Manager	INFLUENCER USER	Reliable delivery	Smooth production flow (output)

The implication is that choice criteria are not chosen randomly or at the whim of the individual. They are often related to the performance criteria used to measure how well each member of the DMU is doing his job. Understanding performance criteria, therefore, gives clues to what is important to each member of the DMU.

Case 5

The Friendly Bank

Synopsis

A savings bank attempts to solve two problems simultaneously. Unprofitable accounts could be eliminated by raising the minimum average deposit to £150, and since this would decrease the number of accounts, congestion and queuing problems would also be reduced. But does this solution ignore other important issues?

Teaching Objectives

1. To show the need to consider a range of options when making marketing decisions.

2. To illustrate the impact of environmental issues on marketing decisions.

Suggested Teaching Approach

This case can be used as a vehicle for discussing how environmental factors impinge upon marketing decisions in a seminar session. Each of the set questions will now be discussed.

1. What other issues should be considered by John Wilson when deciding to recommend this course of action to the bank's board of directors?

The bank would be advised to check the legal position regarding minimum deposits. Depending on the country in which the bank is operating, they may have a legal obligation to offer their services to anyone who wishes to hold deposits.

Assuming that the proposed action is legal, they would need to assess the impact of social forces on the decision. If such action was regarded as socially unacceptable (low income earners being deprived of their banking facilities), adverse publicity in the media would be the likely consequence. This could have a double effect of lowering public perception of the bank, together with the embarrassment of having to reverse the decision under the weight of public opinion.

In the UK some financial institutions impose a charge on small savings accounts, justifying their actions by explaining that they are expensive to administer and are being subsidized by larger ones. One such institution, the Britannia Building Society, suffered adverse publicity in the press when the *Observer* newspaper in October 1994 ran the story under the heading 'Cruel Britannia'.

This teaching note was prepared by David Jobber.

Furthermore, The Friendly Bank would need to examine closely who falls into the category of having accounts of £100 or less each month. Some people, for example, pensioners, may have pressure groups (e.g. Help the Aged) who might respond strongly to such a decision. Others (e.g. young savers) may be attractive as their income grows. It would be short-sighted to alienate them now.

John Wilson has blundered into a solution that could have powerful negative repercussions. He would be well advised to consider other options before recommending this course of action to the board.

2. Should the bank be expected to provide a subsidized banking service to low income customers?

This depends on the bank's objectives. If they are primarily to maximize profits for its shareholders, the answer would be 'no'. If the primary objective were to provide banking services for the whole community, the answer might be 'yes'. However, even in the last instance it would need to consider who provides the subsidy. Is it the shareholders, the other savings account holders, or both? This raises the issue of who pays the costs. Should a small charge be levied on small account holders to cover the extra costs?

3. What alternative strategies might the bank consider?

John Wilson needs to recognize that he has two problems that require two solutions.

Congestion and queuing problems

The major options are:

- Mechanize transactions to speed service delivery: the use of automatic cash dispensers, for example, might reduce queuing.
- Redeploy staff at peak periods: use staff flexibly to cover service points when queues develop.
- Open more branches.
- Train staff to become more efficient.
- Open at more convenient times for their customers: evening and weekend opening (if not already practised) should be considered to spread demand.
- Discourage unprofitable customers from having an account: levy a charge.
- Prevent unprofitable customers from having an account.

As we can see, the action Wilson is considering is only one of several alternatives.

Unprofitable customers

Wilson needs to quantify the problem. How much is the bank losing? How many customers are involved? Who are they? Have they future potential? Only when these questions are answered can the benefits be compared to the inevitable adverse publicity.

The major options are:

- Drop unprofitable customers.
- Charge unprofitable customers.
- Segment unprofitable customers: do not drop or charge young savers, children, or pensioners.
- Reduce services to unprofitable customers: only accept postal transactions.
- No action: accept that the likelihood of bad publicity outweighs the gains.

Case 6

Rouen-Schloss

Synopsis

The European steel abrasives market proved an ideal situation for investigating the nature of information management. Being an industrial market, communication between buyers and sellers tends to be through personal channels. As a consequence, much of the information generated and flowing within this market remains concentrated in relatively few hands, usually with individuals or groups of individuals close to the industry. This situation contrasts sharply with the nature of information dynamics in higher-profile customer markets where much information is communicated through mass media and where pertinent market data are frequently available in published form. In an industrial setting, therefore, the acquisition, processing, and distribution of information is more problematic, and the consequent need for effective information gathering and management more acute.

Teaching Objectives

The objectives of the case will differ depending on which level the case is being used. However, some of the following learning objectives can be realistically obtained.

1. To develop an understanding of a company-specific MkIS and how data is collected.
2. To analyse problems with the data collection and suggest possible solutions.
3. To appreciate the social aspects involved in MkIS development.
4. To become acquainted with the general properties of marketing information systems.
5. To become acquainted with some of the issues and problems discussed in the literature which relate to MkIS development.

Like most case studies, the case can be approached in several ways. Firstly, a discussion of the way in which Thierry tackled the immediate problem might give rise to constructive criticism of what he did and how he might have done it better. This might naturally lead to the second approach, that of the design and implementation of RS's MkIS. In this case, what were the design faults and how might they be overcome? The third approach is to set RS's MkIS in some wider context of MkIS in general, or to discuss more generally the properties of MkIS and the problems of implementation. It is the latter two approaches which will be focused upon in the case discussion. The material is deliberately not written in note form, since past experience with using other authors' cases has convinced the author that problems and misunderstanding can easily arise when a note format is adopted.

The case can be used at a range of educational levels, i.e. introductory, intermediate, and advanced. The easiest way of doing this is to treat the questions as being directed at different levels,

---

This teaching note was prepared by Vincent-Wayne Mitchell, Lecturer in Marketing, University of Manchester Institute of Science and Technology, UK.

i.e. questions 1 and 2 are introductory, questions 3 and 4 are intermediate, and questions 5 and 6 are advanced. The categorization is based upon (1) the level of prior knowledge required by the student; for example, the answers to questions 1 and 2 can mainly be gleaned from the information given in the case (whereas questions 3–6 require some knowledge of the literature), (2) the depth of detail of analysing solutions required, (3) the level of abstraction required by the student. The questions move from the specific to the general. Of course, this suggested division is only for guidance and all questions can be attempted by all levels of students with some degree of success.

Suggested Teaching Approach

The case can be taught through the use of the six questions at the end of the case.

Question 1: Discuss the principal weaknesses of Rouen-Schloss's MkIS and their possible causes.

Three principal weaknesses of the marketing information system at Rouen-Schloss could be said to be:

1. Reliance on a single data source
2. Lack of marketing orientation
3. Underutilization of the marketing database

1. Reliance on a single data source

Due to the general lack of management resources and time, the output of the marketing database was not analysed or scrutinized to any significant extent. Consequently, the deficiencies in consistency, accuracy, and impartiality of these data had not been fully appreciated (although it was generally accepted that no data source could ever be 100 per cent accurate). As a consequence, the need to complement the marketing database with other data sources had not been realized. However, even if this had been the case, the marketing manager would simply not have had the time to engage in the lengthy and often arduous task of searching for these alternative sources, which were frequently disparate. Such a task would require a considerable amount of resources. Numerous potential alternative data sources exist, both within the company and externally. But finding these sources is not sufficient in itself. As they are secondary in nature, most of them would be of limited use or deficient in some way with respect to the use they are required for. Consequently, they would have to be manipulated in some way to increase their utility. This is exemplified by the need to segment the data generated by the RS 34 internal accounting system, whose otherwise aggregated data were of limited use.

However, multiplicity of data sources in itself is only one aspect of MkIS sophistication. Multiplicity of variables is also important. An important weakness of RS's MkIS was its almost total reliance on one variable: the annual steel abrasives consumption of customers and prospects. Such restriction can severely hamper the potential of the MkIS, particularly with respect to developing modelling capabilities. Statistical banks and modelling subsystems typically demand a much richer base of variables to play with. It is such models and their inherent data interrelationships that enable managers to make forecasts. The benefits of these multivariate models can be further augmented by giving users an interactive interface with the system.

2. Lack of marketing orientation

Perhaps the greatest indictment of the management of RS's MkIS was its lack of marketing orientation. Apart from the marketing department, very few of the company's other subunits benefited in any way from the MkIS. Of those that did, the information they received was in a format geared to the needs of the marketing department, and not their own.

3. The underutilization of the marketing database

The lack of MkIS management also contributed to the low relative utility of the marketing database, although in a relatively indirect manner. As national sales managers were largely deprived of numerous potential MkIS benefits, due to the MkIS management's lack of marketing orientation, their interest in the quality of the system was at best limited. Consequently, they felt little compulsion to encourage and supervise their sales staff's data card management, a task which generally lacked any intrinsic motivation for these employees. As a result, the accuracy of the data often suffered.

Nevertheless, even historic data of the sort RS's MkIS was largely dependent on, can be used to produce somewhat crude forecasts through simple extrapolation techniques and time-series analyses. Yet, due to a lack of managerial time and resources, even this was not performed at RS.

Question 2: How might these weaknesses be overcome?

The weaknesses could be overcome by attending to three broad problem areas:

1. Lack of MkIS management
2. Poor salesforce motivation
3. Poor market coverage

1. Better use of MkIS management

Lack of management involvement in the MkIS was leading to numerous opportunities to improve and enrich the system being missed. Clearly, the sheer complexity and variety of issues pertaining to running an MkIS warrant the establishment of a full-time MkIS management capacity. Although the weaknesses identified in RS's MkIS may be common to smaller national operators, their complexity is greatly increased when the system operates on a pan-European or international scale. For example: gathering primary data in many countries creates problems of control and logistics which are exacerbated by the distance involved; the use of secondary data sources is hampered by problems of differing availability and measurement in each country; the demands placed on MkIS management by the need to identify and subsequently satisfy numerous and varied information needs are greatly increased when dealing with a multitude of internationally dispersed subsidiaries.

Rectifying this situation would require a significant amount of managerial resources. The nature of the numerous and diverse information needs throughout the organization would have to be established and the MkIS subsequently modified to meet these needs. This would involve generating new standard reports at the very least. In addition, other changes would almost certainly have to be made such as adopting new variables and measures. Furthermore, this process would have to be on-going in order to adapt to constantly changing information needs. Such a task was clearly beyond the current ability of the marketing manager.

While the appointment of an MkIS manager may be sufficient to overcome the problems of running the marketing intelligence function in a smaller or national company, larger and more internationally dispersed companies are more likely to require a full MkIS management department.

Overcoming the limitations of marketing orientation can perhaps best be achieved by adopting a proactive internal marketing approach to market intelligence management as described by Skyrme (1980). This would involve establishing a full-time, multi-staffed department to handle the multiplicity of on-going activities required:

- Identifying internal target customers and their particular information requirements.
- Defining the department's mission and objectives, and applying these to clearly identified (internal) information customer groups.
- Planning tasks to match the supply of, and demand for, information as efficiently as possible (e.g. to avoid duplication of effort).
- Promoting the department and its services throughout the whole organization so as to ensure that the benefits and value of this organizational subsystem are offered to as large a market as possible, thereby producing economies of scale in this operation.

Better management of the MkIS could have increased its utility by more than simply increasing the accuracy of the marketing database's date.

The MkIS could have been enriched by obtaining a broader set of data from representatives, as identified by Moss (1979).

- Recording and processing customer complaints, preferably by means of a database, covering variables such as the nature of the problem, stage of use of the product at which the problem was noticed and details of the customer personnel affected by the fault.
- Recording volume forecasts based on the anticipated future demand of customers and prospects. In turn, these figures can be apportioned between the various competitors supplying these customers and prospects in order to forecast future market share and competitor sales. The quality of the MkIS could also have been significantly improved if the marketing department had been more involved with the salesforce at a less formal level. Sales representatives should have been encouraged and invited to provide verbal feedback on their impressions of the market, as was the case in the companies investigated by Moss (1979). This could be organized through relatively informal but regular meetings attended by members of the marketing department, national sales managers, and the representatives themselves.

2.   Improved salesforce motivation

The first step in solving a problem is to obtain sufficient understanding of its nature and the related issues. It has already been established that a principal cause of the poor reliability of the marketing database was a lack of salesforce motivation in completing their quota of data cards. Having identified this problem, a better understanding of it can be gained by breaking it down. Here, motivation can be seen to consist of two components:

1.   Coercion
2.   Inducement

The lack of coercion was closely related to the tripartite relationship between the marketing department, the national sales managers, and the representatives themselves, as well as to the lines of authority between them (see Appendix 1 of case). Sales representatives were directly answerable to the national sales managers alone. The formal lines of authority flowed directly from the national sales managers to their own representatives. In other words, the national sales managers were directly responsible for controlling and monitoring their salesforce. In contrast, the marketing department possessed no formal authority over any members of the sales teams, whether national sales managers or the representatives.

Yet it was this department which demanded that sales representatives update and manage their data cards. Consequently, this task was carried out purely out of the good nature of the sales teams and not due to any formal obligation to the marketing department.

The absence of inducements affected motivation at two hierarchical levels. The salesforce received reward for the time and effort spent on managing their data cards. In fact, this actually resulted in a net loss for them as the time spent on filling in the data cards could have been spent in the field generating further sales. It therefore resulted in a loss of potential commission. At the next level in the organization, national sales managers received little more from the marketing database than the salesforce below them. Apart from the annual profile of their national market sent to them after the completion of the annual European Steel Abrasives Market Survey, they received nothing. In Thierry's opinion, this was a key aspect of the problem. Only the national sales managers had the formal authority to 'coerce' the salesforce into better managing their data cards. But as they themselves received very little benefit from the marketing database, they had little interest in doing so. Consequently, they stood to lose little and gain much by encouraging their sales staff to be as swift as possible with the administration of their data cards so as to spend more time in the field. One national sales manager claimed that filling in data cards at the beginning of each year cost his salesforce 23 man days. It would therefore seem that the national sales managers were an important locus for improving the marketing database.

Clearly in this case, motivation by coercion could not work. The only alternative, therefore, would have to be motivation by inducement. This could most easily and directly be achieved by offering the benefits and services of the marketing database to the national sales managers to a much more significant extent. This would necessarily involve a greater level of co-operation and communication between the marketing department as the controllers and prime operators of the marketing database and the national sales managers as potential users of information. Such interaction would be necessary to identify the information needs of the national sales managers effectively. This greater orientation towards users' needs by the marketing department would correspond to the role of Skyrme's (1980) Marketing Intelligence Service.

Such an approach did in fact begin to develop towards the end of Thierry's project. National sales managers were questioned on their particular information needs by the marketing department. It was at this stage that the usefulness of data by sales territory was identified, and the appropriate marketing database report subsequently programmed and generated.

The situation so far described still leaves room for further improvement. Inducement of the national sales managers as described above might lead to eventual coercion of the salesforce. In effect, the marketing department would induce the national sales managers into coercing their salesforce to improve upon the administration of data cards. But motivation by coercion alone is not enough. It yields results in the short term, but because of negative and authoritarian aspects, as well as the general atmosphere of fear and distrust it generates, it risks becoming counterproductive. To overcome this problem, sales representatives themselves should also be offered inducements. This could be achieved by means of an equitable compensation system. The basis of such a system could be the allocation of tangible rewards in proportion to the quality of individual salespeople's data intelligence work. However, developing an appropriate reward system for sales representatives' data card management efforts would be no easy task.

Good sales representatives generally have the basic ego qualities which drive them to sell for personal satisfaction, not just for the financial rewards. Such a task-related motivation towards work is referred to as intrinsic motivation (Dyer and Parker, 1975). Thus, if sales people derive enjoyment from performing job-related tasks, such as influencing their customers and learning more about their company's products, they have an intrinsic orientation towards their work. Such personnel have a deep-rooted desire to sell, and depriving them of the fulfilment of that desire may be hard to compensate for (Sims, 1977). However, this may be overcome by concentrating on the extrinsic aspects of motivation towards work. Extrinsic orientation refers to the attraction of rewards obtained from the environment surrounding work (Dyer and Parker, 1975). For example, if representatives are concerned about the money they earn and other external rewards they receive as a result of doing their job, they have an extrinsic orientation towards their work. As intrinsic and extrinsic orientations are not mutually exclusive (Switzky and Haywood, 1974), it stands that most sales representatives should be susceptible to at least some extrinsic motivators as well as to intrinsic motivators. It follows that extrinsic motivators such as financial and material rewards could be used to encourage sales staff to perform non-sales related tasks.

At the very least, such a reward should compensate any loss of time and income incurred due to time spent out of the field while dealing with data cards. However, merely compensating for this loss would not create a net benefit. In other words, sales representatives would be no better off whether they decided to fill in the data cards or spend the time in the field instead. Keeping the reward at this level would go no further than simply offsetting the disadvantages of data card management. Far better would be to offer a level of inducement resulting in a net benefit. In this way, the salesforce would stand to gain more by administering their data cards than if they spent that time in the field instead.

Such a reward could take the form of a data card management bonus. Bonuses have been shown to be an invaluable means of boosting salesforce motivation in situations where other more orthodox methods such as salary and commission payments do not suffice (Winer, 1976). This bonus could be calculated as a function of the average sales per day of each sales representative and the time spent on filling in the data cards, plus an additional quotient to create a net benefit associated with that task. The reward system would emphasize the importance of the marketing database to the salesforce, and would lead to the task of updating the data cards at the beginning of each year being perceived as something extrinsically positive and worthwhile.

Clearly, quantifying the opportunity cost of data card management (i.e. the cost of not being in the field generating sales as a result of data card updating) would not be an easy task. But an acceptable level of compensation could be established through discussion between the national sales managers, their salesforce, and probably a third-party group such as the human resources department. The important point here is that the system is fair and ensures that each sales representative is better off managing his or her data cards effectively than if he or she spent that time in the field instead.

Inducements of this nature, however, should not be raised to a level where they begin to distract the salesforce from performing their main selling and prospecting duties. This implies that the level of inducement should be balanced. On the one hand it should be sufficient to ensure proper data card management, but on the other it should not be so large as to encourage sales representatives to spend excessive time on this activity at the expense of their other duties.

Although such a bonus system would no doubt increase salesforce commitment to better data card management, it is deficient in one important respect. A key factor in salesforce motivation is establishing a close link between performance and reward (Johnson, 1975; Kearney, 1976). With the proposed bonus system, the reward is linked to the quality of the sales effort forgone, rather than the effectiveness of data card management *per se*. To link reward to performance requires an adequate means of measuring performance. But whereas sales effort can be objectively measured in monetary terms, the quality of card management is much harder to gauge. Although certain criteria such as the number of boxes left blank on each card can easily be measured, other important aspects of the job, such as the accuracy of the estimates, would be much harder to quantify. A task whose attributes cannot be measured objectively cannot be evaluated objectively, and if it cannot be objectively evaluated, it cannot be rewarded equitably.

Here, traditional methods of sales personnel evaluation would be of little or no use. They would not be suited to evaluating data card management as these methods generally deal with quantitative performance standards such as sales volumes and the number of sales calls made (Locander and Staples, 1978). More sophisticated methods such as Management by Objectives (MBO) are more flexible in that they advocate the measurement of a broader variety of performance dimensions (Etzel and Ivancevich, 1974). But even with this method, the central problem of evaluating the quality of salesforce intelligence gathering remains unresolved, as the quality of information does not easily lend itself to objective measurement.

An additional difficulty such a compensation system would encounter would be in coping with different salesforce remuneration packages across different countries. For example, RS sales representatives in France received a much higher proportion of monetary remuneration than their British counterparts, but were expected to purchase their own car, while company cars formed a significant part the remuneration package of British representatives. This imbalance in monetary remuneration would probably affect the perceived impact of the bonus system on French representatives more than on their British counterparts. Consequently, to ensure the same effect, bonuses in France would have to be larger than in Britain. But establishing the precise extent of this additional requirement would again be extremely difficult and subjective. Furthermore, this problem would be compounded by the fact that RS employed salesforces in more than just France and the UK. Clearly, adjusting the data card management bonus in line with differences in remuneration structure across these additional countries would only add to the complications.

Nevertheless, even with its inherent limitations, the bonus system described above would help to improve the quality of the entries on the data cards. As the time spent on data card management would be adequately rewarded, representatives would feel less compelled to rush this activity in order to return to the more lucrative task of selling and prospecting in the field. In addition, the national sales managers' increased interest in the quality of the marketing database would compel them to verify that this updating was performed to the best of each representative's ability.

Although this motivational approach would lead to significant improvements in the marketing database's impartiality, accuracy, and consistency, it must nevertheless be realized that representatives do not possess perfect knowledge, especially concerning competitors. This approach would merely motivate the salesforce to perform better than previously, perhaps even to the best of their ability. But due to cognitive limitations, the data collected would still not be totally accurate.

Such an approach would also be unlikely to overcome problems of data card management by agents. On the one hand, effective coercion would be far less feasible given the geographical distance from the company's main centres of operation and the lack of formal and direct authority over agents. On the other hand, motivating by inducement would also be less feasible. Agents' revenues are usually completely commission based. Consequently, the opportunity cost of their data card updating would be much higher than for RS employed sales staff, whose remuneration was part fixed salary, part commission. As the size of the bonus required may prove prohibitive, another approach to effective data card management would be required in these circumstances.

Increasing the motivation of the salesforce to manage their data cards better would no doubt increase the quality of the data emanating from the known market, i.e. customers and prospects currently covered by the salesforce. In addition, it may even lead to an increase in the salesforce's market coverage. National sales managers may gain an added impetus to push their salesforce further into the field, seeking out new prospects so as to improve further the quality of 'their' marketing database. From an inducement perspective, sales representatives would have an interest in identifying and contacting ever more prospects. This would result in the growth of their data card collection, leading to more time having to be spent on updating, therefore generating a larger data card management bonus. This notion, however, is speculative. Even if it were to prove true, the extent to which market coverage could be increased thereby reducing the extent of non-response as a result, remains doubtful. Either way, because of the sheer variety and number of abrasives users in any market, there would always remain a portion of the market uncovered by the salesforce. This seemingly insurmountable obstacle highlights the need for the total marketing information system to feed off other sources of data, some of which view the market from 'above', based on a broader set of data relating to the totality of markets rather than sourcing from their individual constituents.

3. Improved market coverage

A well-managed and properly motivated salesforce generally provides high-quality market intelligence at a micro level, concerning data specific to individual customers and prospects. However, the motivation of the salesforce in collecting that data and the sophistication of their collection procedures are only a partial guarantee of data quality at the macro level. The quality of that data's representation of the whole market also depends on the proportion of the market's members solicited by the salesforce. In other words, the quality of macro-market intelligence depends on the size of the respondent sample (see Figure 1). Any prospect not solicited by the salesforce will inevitably result in a gap in the representation of the total market. This non-response is inversely proportional to the salesforce's market coverage. Clearly, the smaller the salesforce, the greater the chance of non-response.

While it is virtually impossible to ensure that every prospect in a market is solicited by a company's salesforce, the incidence of non-response may be acceptable in situations where the company enjoys a monopoly or dominant competitive position in the market (a market share of at least 70 per cent) and possesses an extensive national salesforce. Where the company has a much lower market profile, with a salesforce not capable of soliciting the majority of prospects in the market, a much higher level of non-response will invariably restrict the accuracy of the MkIS's representation of the total market. As acceptable sampling frames of industrial customers are rarely available, this problem cannot be feasibly overcome using extrapolation or subsampling techniques. One way to reduce the problem is through the use of as many pertinent alternative market data sources as possible, such as customs statistics, industrial output statistics, and informal industry sources.

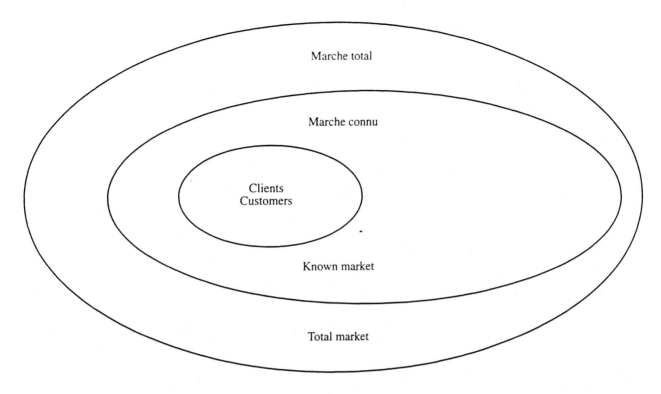

Figure 1

As the extent of a pan-European company's presence and the size of its market share typically vary from one national market to another, this phenomenon can lead to significant discrepancies from one market to another. This was exemplified by differences in marketing database accuracy and error coefficient size between France and West Germany resulting from the different market shares.

Another problem highlighted by considering market coverage is the reluctance of agents to divulge intelligence concerning their markets to their clients. Clearly, agents must be as useful and rich a source of market information as conventional company-employed sales staff. Perhaps reasons for this reluctance should be further studied by commissioning market research study and exploring ways to encourage agents to share this information with their clients more readily.

Question 3: How does RS's MkIS compare with a general model of MkIS? What improvements might such a comparison suggest?

In general, the development and management of an effective marketing information system requires more than just sophisticated hardware and software alone. It consists of three interacting elements:

1. People
2. Equipment
3. Procedures

Satisfying an organization's market information needs depends on a balanced interplay between these three elements. There appears to be a tendency for investment in MkIS to concentrate on equipment and procedures at the expense of people. Clearly, optimum MkIS performance requires that investment in hardware and software be matched by investment in the people who must run and manage them.

31

RS's MkIS included three subsystems:

1. Internal accounting subsystem
2. Marketing intelligence subsystem
3. Marketing research subsystem

1. The internal accounting subsystem

The internal accounting subsystem of RS's MkIS refers to the internal accounting information used by Thierry, i.e. the internal sales information obtained from the RS 34 monthly sales reports. This information was sourced from the invoicing system in the company's order–shipping–billing cycle.

2. The marketing intelligence subsystem

Insofar as it is defined as the set of procedures and sources used to obtain pertinent information about the firm's environment, RS's marketing intelligence subsystem consisted primarily of the marketing database. This system used the company's salesforce personnel to extract information from its customers and prospects, and through these, ultimately about its competitors.

The use of salesforce personnel to collect systematically market data is supported by the findings of Moss (1979), a strong advocate of this source of market intelligence. Yet, when the extensive contact between sales representatives and their customers and prospects is considered, with the wealth of information which can be gleaned as a result, the amount of data formally recorded by RS's representatives on their data cards was surprisingly limited. The companies studied by Moss (1979) obtained a much broader range of data from their salespeople, some of which could have been a useful addition to RS's marketing information system. For example, although RS's sales representatives were always notified of faults and problems associated with their products during visits, this information was not formally recorded within the marketing information system. Clearly a log of such events recorded in a database could yield numerous benefits for marketing, helping improve the product management function, for example. Useful statistics on product failure and quality control problems could be generated, thereby helping improve the final product offering to customers. Ideas for new product development were also not formally recorded by RS sales representatives. This, however, may have been due to the nature of the products being sold. Steel abrasives are a bulk commodity type of product with low technological potential. Any potential developments were usually to be found in their applications rather than in the products themselves. These applications developments were largely the responsibility of the Development and Training centre.

Customer analysis in the companies analysed by Moss (1979) generally went beyond RS's relatively narrow and shorter-term estimations of product consumption during the preceding year. It involved considering a wider variety of factors such as the number and type of machines consuming the products being used, capacity utilization levels, capital investment plans, and company growth patterns. These factors would all influence medium- to long-term future demand. This information was also supplemented by data on the competition in the market place. Again, these data were richer than that collected by RS. Instead of merely covering quantities of products sold to customers and prospects, these salespeople collected data of a broader nature, including factors such as competitor investment plans and details of their marketing mix and strategies where feasible. The companies studied by Moss (1979) concentrated more on future-oriented information, leading to the production of detailed and long-term forecasts. In contrast, by the time RS's marketing database was updated, its data was invariably retrospective.

Another striking difference between RS and the companies in Moss's study (1979) is the importance the latter attach to qualitative information. Although such information does not easily lend itself to being recorded in highly structured and quantitative forms, as was the case with RS's data cards, these companies managed and communicated this information through the use of regular informal meetings between the salesforce and the marketing department. In contrast to this, RS made no arrangements for sales representatives to interact with members of the marketing department or anybody else responsible for the market intelligence function. Consequently, until Thierry's arrival in the company, RS's official marketing information system, comprising solely of the marketing database, was exclusively quantitative in nature, the richness and depth associated with more qualitative data being totally absent. It was only after Thierry began interviewing national sales managers and other relevant executives that qualitative data became an integral part of a broader formal marketing intelligence subsystem. Clearly, the salesforce, as a source of important market intelligence, was being underutilized.

3.   The marketing research subsystem

A marketing research subsystem also formed part of the company's total marketing information system. When the need for intelligence was identified, consultants and market research firms were hired, as was the case with the study of the French diamond-tipped tool market. In addition, employing students to carry out specific projects was also common. In France, the convention for hiring students stipulates that they should be paid no more than the statutory minimum wage, supplemented only by coverage of any project expenses. However, adopting such an approach can have its drawbacks. In the majority of cases, students are only available for a few months at most, being required to return to their teaching institutions. While this poses no problems when the duration of the project is known in advance and is of a relatively short-term nature, when the length of a project is not predictable from the outset and possibly prolonged by certain unpredictable events, the student may find him or herself having to leave before the project's completion.

At RS, hiring students for compiling the annual European Steel Abrasives Market Survey raised two problems of a different nature. First, as a different student was hired the broad methodology adopted would differ from year to year. Each student would have his or her own particular style. The manner in which ambiguities were resolved and assumptions made would consequently vary, being subjective in nature and therefore open to personal bias. This inevitably led to inconsistencies in the quality of the data year on year, undermining the reliability of any trends identified. Secondly, the learning curve associated with the project was broken every year as each new student had to familiarize him- or herself with every aspect of the company and the project from scratch. The project typically took three to four months; however, a significant proportion of this time was taken up by training and the general process of familiarizing the student with the company and the project. If the survey was executed by the same person each year, the time required could be cut by at least half. The experience thus gained by this individual would also lead to fewer mistakes being made, resulting in further time savings. Using the same person in this way would also help overcome the problem of inconsistent methodologies described above. The consistency of the work carried out year on year would be significantly improved, thereby improving the quality of any trend analyses.

4.   The analytical marketing subsystem

The company's marketing information system did not possess a formal analytical marketing subsystem. First of all, it did not include a statistical bank. Formal statistical techniques were not used, supporting the findings of Johnston and Woodward (1988) who claim that this tends to be due to both a lack of systems geared to the formal analysis of relationships between different sets of data on the one hand, and poor managerial abilities in informal statistical techniques on the other. Here, although RS did possess a formal database, the use of statistical techniques was limited due to a lack of managerial ability in statistical techniques. Only basic calculations, such as determining market shares, were made. Neither was the computer system programmed to perform any sophisticated statistical functions such as cluster and correlation analyses, nor were managers trained to engage in these.

However, attempting to establish such a subsystem would have met numerous difficulties, largely due to the limited number of variables covered by the company's marketing information system. It was dominated by one variable: sales of steel abrasives in tonnes; the only other variable included was the output of certain industrial segments, in tonnes, and revenue, obtained from the industrial output statistics directory. Although attempts were made to establish a relationship between the sales of steel abrasives to these sectors and their output, no further multivariate analyses or any other formal statistical techniques were adopted. Clearly, if a statistical bank capable of establishing numerous important relationships was to be developed, a broader variety of variables would have to be covered by the MkIS. In this light, useful internal data could include unit price and cost, while external data could include national GNP growth, interest rates and other publicly available macroeconomic indicators. Suitable statistical techniques could then be used to establish the nature of relationships between certain of these variables. For example, establishing the relationship between price and sales could help determine the price elasticity of demand for the company's products. This would be useful in determining pricing policies or formulating market penetration strategies. In addition, the relationship between GNP growth and market volume would be a useful tool for forecasting demand.

RS's MkIS was also characterized by the absence of a model bank, inasmuch as the output of the system was a static representation of the European steel abrasives market, presented in tabular form. Although this did constitute a set of interrelated variables representing a real situation, this model was severely limited. The best models are interactive in nature. That is to say that they enable a user to analyse the effect that different inputs have on the output of the model. These inputs, known as independent variables, can be from either the organization's internal or external environments. These could include variables such as unit price and the number of different products offered in the case of the internal environment, and market size, the number of competitors and their product prices in the case of the external. The output, or dependent variables, could represent sales volume or market share. Such models allow managers to pre-empt the effect of different strategies before actually putting them into action. Such scenario analyses permit managers to identify those strategies or courses of action most likely to provide the required outcome. These kinds of models are used for tasks such as new product sales forecasting (Silk and Urban, 1978), sales call planning (Lodish, 1971), and marketing mix budgeting (Little, 1975). With such models, the emphasis is distinctively on anticipating the future.

No such facility existed in RS's MkIS. It was limited to the more basic collection, processing, and compilation of data, and was incapable of performing such interactive 'what-if' scenario analyses. Consequently, an important means of generating future-oriented data was ignored. The information generated by the MkIS was largely retrospective, its principal task being to generate as accurate and detailed a picture of the market over the preceding year as possible. This supports the findings of Johnston and Woodward (1988) who claim that most managers rely on looking at historical sales figures and a feel for the market gained through diverse information sources, instead of adopting formal forecasting techniques. Yet even such historical data could have been used to produce forecasts by analysing trends and performing various time series analyses.

Question 4: Discuss where you would place RS's MkIS on the EDP–DSS continuum.

The marketing database fits Jobber and Rainbow's (1977) definition of a formal marketing information system as one in which information is formally gathered, processed, stored, and distributed to managers in accordance with their informational needs on a regular and planned basis, although in actual fact the satisfaction of third-party information needs left much room for improvement as has been discussed.

Although customers and prospects were the only source of information for the database, other sources, not part of this system, were used by Thierry for the purposes of the market survey. These were formally addressed, managed, and co-ordinated in conjunction with the marketing database. This broader information system, managed by Thierry, conforms to other definitions of MkIS, such as those of Smith, Brien, and Stafford (1976), Schoner and Uhl (1975), Buzzell, Cox, and Brown (1969), Churchill (1976), Eskin and Labbak (1969), and Bellenger and Greenberg (1978), which all focus on the management and organization of multiple information sources, as well as making the distinction between *ad hoc* marketing research and more continuous scanning and storage of marketing information. On this point, however, RS's MkIS fell somewhat short of the continuous scanning function described above. Data for the marketing database was updated once a year only, and the other sources within the broader MkIS had only been adopted since Thierry's arrival in the company. This multi-source approach was superior to that described in the large number of companies surveyed by Jobber (1977) and Fletcher (1983), which could not supply information on the environment.

The marketing intelligence system at RS would also seem to support Johnston and Woodward's (1988) view that the concept of the computerized, instant-access MkIS is applicable only to the largest and most sophisticated companies. At the time of the research, Rouen-Schloss was the largest supplier of steel abrasives in the European market, with dominant market shares in most of the countries it supplied. In fact, one of the prerequisites for a successful marketing database is extensive market coverage by the company's salesforce in each national market.

Interactive facilities are an important attribute of formal decision support systems as described by Sprague and Watson (1979). But due to its inherent deficiencies in terms of both statistical and model banks, Rouen-Schloss's MkIS was distinctly lacking in decision support facilities. If viewed in terms of Sprague and Watson's (1979) continuum, it would probably spread from pure electronic data processing to about midway between this and decision support system status. At the EDP end of the spectrum, basic data were obtained directly from the internal accounting system, such as tonnage of steel abrasives sold, sourced from the RS 34 reports, and were obtained through basic electronic data-processing techniques. This categorization is further vindicated by the fact that such data were frequently used at the lower, operational levels of management, and, additionally, were highly accurate, detailed, quantitative, current, and internal. Other, broader aspects of the MkIS would position it further towards the right of the continuum. The MkIS's externally focused data included that obtained through the marketing database as well as that obtained through the other three externally oriented sources: national customs and industrial output statistics and information derived from the national sales managers. National sales managers were in addition a source of more qualitative data.

Integration, one of Sprague and Watson's (1979) requisite characteristics of decision support systems, was present in RS's MkIS in two important respects. First, data from varied sources, i.e. from numerous national markets, were contained and integrated centrally within the marketing database. Secondly, data from the alternative sources were processed, managed and integrated with data from the marketing database by Thierry himself.

However, RS's MkIS fell short of full DSS status for a number of reasons. Firstly, Sprague and Watson (1979) argue that a pure DSS serving strategic management should comprise an integrated system in which the decision makers, decision models, and the database are linked in an interactive manner. Clearly, the MkIS at RS did not satisfy this criterion. Secondly, as the MkIS was on the whole controlled and managed solely by the marketing and computer departments, many important decision makers did not interact directly with the MkIS. Most were simply passive recipients of MkIS data. This situation does not agree with the view of decision support systems put forward by Fletcher, Buttery, and Deans (1988) who argue that a DSS should allow direct interaction between the decision maker and the information base. Thirdly, although the MkIS did include a sophisticated database, beyond the simple static tabular representations of each market contained in the survey report, no sophisticated modelling facilities were available, either inherent in the computer system, or developed managerially outside of it. This limited the availability of future-oriented information which, according to Keen and Morton (1978), is another important attribute of DSS. Instead, the data included in the MkIS was largely restricted to estimates of tonnages of steel abrasives sold by various suppliers over the previous calendar year. It did not include future-oriented estimates of this variable or other broader economic variables, such as interest rate, industrial output, and exchange rate predictions, which, in addition, could have provided the basis for more sophisticated scenario-based interactive and real-time forecasting models.

Question 5: What are some of the social and organizational issues involved in RS's MkIS?

In general, little evidence was found of any social or organizational resistance affecting the operation of development of the marketing database as generally highlighted by Piercy (1980). The nature of interdepartmental relationships affecting the marketing database posed few problems. This was largely due to the fact that it was controlled primarily by only two organizational subunits: the marketing department and the computer services department. The relationship between this and the computer department certainly goes against the findings of Walton and Dutton (1969) who view the nature of the interface between user managers and systems personnel as a source of potential conflict. Although the marketing department was highly dependent on the computer department for the use of the marketing database, the close relationship between the two departments resulting from their virtual monopoly over the system ensured that both generally spoke the same language, greatly reducing the potential for error due to poor communication. The only friction which occurred between these two departments was due to the marketing department occasionally placing unrealistic timeframes on data requirements which the computer department could not meet due to its obligations to other parts of the organization. However, this was kept to a minimum as a result of both the general quality of communications between the two departments and good planning on behalf of the marketing department.

The virtual duopoly over the marketing database shared between the computer department and the marketing department also precluded other organizational problems associated with MkIS in the literature. For example, the fears associated with retraining highlighted by Dalal (1980) did not affect many information users as they were not directly involved with the operation of the system, merely receiving their information from a third party instead. Furthermore, as the information from the MkIS divulged to these other managers tended to be restricted to the annual publication of the European Steel Abrasives Market Survey, the information tended to be the same for everyone. This greatly reduced the incidence of imbalance in status and power developing between individual subunits as identified by Carper (1977).

Although the rather centralized and 'dictatorial' nature of the MkIS management and operation overcame many of the problems adequately, MkIS management at RS was very much run according to what might be termed the 'production concept'. This holds that customers favour products that are widely available and low in cost. Management concentrates on achieving high production efficiency and wide distribution coverage, without paying due respect to customer needs. Clearly, the management of the MkIS needed to concentrate more on satisfying the numerous and diverse information needs of users. This lack of marketing orientation was largely responsible for the marketing database's unreliability.

As the MkIS's management becomes more customer oriented, the demands placed upon the MkIS will increase and this pressure may in turn adversely affect the relationships between the marketing and computer services departments.

Question 6: Describe some of the general problems of MkIS implementation and development.

The relatively limited development of marketing information systems in many industries has been confirmed by Fletcher and Wheeler (1989). This has been partly explained by social and organizational problems (Cox and Good, 1967).

Marketing information is directly related to factors that affect people's work, security, motivation, and organizational status. Consequently, the introduction of an MkIS may have severe repercussions, both at an individual and subunit level, which may affect its successful adoption. For example, user managers may associate the innovation with fear of the unknown, fear of technology, fear of retraining and changing direction, fear of dependency, and fear of criticism (Dalal, 1980). Retraining, no matter how minimal, creates the fear of having to master something new, and in some extreme cases, the fear of rejection for poor results during the retraining period. The system may also be seen as threatening to status or power, causing job role ambiguity and changes in interpersonal relationships and work patterns (Carper, 1977). Markus (1979) adds that these factors may lead to deliberate attempts to bring about system failure. The nature of the interface between user-managers and systems personnel has been identified as a potential source of conflict (Walton and Dutton, 1969). In situations of high mutual dependency between these two groups, the potential for conflict will be increased. Another potential source of conflict between user-managers and systems personnel arises from the difference in language used by these two groups. Both have their jargon and terminology which is unfamiliar to people outside their respective professions.

The establishment of an MkIS may also affect the distribution of power between subunits. It may confer additional power on the marketing subunit by improving its ability to cope with uncertainty, for example by allowing quicker response to environmental change. Clearly, possession of information can boost a subunit's ability to influence some part of the organization's decision-making process. This may result in instances where departments and individuals resist the development of certain types of information and therefore power and control over others (Piercy, 1979). Jobber and Rainbow (1977) found that in half of the companies they studied which did not possess a formal MkIS, managers claimed that the dynamics of the industries in which they were involved did not call for the development of formal information systems.

The use of formal techniques by marketing executives appears to be very limited. This was due to managers' lack of knowledge of statistical techniques, lack of expertise in the interpretation of the results, and lack of time. Attitudes towards forecasting techniques were particularly sceptical (Johnston and Woodward, 1988). There seemed to be a tendency for raw, unprocessed data to be passed straight to managers who were left to assess the sources and evaluate the data. They warn that this problem is likely to get worse as companies improve their information-gathering capabilities. One possible solution to this problem would involve setting up a separate information department which could perform the necessary analytical processes which managers seem so reluctant to use or incapable of performing. This is partly vindicated by their research which found that companies in which the MkIS appeared to work most effectively were those where responsibility over the system was given to a specific individual or group of individuals.

Beyond organizational considerations, the reluctance of marketers to use information systems has been largely due to the nature of the marketing decision making process. While some functions require a simple database and retrieval service, more strategic marketing decisions require much more sophisticated systems capable of handling qualitative data and 'guestimates'. The majority of information systems used by firms cannot cope with this degree of complexity (Fletcher, 1983). A study by McLeod and Jones (1986) found that computer reports formed less than 3 per cent of top executives' informational inputs, with greater preference being given to oral communications, brief memos, and letters. Informal systems were also preferred over formal systems, and when computer reports were used, they were frequently rewritten into 'non-computer' form.

This highlights perhaps the most crucial aspect of successful MkIS development, namely the need to match the information system to the user, rather than force the user to fit the system. Yet even when this condition is met and management receive pertinent information as a result, MkIS development may still run into obstacles. The intangibility of the benefits of an MkIS makes the justification of allocating extra resources to it problematic. This problem becomes more acute the higher the level of management, as the return on decisions with long time horizons, based on qualitative externally focused data is virtually impossible to establish, especially in the short term. Consequently, there is often the risk that MkIS development projects may appear unattractive in comparison with other projects producing more immediate and tangible results.

REFERENCES

Bellenger, D. N. and Greenberg, B. A. (1978) *Marketing Research—A Management Information Approach,* Irwin, Homewood, Ill.

Buzzell, R. D., Cox, D. F. and Brown, R. V. (1969) *Marketing Research and Information Systems.* McGraw-Hill, New York.

Carper, W. (1977) Human factors in MIS, *Journal of Systems Management,* vol. 28, no. 11, pp. 48–50.

Churchill, G. A. (1976) *Marketing Research: Methodological Foundations*, Dryden Press, Hinsdale, Ill.

Cox, D. F. and Good, R. E. (1967) How to build a marketing information system, *Harvard Business Review*, May–June, vol. 45, pp. 145–154.

Dalal, J. (1980) Management change, *Journal of Systems Management*, vol. 31, no. 4, pp. 32–36.

Dyer, L. and Parker, D. F. (1975) Classifying outcomes in work motivation research: an examination of the intrinsic–extrinsic dichotomy, *Journal of Applied Psychology*, vol. 60, pp. 455–458.

Eskin, G. J. and Labback, R. (1969) Towards a planning-oriented marketing information system, in *Marketing in a Changing World*, Morin, B. A. (ed.), American Association, Chicago.

Etzel, M. J. and Ivancevich, J. M. (1974) Management by objectives in marketing: philosophy, process, and problems, *Journal of Marketing*, vol. 38, pp. 47–55.

Fletcher, K. (1983) Information systems in British industry, *Management Decision*, vol. 21, no. 2, pp. 25–36.

Fletcher, K. and Wheeler, C. (1989) Market intelligence for international markets, *Market Intelligence and Planning,* vol. 7, no. 5/6, pp. 30–34.

Fletcher, K., Buttery, A. and Deans, K. (1988) The structure and content of the marketing information system: a guide for management, *Market Intelligence and Planning*, vol. 6, no. 4, pp. 27–35.

Jobber, D. (1977) Marketing information systems in United States and British industry, *Management Decision*, vol. 15, no. 2, pp. 297–304.

Jobber, D. and Rainbow, C. (1977) A study of the development and implementation of marketing information systems in British industry, *Journal of the Market Research Society*, vol. 19, no. 3, pp. 104–111.

Johnson, W. H. (1975) *Sales Management: Operations, Administration, Marketing*, C. E. Merrill, Colombus, Ohio.

Johnston, S. and Woodward, S. (1988) Marketing management information systems—a review of current practice, *Market Intelligence and Planning*, vol. 6, no. 2, pp. 26–29.

Kearney, W. J. (1976) The value of behaviourally based performance appraisals, *Business Horizons*, vol. 19, pp. 75–83.

Keen, P. and Morton, S. (1978) *Decision Support Systems: An Organization Perspective*, Addison-Wesley, Reading, Mass.

Kotler, P. (1984) *Marketing Management: Analysis, Planning and Control*, Prentice-Hall, Englewood Cliffs, NJ.

Little, J. D. C. (1975) BRANDAID: a marketing mix model, structure, implementation, calibration, and case study, *Operations Research*, July–August, pp. 628–673.

Locander, W. B. and Staples, W. A. (1978) Evaluating and motivating salesmen with the BARS method, *Industrial Marketing Management*, vol. 7, pp. 43–48.

Lodish, L. M. (1971) Callplan: an interactive salesman's call planning system, *Management Science*, December, pp. 25-40.

Markus, M. L. (1979) Understanding information systems use in organizations: a theoretical approach, unpublished doctoral dissertation, Case Western Reserve University.

McLeod, R. and Jones, J. (1986) Making executive information systems more effective, *Business Horizons*, vol. 29, no. 5, pp. 29–37.

Moss, C. A. (1979) Industrial salesmen as a source of marketing intelligence, *European Journal of Marketing*, vol. 13, no.3, pp. 94–102.

Piercy, N. (1979) Low cost marketing analysis, *Retail and Distribution Management*, vol. 7, no. 3, pp. 23–27.

Piercy, N. (1980) Marketing information systems: theory vs practice, *Quarterly Review of Marketing*, Autumn, pp. 16–24.

Schoner, B. and Uhl, K. P. (1975) *Marketing Research—Information Systems and Decision Making*, Wiley, New York.

Silk, A. J. and Urban, G. L. (1978) Pre-test market evaluation of new packaged goods: a model and measurement methodology, *Journal of Marketing Research,* May, pp. 171–191.

Sims, J. T. (1977) Industrial sales management: a case for MBO, *Industrial Marketing Management*, vol. 6, pp. 43–46.

Skyrme, D. J. (1980) Developing successful marketing intelligence: a case study, *Management Decision*, vol. 28, no. 1, pp. 54–61.

Smith, S. V., Brien, R. H. and Stafford, J. E. (1976) *Readings in Marketing Information Systems*, Houghton-Mifflin, Boston.

Sprague, R. and Watson, H. (1979) Bit by bit: towards decision support systems, *California Management Review*, vol. 22, no. 1, pp. 61–68.

Switzky, H. N. and Haywood, H. C. (1974) Motivational orientation and the relative efficacy of self-monitored and externally imposed reinforcement systems in children, *Journal of Personality and Social Psychology*, vol. 30, pp. 360–366.

Walton, R. E. and Dutton, J. M. (1969) The management of interdepartmental conflict: a model and review, *Administrative Science Quarterly*, vol. 14, no. 1, pp. 73–84.

Winer, L. (1976) A sales compensation plan for maximum motivation, *Industrial Marketing Management*, vol. 5, pp. 29–36.

Case 7

Weatherpruf Shoe Waxes

Synopsis

Weatherpruf (a family-owned firm) have dominated the market for quality solid shoe waxes from the 1930s but are now facing aggressive competition and a technological change affecting their position. Students are initially directed to estimating demand for the next year. The analysis reveals, however, a deeper set of problems facing Weatherpruf.

Teaching Objectives

This case has been used successfully at undergraduate, MBA, and post-experience levels to illustrate the significant roles marketing segmentation and positioning play in developing a marketing plan.

Suggested Teaching Approach

The case can be used as an introduction to market segmentation and planning or as a means of summarizing and illustrating issues already made. It is short enough to allow in-class reading and use with little prior analysis.

1. Forecast future demand for Weatherpruf shoe waxes

The market is clearly segmented by product use into three main segments: the protection segment use shoe wax to protect footwear; the appearance segment use the product to enhance the appearance of their footwear; and adults use the product to revitalize children's shoes. Overall the market is mature, with decline experienced in the appearance market and growth in the children's segment.

The forecasting is mechanistic using the data supplied in the case. Table 2 uses that data. Some tutors may prefer to give students Table 2 with the case. This saves time calculating the figures. For the appearance segment it is assumed that liquids will go to 30 per cent of the market next year (i.e. $0.3 \times 85 = 25$) due to their current rate of growth and the move towards non-leather shoes. The children's segment takes the remainder of predicted demand. Projecting further ahead than one year and the decline in wax becomes even more marked.

Demand for Weatherpruf Waxes can be estimated under at least two different scenarios:

Scenario 1: Weatherpruf hold share of solid waxes. (There is not much evidence that they will be able to!)

This teaching note was prepared by Professor Graham Hooley, University of Aston, UK.

Table 2

| | Current | | | Predicted future | | |
	Total	Wax	Liquid	Total	Wax	Liquid
Total volume	300	200	100	300	180	120
Protect	100	100	0	100	100	0
Appear	100	75	25	85	60	25
Kids	100	25	75	115	20	95
Total value	100.00	50.00	50.00	105.00	45.00	60.00
Protect	25.00	25.00	0.00	25.00	25.00	0.00
Appear	31.25	18.75	12.50	27.50	15.00	12.50
Kids	43.75	6.25	37.50	52.50	5.00	47.50

A 50 per cent share of the predicted 180m unit market gives Weatherpruf expected sales of 90m units valued at £22.5m (25p × 90m) retail and a gross contribution of £4.5m. Note that this is 10 per cent down on the current year.

Scenario 2: Bloom continues to increase share. (This is more likely given the stated objectives of Smart Shoe and their more healthy cash position—see below.)

This could be at the expense of the speciality wax manufacturers. There is bound to be, however, a significant effect on Weatherpruf as market leader and that is where Bloom's growth to date has come from.

Assuming Weatherpruf share declines to 45 per cent, sales will be around 80m at £20m retail and a contribution of £4m. A drop in share to 40 per cent would result in sales of 72m units at £18m retail with a contribution of £3.6m.

Given the current strategy, or lack of one, a reasonable prediction would be 75–90m units depending on the strength of attack by Smart Shoe.

Note the poor state of the Weatherpruf product portfolio—only one product, in a declining market segment, and the strong possibility of further loss of share.

Smart Shoe profitability

Smart Shoe is in a much healthier position. Bloom has 30 per cent of the shoe wax market (60m units at £15m retail and a contribution of approximately £3m—though this may be less as costs could be higher than Weatherpruf's due to smaller scale of production). In addition, however, they have Scuffer with 70 per cent of the liquid shoe polish market (70m units at £35m retail and a contribution of £7m). In total Smart Shoe currently have nearly twice the contribution of Weatherpruf and are prepared to plough it back in to gain position. Next year, with the growth in liquid polishes, predicted sales of Scuffer (on current market share) could yield a contribution of £8.4m and Smart Shoe's total contribution could rise 10 per cent to £11.1m.

Note how much more profitable liquid polishes are:

1. The contribution per unit is twice that of wax
2. The greater frequency (1 wax = 1.5 liquids) makes them three times as profitable.

Conclusions

1. Given the decline in waxes, even holding position will result in reduced contribution for Weatherpruf—will Mr Thomas remain 'well pleased'?
2. Compound on this the aggression of Smart Shoe in the market. They have cash generated from Scuffer which they can use to blitz the market for waxes to get to number 1. Weatherpruf's contribution is vulnerable to changes in market share and overall market movements.
3. Weatherpruf, therefore, needs to rethink its overall strategy from basics.

2. Developing a marketing plan for Weatherpruf

Using the marketing planning framework given in Figure 2.1 Weatherpruf can tackle the key issues which are:

- Define the business mission
- Conduct a marketing audit and SWOT analysis
- Generate and evaluate the strategic options
- Set marketing objectives
- Develop the core strategy
- Design a marketing mix
- Organize and implement
- Control

Define the business mission

1. What business are we in?

By default Weatherpruf have defined their business as shoe waxes. This is a technology-based definition which could lead them to ignore or miss new developments in the market.

2. What business do we want to be in? (or do we need to be in?)

To answer this question we need to pose three others:

- Who will we serve?
- How will we serve them better than the competition?
- What will we serve them with?

This raises three alternative ways of defining the business:

- By market (the segment or segments that will be served)
- By needs (the benefit the target market received)
- By technology (the product form or forms on offer)

The process of marketing planning may lead to a redefinition of business mission (see section 4).

Marketing audit and SWOT analysis

1.   Company analysis

Strengths	Weaknesses
Positive current contribution Reputation for good quality Efficient production Current market leadership in waxes Cost advantage over liquids	One product company Poor availability in multiples (growth sector) Lack of aggression Not in growth segments

2.   Competitor analysis

Smart Shoe	Cash rich, aggressive, out to dominate the market adopting a Differentiated Marketing Strategy (different products in different segments) Innovative (liquids—multiples—customer pull).
Patent Leather Co.	Not a direct (wax) competitor but a rival, especially in the appearance segment
Independents	Highly focused, not losing out to Smart Shoe and less vulnerable to attack

3.   Customer analysis

Clearly segmented market. Weatherpruf currently sell in two of the segments but are increasingly under attack both from liquids and from Bloom.

4.   Distinctive competencies

The strengths of Weatherpruf are reputation and quality. The strengths of SS are distribution (multiples), customer satisfaction (colours), and customer pull (media advertising).

Weatherpruf are relying on the distinctive competencies of yesterday. SS have today's distinctive competencies. What will be the distinctive competences required tomorrow?

5.   External analysis summary

Opportunities	Threats
• Develop liquid polishes (Merger/JV with Patent?) to attack SS in cash generator • Product development of waxes to offer superior benefits (e.g. easy application, more colours, etc.) • Distribution development into the multiples	• SS may enter Protection segment with improved product delivery • Increased pressure from Bloom in Appearance segment

Generation and evaluation of strategic options

Alternatives include:

Convert new users: Unlikely to show much success as the market is mature. If there is any mileage it may be in the children's segment.

Increase usage rate: This is currently high, however use of liquids is greater than waxes. Promote regular waxing patterns if research proves this to be sporadic.

Promote new uses: Look to the leather treatment market or other uses for the 'shoe' wax. Long term this makes much sense but requires getting to know the new markets (and the competition) this will entail.

Develop new products: Here the opportunities are more exciting. Need to develop better solutions to the shoe protection and appearance needs of the customers. Creams? Sprays? Applicators? Use core competencies (wax technology?) to create superior products to attack Scuffer and Bloom.

Win competitors' markets: It is unlikely they will make much ground against SS without product development (see above). There may be more scope for taking from specialist (niche) players but still limited.

Buy competitors: May be more of an option with Patent or with specialists. Purchase of Patent could get them quickly into the market against Scuffer and might also open longer term markets. Don't know anything about the financial strength of Patent, however. It is possible they could move on Weatherpruf!

Strategic alliances:	SS will not ally (nothing to gain). Maybe with a shoe manufacturer (e.g. free sample with the shoe when purchased, endorsement by manufacturer). Maybe with a multiple to supply own label. Danger here for a market leader in attacking its own brand but given limited distribution through multiples may be sensible. Maybe with a shoe retailer (tend to be the manufacturers so see above).
Increase price:	In segments where wax is competing with liquids (e.g. children's segment) the price differences in usage rate, makes wax very cheap. However, in the rest of the market price differences between waxes is more important. Given the attack by Bloom a price increase would not appear to be a sensible option.
Reduce costs:	No evidence available that costs are particularly high but should always be trying to keep them down.
Rationalize the product mix:	Already too limited—only one product!

Marketing objectives

These can be delivered in terms of strategic thrust and strategic objectives (see Chapter 2).

1. Strategic thrust.

The alternatives can be summarized using Ansoff's Matrix:

	Current Markets	New Markets
Current Products	**Market Penetration** Wax for *protection* and *appearance* segments	**Market Development** Wax for other uses, e.g. leather, wood treatment
New Products	**Product Development** Liquids or other new product forms for *protection* and *appearance* Segments	**Diversification** New product forms for children's and other new markets ?????

This analysis may lead to a redefinition of the business mission. The Product Development route keeps the company in the markets that they know and that know them. This effectively defines their business in market terms. The Market Development option keeps them in the technologies they know and opens new (but currently totally unknown) market opportunities. In the short term at least, the Product Development route makes most sense, keeping to their traditional markets but seeking better ways of serving those customers. In the long term a wider business definition to exploit their technologies in new markets should be considered.

2.   Strategic objectives.

These will vary by market segment. They should defend (aggressively!) in the protection and appearance segments through product development in waxes and possibly developing (or buying into) liquids.

Core strategy

Customer targets: Need to retain protectors and pursue appearance market more aggressively. With a liquid in the portfolio they could also attack the children's market.

Competitor targets: SS has targeted Weatherpruf. They have no alternative to fighting other than capitulation. Emphasis on the protection segment makes speciality wax manufacturers a secondary target.

Competitive advantage: Continue to exploit quality image and reputation while developing new products. Forge strategic alliances with shoe manufacturers and retailers.

Marketing mix decisions

Product: The range must be expanded to include other colours (should be easy and cheap to do) and other forms to lead the market and regain the initiative from SS.

Price: Little evidence to suggest any change to pricing strategy—beware the temptation to fight Bloom by a price war as SS have cash from Scuffer to win such a war.

Promotion: Current emphasis on selling needs re-evaluation, especially if they are going into the children's market. There could be an argument in favour of media advertising to create more customer pull and loyalty. Other promotions (in-store) should be considered (a multi-pack with various colours included?) together with piggy-backing shoe sales.

Place: Essential to pursue the grocery multiples vigorously (this is where 80 per cent of sales go).

Organization and implementation

Need a sharper awareness of changes in the market place and how they affect the business. Need for marketing (rather than sales) person if they move to more above the line activity and NPD.

Control

Look especially at market share by segment and product contributions. The current position has arisen from a lack of focus on market share.

If all else fails Mr Thomas should sell the business to Smart Shoe and live in the Bahamas!

End of Module Case

Electrolux in Iran

Synopsis

Multinational corporations (MNCs) are always faced with the problem of political actors in the business relationship. Sometimes the influences are supportive and sometimes coercive. This case illustrates a changing environment, i.e. from supportive to coercive and from coercive to supportive. The case provides evidence about the impact of the political and social factors on a MNC's operations in a foreign market. The Swedish MNC, Electrolux, over a period, was enjoying prosperity in the market. Sales were increasing as well as market commitment. An unexpected political crisis required drastic changes in decisions, a condition that was never included in their plans. The decision to leave the market would result in a huge loss in the investment, and staying in the market was combined with uncertainty about future market turbulence and risks for the lives of personnel. The case provides evidence about the impact of the political and social factors on the MNC's operations. It also is about marketing decisions where environmental factors are changing.

Teaching Objectives

1. To introduce readers to the general and specific influences of political factors.
2. To understand the impact of those political factors on marketing activities.
3. To appreciate the type of political actions as well as business actions necessary under supportive or coercive conditions.
4. To understand how managers make rapid decisions in a crisis where there is insufficient time for information gathering.
5. To consider a real world far removed from the concepts presented in traditional marketing studies.
6. To encourage students to consider a range of alternative decisions for the future. Each alternative contains market operations and costs drastically different from the others.
7. To understand how macro-environmental factors, i.e. the economic, political and social factors, directly influence the international firm.

Suggested Teaching Approach

The case can be discussed in one or even two sessions. The core issue is about environmental influences on marketing. It specifically deals with relationships between the political and business actors in the market. It is also concerned with the cultural and social differences in doing business with developing countries. In other words, the case divides the environmental factors into political and cultural components. The main issue is the instability in the nature of these components and also

---

This teaching note was prepared by Dr Amjad Hadjikhani, Director of Marketing, Uppsala University, Sweden.

the uncertainty of business behaviour. The decision makers are faced with drastic and rapid changes having no idea about the future.

Accordingly, it would be interesting to direct the students to discuss the management of uncertainty in such turbulent environments. In this book, Chapter 2, Marketing Planning, is a good chapter to start the debate. For example, Figures 2.2 and 2.3 provide a useful basis to initiate the discussion. A comparison of the literature dealing with marketing decisions in a dynamic environment and the case would provide students with comprehensive knowledge about the similarities and dissimilarities between the two. The primary teaching objective is to understand marketing behaviour in a critical condition. Rapid decisions are required far from so-called rational behaviour. The case can be analysed by referring to Chapter 5 which deals with the marketing environment. The case discloses how the macro-environment comes closer to the business core and disturbs the macro-environment as well as the business operation. There are several different ways to study the case. One way is to compare Figure 2.2 with Figure 5.1.

1. **Do you find it reasonable the way in which Electrolux has dealt with this market reasonably until 1980? How would you describe its former and existing marketing and financial problems?**

The question should divide the students into two categories supporting and criticizing EL's decision to stay. Some students may claim the decision was correct because they have invested in the country and they need to defend it. The next group may claim the decision was wrong because market turbulence is high and risky. The future is unclear and any further financial investment or market operation would cause an increase in costs. It would be interesting to penetrate further and discuss the reasons and further consequences of the decision for future marketing. Each decision (stay or leave) is associated with advantages and disadvantages both in the form of market investment and market operation. The tutor may have a chance to speculate on other kinds of market operation, e.g. exporting. Dividing students into the yes/no groups needs to be related to some of the issues in the book. The planning framework presented in Figure 2.1 may be used by the 'no' group, and the concepts presented in Chapter 5 may support 'yes'. Students should consider their answers with theories presented in the book.

2. **With the help of studies on risk management (traditional ones explaining high-risk leads to exit from the market) analyse the situation for the period 1970–1980. What would your analysis look like and what would your decision be?**

The literature on risk management tries to quantify marketing probabilities and therefore puts forward detailed plans for the future. The risk in market operations and investment is well discussed in the marketing literature. It mainly focuses on information gathering, strategy formulation, planning, and action. In such studies, risk can be estimated and uncertainty can be reduced by accumulation of information. This means that risk and uncertainty can be managed. According to this method, the company should have left the country a long time ago, perhaps in 1978. The question is how and why the evaluation by the course participants varies from the risk management literature as well as among themselves. This can also be related to Figure 1.4 in Chapter 1 of this book.

Students may refer to their general understanding of risk management and discuss the exit of the firm from the market. In reality we know that this did not happen. The firm really did not have any market operation strategy other than being in the market, despite the fact that it was expensive to the firm and the future was uncertain.

3. Concerning personal relationships and trust development, what would you recommend to Electrolux's manager?

An interesting matter is to help the participants to understand trust and also the dynamism in that trust. Moreover, they should also analyse trust at different levels, such as trust at the country, company, and individual levels. This can be connected to Chapter 4, Relationship Marketing, where trust is one of the fundamentals in any relationship. One specific and interesting area for this question is to examine trust at different levels. For example, the case shows trust at the country level (the neutrality of Sweden), at the firm and product levels (the high quality of the products), and at the individual level (the honesty of the Swedish managers in doing business).

4. Do you think it is an advantage or disadvantage to introduce a new person in this situation when considering the nature of the Islamic revolution?

The answer can be related to the question above. Since all business exchange was interrupted, the matter of trust had come under focus: the trust of the religious groups in the company and the personnel. Sending a new man required (a) a start from zero in the market, and (b) investment in the establishment of a new contact. Keeping the former manager may have reduced the costs for establishing new contacts but, on the other hand, it may have had other shortcomings. This question interrelates the concepts in Chapter 5 and Chapter 4. On one hand the matter of religion and culture is related to the environment in Chapter 5. On the other hand the issue of trust and behaviour is considered in Chapter 4. (Students can also compare the issue with other studies on social relationships, relationships marketing, business network studies.)

5. Do you think that the decision of the headquarters in reactivating marketing activities is correct?

The market is changing continually. The revolution is continuing and there is a war. There is lack of trust. A comparative answer would be interesting to understand the costs and benefits of such a decision in terms of market loss and market opportunities. In Chapter 5 there is a discussion of environmental change. The case can show the similarity of the case and the concepts in this chapter. The strategic decisions are also discussed in the book. The task is to relate concepts regarding such decisions to this case.

6. What is your strategic proposal for the future? What is your opinion about leaving the market given that the number of problems are increasing?

The company is faced with a high degree of uncertainty. It has difficulty managing it because conditions are always changing and also the manager has not much power in the market. Accordingly, the question is what to do so that the company does not lose too much. The question provides an opportunity to relate concepts discussed in Chapters 2 and 5 to the case. A comparison of students' answers with what actually happened can be made by reference to the next section in this teaching guide.

What really happened after 1984

The manager followed the local personnel to the local organizations to show his interest in the problem. It was also necessary to negotiate with the departments and convince the authorities about the need for and quality of the components. Since the personnel in these departments were new and had no deep technical knowledge, the problem was to make them understand the relationship between price and quality. Also each department revised the application from its own point of view, leading to contradictions.

During 1982–91, almost all the local managers in Savalux had had a university education. The problems were about their low level of business experience and their specific knowledge about home appliance products. But the fundamental problem was related to the management changes which specifically affected trust.

In every change at the managerial level, the business rules were different to the earlier ones. Sometimes they were contradictory. The manager had to start from the beginning with every new group. There were several reasons why every new manager established a positive relationship with the Swedish manager: (1) his residence in Iran when there was a war, (2) his enthusiasm in learning the language, and (3) his showing of interest in their business problems and assisting them. But still the local managers were a little suspicious about EL. The business could continue because of EL's local office in Iran.

However, the local manager succeeded in purchasing all the components for the refrigerators from local suppliers and after a short period became independent of EL. For the vacuum cleaners, they succeeded in reducing the value of the imported components from 80 per cent in 1978 to 50 per cent in 1990. The main components exported to Savalux were the motors. The managers gained such independency because (a) EL itself buys components from other suppliers, EL only produced motors and a few other important components; (b) purchase within the country led to a lower level of dependency on foreign exchange, which consequently increased the production and selling for Savalux, this resulted in more purchases of motors from EL; (c) the most valuable part of vacuum cleaners is the motor. Even for this component, Savalux was able to resort to local suppliers and became completely independent from EL. But Savalux was not able to gain access to the latest technology and also could not use EL's brand name. EL in 1989 introduced at Savalux a new technology for the production of vacuum cleaners.

The manager, by having Savalux as a point of departure, succeeded in expanding its contracts with several other firms. One of the firms, Arj, which specialized in the production of home appliances, was nationalized after the revolution and functioned under NIIO. The Swedish manager came into contact with Arj's leader in 1985 seeking a new production technology. When Arj's leader left the firm, the project became inactive, but the Swedish manager continued his contact with Arj's manager in NIIO. After a period Arj's manager became appointed by NIIO to lead another big home appliances company, called Pars Khasar, specializing in products like fans. The company lacked the technology for the production of refrigerators and the new manager asked the Swedish manager to sell the production process and also the main components. After negotiations with several state departments in 1989–1990, the first approval for the project, as well as foreign currency, was received. The production of refrigerators began in Pars Khasar but output was lower than at Savalux. It would take several years before Pars Khasar could reach the same production level as Savalux. EL had a five-year delivery contract with Pars Khasar.

The Swedish manager, meanwhile, also tried to expand EL in other business areas. In 1984 two Iranians visited Sweden and asked for industrial cleaning products. They were well-educated and knew the market. Their firm, Armita, had its major business in communication and electrical products. Before they travelled to Sweden, they had already met the manager in Iran. They had also discussed the matter with EL's international divisional manager when he was at the 1984 Tehran exhibition. Until 1984, they had no business relationships with EL but they knew about EL and their products. They knew about the market and wanted to fill the empty space in the market with EL's products. The divisional manager visited their premises and selling facilities, which were similar to firms in Western countries. On the recommendations from the manager in Iran and the divisional manager, Armita won the agency and began marketing. It was clear that EL, for the marketing of these products, needed a local organization which followed the political changes and had the necessary managerial and technical ability. Armita had already established relationships with public and industrial organizations for other products. The selling value was very low for the period 1984–1988 because of the war. But during the last years (1988–1991) sales had increased 5 per cent every year. From total sales of 560 MSEK in 1991, about 35 MSEK was for EL's products. This value was 70 per cent of the total annual import of the industrial and public cleaning appliances. In 1991, Armita was the best seller for EL's industrial cleaning products in the Middle East. From the beginning of the relationship the chief manager in Armita travelled to Sweden 2–4 times each year. The same principle was used for the engineers and technical service personnel.

As mentioned earlier, during the years 1984 and 1985 there were no foreign competitors in the country, the products in the market were supplied by local firms and the import was organized by private financiers. The competitors from Germany, Italy, and Japan used to send managers occasionally to check the market. The market was evaluated as risky and uncertain. Especially when Iraq was bombing Tehran, foreigners became frightened of staying in Iran. After the war, competitors returned. Reluctantly, even American firms came back to Iran. Armita's old established relationship with the buyers, together with the supply of a fully dedicated system of cleaning and food services by EL products, strengthened its market position. Providing a total system, including service and training, gave a strong competitive advantage. The competitors were new and had mainly focused on selling individual products and not the whole system.

Until 1991, the selling of home appliances was managed by the Swedish manager. As mentioned earlier, during 1980–1982 there was no selling. In 1993, the manager succeeded in entering the market and became familiar with the new marketing rules. Consequently, sales increased. With assistance from subsidiaries in the neighbouring countries, especially Dubai, he succeeded in increasing the selling quantity to more than 50,000 in 1984–1985. After this period the number of competitors following the same approach had increased. The shortage of foreign-currency led to very turbulent selling. Sales in 1987 were satisfactory but fell in such a manner that in 1988 and 1989 sales were very low. In 1990 and 1991 the government changed the rules. The import of these home appliances became free. This freedom was given only to the Iranian firms. The foreign firms were refused permission to enter into such business. The Swedish manager was looking for a partner.

Veraste was back in Iran because of the general amnesty in 1990. The amnesty was for all rich and non-political people who had left Iran after the revolution. The government, which had nationalized Varaste's ownership in Savalux, started negotiations with Varaste about his shares. His share in the firm had dropped to 12 per cent because of the costs paid by the new owners. EL's ownership had also dropped to 6.5 per cent for the same reason. This meant that in reality there were very few changes in Savalux's ownership. EL had kept its ownership; Ebba's ownership, which belonged to the government in the Shah's time, was now managed by another state department, Omran Nosazi; and Varaste's ownership was under revision.

Varaste had a contact with another firm, Mesbahi. The Swedish manager became acquainted with the two managers in Mesbahi who were well-educated and had good knowledge of the market. In 1991 they became EL's agent for selling home appliances. The Swedish manager left Iran since the agencies were to undertake his duties. This meant that the manager during his residence had succeeded in expanding EL's sales in the market. The main reason for success was having a local office during the crisis. Once the political situation had improved, the manager could meet some of the managers socially and build personal relationships.

By 1990–1993, there were several competitors for home appliances. Besides products from Germany, Italy, Switzerland, England, Japan, and South Korea, American products were also available in the market. There was hard competition among these firms. The price of some of the products was 20–30 per cent lower than EL's products. Mesbahi had paid attention to service and Swedish quality. The firm had become active in the last 6 months and had made some selling progress. But now it was faced with selling problems, mainly because the firm was new and small. It also focused on private buyers with changing behaviour. The competitors had a lower price and a high level of advertising and service. Firms selling Swiss, Japanese, and German products received intensive backing from their parent companies for service and marketing.

Figure 2 illustrates the sales during 1972–1982.

For the years 1983–1990 there are no specific numbers. But in general the sales were as follows for EL's products:

1983	fair	1992	better than before
1984	very good	1993	worse because of the financial crises
1985	very good		
1986	good		
1987	bad		
1989	bad		
1990	relatively good		
1991	relatively bad		

	Refrigerators	Vacuum cleaners
1972	0	0
1973	0	0
1974	4000	1000
1975	5000	3000
1976	7000	10000
1977	8000	15000
1978	8000	30000
1979	0	10000
1980	50000	8000
1981	0	0
1982	0	0

For the components

	Refrigerators	Vacuum cleaners
1978	0	36000
1979	0	12000
1980	50000	11000
1981	0	0
1982	0	0

Sales in Savalux

	Refrigerators	Vacuum cleaners
1977	0	0
1978	0	35000
1979	0	20000
1980	15000	50000
1981	0	0
1982	0	0

Figure 2 Sales for the fabricated items.

Case 8

Wetsuits

Synopsis

Gul, the UK's leader in wetsuits, is facing a strategic problem. After some 30 years of steady growth, particularly throughout the consumer boom of the 1980s, sales are plateauing. As part of its response the company has expanded its product range into related areas hopefully attractive to its existing customers, e.g. clothing, neoprene boots, gloves, hoods, water-resistant watches, body boards, etc.

However, Gul is facing increasing competition both from other UK suppliers (Sola, Typhoon, Spartan, etc.) and imports O'Neal (USA) and Billabong (Australia). A decision has to be made as to how to respond to this increasingly competitive position in a mature market.

Teaching Objectives

1. To develop an understanding on what fundamentally causes markets to grow, be in maturity, or decline.
2. To identify and evaluate appropriate marketing objectives and actions for a brand leader in a mature market.
3. To identify and evaluate appropriate marketing objectives and actions for a brand follower in a mature market.

Suggested Teaching Approach

When asked what causes a market to grow, students will frequently offer a technological response pointing to an increase in sales, marketing mix activities pushing the demand curve to the right, and perhaps the emergence of a new market segment.

- If the number of consumers in any given market is increasing, and furthermore they are, per head, increasing their usage/consumption of a product, a market is likely to be in *growth*.
- If the number of consumers in any given market is about static, and furthermore they are, per head, consuming the product at a replacement level only, a market is likely to be in *maturity*.
- If the number of consumers in any given market is decreasing, and furthermore they are, per head, decreasing their usage/consumption of the product, a market is likely to be in *decline*.

Using this type of argument, students can be asked if they think the UK wetsuit market really is in maturity, or whether the current level of sales is a temporary phenomenon. What kind of

---

This teaching note was prepared by David Cook, Lecturer in Marketing, University of Bradford Management Centre, UK.

environment change might reactivate UK demand? Is it possible for Gul to do anything to trigger such a change, e.g. lobbying the government to legislate that all lifeboats carry not only life-jackets but fully protective body suits for survivors of any capsize or sea disaster? Naturally enough, such a new market opportunity would require product adaptation especially concerning the ease with which the suit could be put on in adverse conditions.

1. Strategic objectives

A useful general paradigm for strategies in mature markets is shown below:

		Business positions in key segments	
		STRONG	WEAK
Industry Environment			
Rate of sales growth or decline. Existence of strong pockets of demand	FAVOURABLE	BUILD OR HOLD 1	HARVEST OR EXIT 2
Degree of price/ margin pressure	UNFAVOURABLE	HARVEST OR EXIT 3	EXIT 4

Students can be asked where they would classify Gul on such a matrix. In the majority of cases they will opt for Cell 1 with a consequent strategic objective of either *build* or *hold*.

If students assess the maturity to be caused by limitations in the company's present marketing activity, a *build* strategy would be logical. It would be possible either to increase share in a static market, or, via revitalized marketing, restart the market into a further growth phase (as shown in Figure 3).

Possible options here could include:

- Converting non-users
- Increasing multiple ownership
- Increasing the frequency of use and, in the longer term, replacement demand.
- Development of underdeveloped product/market sectors, e.g. by geography/overseas markets or alternative new uses
- Persuading competitors' customers to switch brands

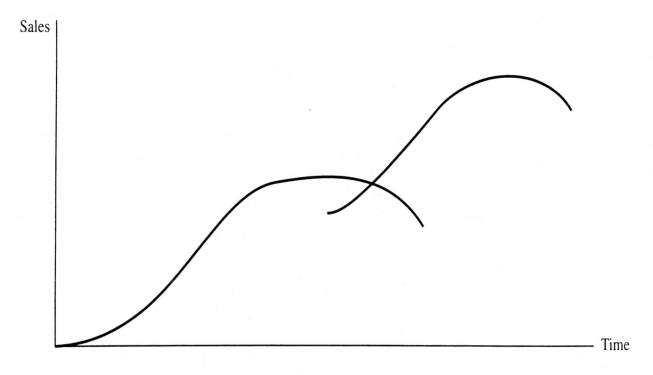

Sales

Time

Figure 3

If students assess the maturity to be structural, and think competitors are unlikely to yield their customers, a *hold* strategy would be logical.

2. Generic strategy: Differentiation/low cost

The case also provides an opportunity to introduce the idea of generic strategies.

Hall, in his study of eight mature industries, pointed out that the two leading firms offered either high relative produce differentiation or the lowest delivered cost. In most cases, the industries' ROI leader opted for one of the strategies, while the second ROI leader placed company followed the other. It is not impossible (cf. Heinz) but difficult to follow both simultaneously. It is likely that the larger margins probably associated with a low-cost generic strategy would not support medium/long-term differentiation.

Students can be asked to consider how each of the classic ways to achieve differentiation and low cost might be applied to wetsuits.

(i) Differentiation

Possible method	Possible application
Functional performance	• Make the suit stronger/warmer via the use of titanium-lined neoprene; ankle and wrist straps; 100 per cent waterproof zips and neck seals; heat-sealed blind stitch; taped seams, etc.
Durability	• Heavy-duty brass non-corrosive zips; fitting heavy-duty knee pads.
Conformance to specification	• Commitment to quality control by clearly showing a label stitched into the suit showing the name of the inspector and the date of inspection.
Reliability	• Build quality attributes into the product and brand name over time, e.g. Gul—The Original Wetsuits—Bathe in the Suit on the Cornish Atlantic Coast.
Serviceability	• Offer a warranty scheme with every purchase and ensure a fast, responsive, and accurate repair service. • While suit is away being repaired, offer the opportunity to hire a nearly new suit.
Fit and finish	• Ensure specification adhered to via quality control. • Display product design to ensure suit is distinctive and yet fashionable. • Pay attention to the thickness (2, 3, 4 and 5 mm normally) and smoothness of materials. • Design-in comfort especially under the arms and around the forearms. Both these areas are critical to windsurfers.
Brand reputation	• Pay particular attention to the communication mix, i.e. — sponsorship of key sailors — advertising in specialist magazines — attendance at exhibitions, e.g. The Boat Show — ensure sales literature and leaflets available in the retail outlets.

(ii) Low cost

Possible method	Possible application
No frills product	• Offer a basic non-fashion product aimed at the price-conscious consumer, perhaps as part of an introductory kit offer for a sport, e.g. wet-suit, buoyancy aid, plus skis for water-skiing.
Innovative product design	• Develop a low-cost design e.g. perhaps a one piece moulded suit not requiring joins.
Innovative production	• Perhaps linked to product design and for manufacturers overseas. Retain the value-added design skills, but subcontract manufacture. This approach is used both by windsurf sail manufacturers (made in Hong Kong/China) and squash racket manufacturers (made in Taiwan).
Low cost distribution	• Concentrate on larger key accounts in a highly fragmented retail industry.
Reduce overhead	• 'Me too' products: new product ideas/innovations developed by others because of the absence of patent protection and low technological barriers.

3. Share leader—build strategic objective

Gul has three basic options to enact a build strategy:

• Increased penetration of the existing actual and potential market
• Persuading existing users to use their equipment more frequently
• Seek new customer groups either by use or geography

The volume of sales in a given target market is a function of the number of potential customers, the penetration of the potential customer base, and the number of times the product is used. Using this type of thinking it would be possible for Gul to argue that:

• All those who participate in windsurfing or water-skiing but do not own a wet-suit, represent potential as compared to existing demand.
• One possible way to contact these potential customers would be while they were in the learning stages, i.e. on an introductory course. If a hire charge for a Gul suit were included as part of the course fee, potential customers would not only be introduced to the brand name and the benefits of a Gul suit but also at the end of the course the hire charge could be offset against the purchase price. Such practice is regularly used by manufacturers of snow skis and musical instruments.

- On successful completion of their introductory course, students could be given an introduction to their local club which would encourage attendance at club evenings, days, and events and consequently equipment usage.

For existing non-Gul wetsuit owners the 4-Ps need to be designed to deliver sufficiently strong reason (differential advantage) to switch brands in the rebuying situation. As a wetsuit with average use may be expected to last for 3–5 years minimum, the use of an annual update of the product range using design, fashion, and new product features should be considered to encourage repeat purchases and brand switching. An additional way of acquiring competitor's customers is to acquire the competitor!

To encourage extended use it is necessary to know why owners of wetsuits leave them hanging up in a cupboard rather than actually deploying them both on and in the water. Beyond conducting formal market research to establish reasons for non-use, the names generated by the returns of guarantee cards could be used as an appropriate database for relationship marketing techniques. Specifically reminder joint promotions and newsletters could be used alongside such organizations as the RYA (Royal Yacht Association), the UK Windsurfing and Water Skiing Associations, the BTA (British Tourist Association), sailing resorts, and locations around the UK, including recognized teaching schools such as West Wales Windsurfing and Sailing at Dale and Plan Menai at Menai Straights in South and North Wales respectively.

Market expansion could include seeking new geographic markets (globalization), identifying new segments, e.g. persuading ocean-going, and particularly dinghy, sailors to wear maybe a modified wetsuit, and possibly entering the own-label market, e.g. Olympus.

4. Share leader—hold strategic objective

To pursue a hold strategy, Gul would need to enhance customer satisfaction/loyalty and consequently encourage/supply repeat purchases. This could be attempted either via the differentiation or the low-cost route. The former is likely to involve such activity as, *inter alia*, stressing quality control, the search for product improvements, emphasis on the brand name via advertising, trade promotion, sponsorship, etc., and the strengthening of customer service, for example via on-time delivery, in-stock availability, and retailer training. The latter clearly would involve all ways to achieve low delivered cost including process improvements/material substitution, but not to the disadvantage of customer perceived quality, overhead control, etc.

Whichever route to achieve a hold strategy was followed it would be vital to guarantee that the brand was within a customer's evoked set whether an original or repeat purchase was being considered. While the role of word of mouth would not be discounted, effective distribution incorporating retailer support, stock availability in store, supplies of sales literature/product information with appropriate pre-announcement of new season product lines/fashions, colour, logo, and technical specifications would be vital. This would need to be supportive to any magazine advertising and promotions at special events/exhibitions.

Should Gul as leader be affected by a low-cost supplier, then the two most likely responses would be either direct competition or flanker.

Possible applications for a confrontation strategy could include:

- New product development

  — extra thermal protection via the use of new materials, zips, sealing methods, etc.;
  — increased comfort;
  — the inclusion within the wetsuit of an integrated thermal bed for winter;
  — the design into the wetsuit of an SOS device to assist in any search and rescue mission. (Such devices are designed with some snow suits made by Hevica.)

- Revitalized marketing by Gul which may include:

  — the use of new distribution channels, e.g. mail order with trails and advertisements on alternative media channels, e.g. Sky Sports and perhaps eventually BBC Radio 5;
  — the redesign of the channels of distribution using franchised stores at selected holiday/course/event venues;
  — sponsored events;
  — joint ventures/promotions with other major suppliers to the windsurfing industry, e.g. Mistia or F2 (boards), Tushingham (sails).

A flanker strategy could include the development of a new type of sail for a new use, e.g. a one-piece suit to protect the skin against corrosive materials, or the development of an undersuit for skydiving and parachuting.

5. Share follower

If the share follower companies are of the view that the share leader is aggressive, dynamic and highly likely to respond strongly to any direct challenge to its market share position, a head-on challenge strategy would not be viable. Logical strategies to consider would include:

- Niche
- Guerrilla
- Follower

Case 9

Alcan

Synopsis

This case study focuses upon the development and launch of a major new initiative designed to increase the public's awareness of the benefits of recycling aluminium cans.

Teaching Objectives

The case can be used to illustrate a variety of issues including:

1. The development of a new marketing strategy.
2. Measures of success.
3. The characteristics of the customer innovation process.
4. Dimensions of environmentalism.
5. The ways in which a competitor (in this case the steel can makers) might possibly respond to a major push from the aluminium industry.
6. The significance of an innovative and entrepreneurial managerial culture and the problems that might possibly arise in grafting this on to the organization that traditionally has reflected a strong production orientation.

Suggested Teaching Approach

The sorts of areas that might be covered in order to stimulate discussions are:

1. Identification and evaluation of AACR's marketing strategy during the period covered by the case

The strategy was made up of five principal strands:

- The initiative aimed at the individual consumer which was designed to encourage them to collect cans over several weeks or months and then take them either to a buy-back centre or to a mobile van collection point in return for cash.
- A campaign that was targeted at schools, charities and other groups which illustrated how can collecting could raise significant sums of money for items that they might otherwise not be able to afford.
- Links with retail chains to increase the number of collection points, thereby making the task of recycling easier for the consumer.

This teaching note was prepared by Colin Gilligan, Professor of Marketing, and Lanchezar Christoff, Research Assistant, Sheffield Hallam University, UK.

- The development of a network of third-party collectors whose role was to collect aluminium in various forms for baling and sale to Alcan.
- A major initiative that was aimed at can fillers in order to encourage them to shift from steel to aluminium on their filling lines.

Using this framework as the starting point, tutors might ask the group to identify how the potential and value of each target group might possibly be identified. They might then move on to a discussion of the sorts of problems that might be encountered in co-ordinating a marketing programme across these five areas. In doing this, it should become apparent that the co-ordination of the marketing effort aimed at the first two of these (individual consumers and groups of consumers) should be relatively straightforward, since the motivations are broadly similar. Quite obviously, a degree of message tailoring will be necessary, but this should not create any real difficulties once the idea of cash for cans has been communicated. The initiative aimed at the retail chains should follow on from this but is only really likely to succeed if retailers have firm evidence over a sustained period that reasonably large numbers of consumers are committed to the idea of aluminium can recycling. Without this evidence, it is almost inevitable that they would be unwilling to get involved. Students might therefore be asked about the sorts of factors that are likely to motivate each of these groups. The sorts of points that might emerge include:

- *Individuals:* the financial return that comes from collecting cans that would otherwise be thrown away and/or a belief that in a world of scarce resources we should do whatever we can to help the recycling movement (there is some evidence that the first of these is more important for people from the poorer socio-economic groups).
- *Groups:* a unity of purpose, a tangible end result (product that the group would not otherwise be able to buy), and in the case of schools, a demonstration of the benefits and importance of recycling.
- *Retailers:* a public statement of the organization's commitment to socially responsible behaviour.

In the case of the third-party collectors, the primary motivation is almost inevitably commercial. For Bronze collectors, the price guarantee given by Alcan is an obvious attraction, while for the Silver and Gold collectors, the various additional benefits of dealing with AACR are an added and significant bonus.

The initiative aimed at the can fillers is obviously crucial, since the larger the number of cans in circulation, the greater the scope of any recycling operation. Students might therefore be asked to identify and consider the sorts of factors that might encourage a filler to shift either totally or partially from steel to aluminium. The sorts of points that should emerge from this include the comparative costs of the two materials; whether there are any differences in the ease of filling; the relative weights and transportation costs; any possible storage problems (might the lighter weight of the aluminium lead to it denting more easily?); the implications for printing on the can; and the filler's commitment to environmentalism.

2. Measures of success

The success of the programme can be measured in a variety of ways, including the proportion of cans that are put into the recycling loop; AACR's market share of this; the growth of the operation (the numbers of buy-back centres, third-party collectors, retail outlets, etc.); the publicity given to Alcan's environmental initiative; the extent to which the capacity of the Warrington recycling plant

66

is used; and, of course, the profitability of the operation. In discussing these points, one comment that must be made is that the case study covers the period from the launch in 1989 through to 1993. Given the long-term nature of most marketing campaigns and Alcan's stated commitment to recycling, students should recognize that short-term and long-term objectives are likely to differ and that any measures of success obviously need to reflect this.

3. The characteristics of the customer innovation process

We have already touched upon some of the motivations of those involved in recycling aluminium cans. However, the discussion can be taken a step further by asking students to consider whether the diffusion of innovation curve that was developed by Rogers and which classifies people as innovators, early adopters, the early and late majority, or laggards is at all useful in helping to explain patterns of behaviour and attitudes to recycling.

In the very broad terms, the evidence that exists seems to suggest that it was the young rather than the old who were the first to become concerned about environmental issues and who have shown the greatest sustained commitment to recycling. Students might therefore be asked how this should be reflected in any subsequent marketing programme and how factors other than age might be of significance (social class, peer group behaviour, etc.). This might then lead to a discussion of how environmentally friendly behaviour might be categorized (e.g. dark green consumers who have a very strong commitment to environmentalism and who reflect this in nearly every aspect of their buying behaviour, through to light greens).

4. Dimensions of environmentalism

This should follow on fairly logically from the previous section, with students being asked to identify examples of good and bad environmental practice, and how, if at all, organizations might be expected to make a trade-off between environmentally sensitive behaviour and profit.

5. The ways in which the steel can manufacturers might respond

With the aluminium industry having taken the initiative in the recycling debate, the steel industry is in the position of having to fight back aggressively or risk losing the battle completely. However, whether the steel can makers would see this to be a *really* important battleground has been questioned, since cans represent a less important market for the steel industry than for the aluminium companies. Assuming that they do decide to fight back, any campaign would probably need to focus upon the lower energy costs involved in producing a steel can. The aluminium industry might feasibly then respond by highlighting lifetime costs (their claim that it is easier to recycle aluminium without any degradation of the material, the lower transportation costs, etc.). If the steel industry wanted to engage in a 'dirty tricks' campaign, they might possibly resurrect the controversy that emerged in the 1980s about the possibility of a link between aluminium and Alzheimer's disease. However, the aluminium industry could then respond to this by highlighting that aluminium cans have an internal lacquer so that the food or drink that the can contains does not come into contact with the aluminium, and that the link has not been proven anyway.

6. The significance of an innovative and entrepreneurial managerial culture

With any new initiative, particularly if it is being taken by a division of a far larger organization, there is always a danger that bureaucratic demands and inertia will inhibit creativity and entrepreneurial behaviour. Students might therefore be encouraged to identify what is meant by innovation and entrepreneurialism and how the structure and patterns of behaviour in large organizations tends to work against these. The sorts of issues that might realistically be raised include managerial risk aversion, a commitment to existing procedures, a lack of an obvious focus, etc. Students should then be encouraged to consider how these barriers might possibly be overcome. This might then be used as the basis for a discussion of the role of product champions, venture teams, the importance of the attitudes of senior management and their commitment to innovation, the development of a risk-taking culture, a willingness to experiment, flatter hierarchies, a greater degree of employee empowerment, the clear allocation of funds for new product/service and market development, and a recognition of the problems of short termism.

Case 10

Hansen Bathrooms (A)

Synopsis

A traditional bathroom manufacturer has a pricing problem. A new bathroom range coated with a substance that repels grime and grease is to be launched after extensive product testing. Hansen's usual pricing formula produces a figure below that charged by their competitors.

Teaching Objectives

1. To discuss the limitations of cost-based pricing.
2. To explore the role of price in positioning a product in the marketplace.
3. To examine the influence of marketing-oriented factors on the pricing decision.

Suggested Teaching Approach

This case can be used as part of a seminar session or at the end of a lecture on pricing to crystalize the concepts discussed.

1. If you were Susan, would you agree or disagree with Rob Vincent's proposal?

Vincent seems set on charging a price less than the competition but his focus is on costs rather than customers' willingness to pay. Customers do not evaluate products on how much they cost to make but the value they receive from them.

Marketing research has shown that the coating extended the period between cleaning from two weeks to three months, a change that delighted customers. This is an example of a *differential advantage* and Vincent needs to consider the extra value compared to the competition. It would appear that the added benefits offered by the coating would justify a higher price. Susan should suggest that Rob should pause to consider other issues that may affect the pricing decision.

2. What other factors should be taken into account?

Figure 10.2 'Marketing-orientated pricing' provides the framework for answering this question. Each factor will be briefly addressed.

Marketing: The bathroom range needs to be carefully positioned in the marketplace. This means deciding the target market and establishing the strength of the differential advantage. The target

This teaching note was prepared by David Jobber.

market would appear to be those people who value the benefits of cleaning the bathroom every three months rather than every two weeks. Households with both partners in paid employment is one obvious target segment. Since they have two incomes, they are likely to be able to afford a premium price. In qualitative terms, the differential advantage would appear to be very strong for them.

Value to the customer: The benefits of the coating do seem to confer added value.

Price–quality relationships: A low price (compared to competition) may infer low quality. A premium price is consistent with the positioning of the product as providing added value.

Explicability: Since the coating is exclusive to Hansen, it is not unreasonable to suppose that the bathroom costs more to produce than the competition. Therefore the price is easily 'explained'.

Product line pricing: Vincent and Clements need to price position the new bathroom suite carefully within their existing product range.

Competition: They also need to take into account competitors' prices and reactions. A price lower than the competition and yet giving a differential advantage may cause rivals to lower their price to become competitive, thereby reducing the attractiveness of the market.

Negotiating margins: A high list price to retailers provides negotiating room to bargain with powerful retailing groups.

Affect on distributors and retailers: A high price gives them a bigger absolute profit margin.

Political factors: Not likely to be relevant.

Costs: The cost of producing the bathroom suite may be lower than the competition perhaps because the coating is inexpensive to produce and Hansen benefits from greater economies of scale than its rivals. However, this is an opportunity for large profit margins rather than a signal that it should charge a lower price.

3.   What alternative strategies exist, if any?

The alternative strategies are given in Figure 10.4 'New product launch strategies'. Given the above analysis, the large target market and the need to communicate the benefits of the coating, a rapid skimming strategy would appear to be the most sensible approach assuming that Hansen Bathrooms has sufficient resources to support it.

Case 11

The 'Green' House

Synopsis

A different type of house was offered on the market by a small building firm: one that was environmentally friendly. The house included many energy-saving features that were both good for the environment and saved money.

Teaching Objectives

1. To show the relationship between target audience, development of an advertising platform, and advertising execution.
2. To provide an opportunity for students to create an advertisement unencumbered by the need to create visuals to support the headline and body copy.

Suggested Teaching Approach

Students can be asked to answer the questions at the end of the case in syndicate groups. This can be followed by classroom presentations. Alternatively, the case can be used as an individually assessed assignment.

1. Who is the type of buyer likely to be interested in buying a 'green' house?

The key issue here is whether there are sufficient numbers of people willing to buy this house for altruistic (environmentally friendly) reasons only. It is more likely that most people who may be interested in the house would do so for a combination of personal (cost saving) and altruistic reasons.

The type of buyer is, therefore, likely to want the benefits of saving money while at the same time experience the 'feel good' factor of helping the environment. This was not immediately appreciated by the builders who initially advertised the house (unsuccessfully) on a solely environmentally friendly basis.

2. Develop an advertising platform to appeal to them.

The advertising platform is the foundation on which advertising messages are built. It should be important to the target audience and communicate competitive advantages.

This teaching note was prepared by David Jobber.

The platform for advertising this house should be based on cost saving and its environmentally friendly attributes. Both are important to the target audience and since the house was the only one of its kind in the area, the platform communicated its competitive advantages.

3. **Bearing in mind that the funds restrict the advertisement to a maximum of 8 cm high × 10 cm wide, design an advertisement for the house. Note that space precludes the use of a photograph.**

The headline and body copy need to reflect the advertising platform. The headline is the attention getter and should therefore include both appeals. 'THE HOUSE THAT'S FRIENDLY TO THE ENVIRONMENT—AND YOUR POCKET' is one option.

The body copy should support the headline by presenting the evidence, and should contain essential information. Given the limited space, decisions have to be made regarding what information must be left out of the advertisement and included in the supporting literature which will be given to interested people. For example, 'the loft has 30 cm of non-irritant brown cellulose, made from recycled newsprint. Under the floor there is a 10 cm layer of CFC-free polystyrene' may have to be reduced to '30 cm of loft and 10 cm of underfloor insulation using environmentally friendly materials'.

By rewording the product features, students will be amazed at how much relevant information can be contained in an 8 cm × 10 cm advertisement.

The issue of the choice of media may also arise. Some newspapers are more likely to be read by people concerned with the environment than others (e.g. *The Guardian*). The problem is that using national newspapers (even those that allow regional advertising) is costly and wasteful since many readers will be located outside of the local area from which a buyer is most likely to be found. The builders actually advertised in *The Guardian* initially but received no enquiries. The successful formula was to advertise in the local newspaper with an advertisement based on the twin appeals recommended in this teaching note.

Case 12

Selling Exercise

Synopsis

A customer enters a shop to buy a torch. The salesperson has a range of six torches with very different product features and prices.

Teaching Objectives

1. To give realism to the principles of selling discussed in Chapter 12.
2. To provide an opportunity for students to practice personal selling skills.

Suggested Teaching Approach

This exercise has been used very successfully with undergraduates, MBA students, and delegates on post-experience courses. Although the situation is a retail outlet, the exercise can be used to teach selling skills for almost any sales situation since the principles remain valid.

The approach taken by the author is to ask for three volunteers to act as salespeople, with the instructor acting as the customer. Each sales interview is video-recorded privately and then each recording is played back to the whole class. Discussion begins by asking the salesperson to describe their strengths and weaknesses before opening the analysis to the rest of the class.

A well-tried approach is for the customer to answer the question 'What is the torch to be used for?' by stating that it is for his/her son who has won a painting competition. The prize is a camping holiday and the torch is to be used for camping.

The key issue is that the customer wants a spread beam so that his/her son can see the guy ropes when walking between tents at night. It is the salesperson's job to identify this need by appropriate *questioning*.

Once this information is revealed a salesperson with good *product knowledge* (they are allowed to keep the product details with them in the role play) will know that torches A and D fulfil those needs. Invariably they will start by suggesting A (possibly because it is more expensive).

This provides the opportunity for the customer to raise the *objection* 'I have one of those in my car. I could give my son that one for the weekend instead of buying one.' The look on the salesperson's face at this point can be quite amusing!

This teaching note was prepared by David Jobber.

By rejecting torch A (because it is too bulky) the customer leaves the salesperson with one suitable torch, D. The customer then asks 'It's not made in the Far East is it?' This is designed to illustrate a situation when the salesperson should *question the objection* (e.g. why is that a problem?). This then identifies the underlying issue: there can be a number of potential reasons for the objection/question (e.g. product unreliability, relative of a World War II prisoner, exploited labour). Until the salesperson knows the answer he/she cannot deal with it. By stating product unreliability as the issue, the salesperson has the opportunity to use an *agree and counter with a reference sell*, i.e. 'Yes that used to be the case a few years ago but Far Eastern products are extremely reliable now. I have sold dozens of these torches and have never had one complaint.'

The salesperson should then issue a *buying signal* (e.g. 'that looks fine'). Whether the salesperson *closes the sale* at that point is often a discussion point (as is the question of whether batteries are sold with the torch).

The instructor should plan to raise two or three learning points with each video-playback. The session can be drawn to a conclusion by stating that successful selling does not rely on slick, fast-talking showmanship, but a concern for understanding customer needs, and the willingness to help solve customers' problems (i.e. to find a suitable torch) based on questioning skills and product knowledge. With practice this exercise can be highly successful when teaching newcomers the art of selling. With three volunteers the playback session usually takes one-and-a-half hours.

        Case 13

        Tetley Bitter

Synopsis

The Joshua Tetley Brewery, based in Leeds, is part of Carlsberg-Tetley and is most famous for its leading brand Tetley Bitter, which has high penetration levels in the North of England, particularly Yorkshire. This position is not mirrored in the Midlands and South of the country. The case study illustrates the use of sports sponsorship to develop awareness of the brand in new geographic markets.

Teaching Objectives

The case is designed to highlight the differences between advertising and sponsorship, and stresses the need to secure a fit between the image or products of the sponsor and the sponsored activity. Sponsorship programmes are optimized through the application of a systematic framework for their management, and students are encouraged to identify the key steps in this process.

Suggested Teaching Approach

1. Is sponsorship just another form of advertising?

Although advertising and sponsorship are both elements of the communication mix, sponsorship offers benefits which are difficult to achieve by advertising alone. Differences between advertising and sponsorship have been identified in the literature in relation to issues of control, message, implementation, motivation, and audience reaction. While advertising is viewed by the public as solely benefiting the company, sponsorship offers tangible benefits for sport, arts, community, etc., which generate feelings of goodwill towards the sponsor. Figure 4 highlights several features of sponsorship which provide added value and enhance mainstream advertising.

The flexible nature of sponsorship is such that it can fulfil multiple simultaneous objectives in relation to a broad range of target constituencies. It is this versatility which has presented difficulties in classifying it within the marketing mix and locating it within the organization's functional areas of operation.

A key distinction between advertising and sponsorship is the degree of leverage necessary to optimize its effectiveness. The sponsorship fee invariably represents the starting point and additional promotional activity is necessary to exploit the relationship.

This teaching note was prepared by Des Thwaites, Senior Lecturer in Marketing, School of Business and Economic Studies, University of Leeds, UK, and Nicola Eastwood, Marketing and Sponsorship Assistant, Carlsberg-Tetley.

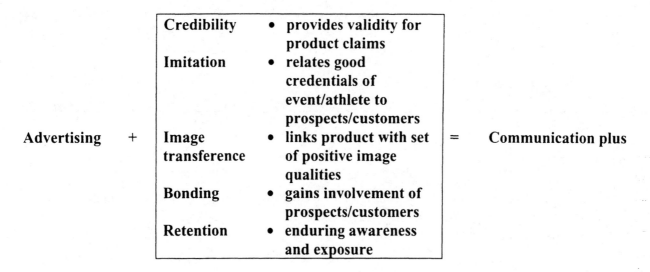

Figure 4 Adding value through sponsorship. (Source: adapted from Marshall, 1993.)

2. To what extent is there compatibility between the Tetley Bitter brand and cricket?

The choice of the activity to sponsor is fundamental to the ultimate success of the venture. A body of research evidence suggests that the company and the sponsored activity should be compatible. This degree of fit can occur at various levels:

Product linkage: The product is related to the sponsored activity. For example, an oil or tyre company sponsoring motor racing or a sports drink or energy food company sponsoring an athletics meeting (Mars and the London Marathon).

Product image linkage: The image created by the product relates to the sponsored activity. For example, a jeans manufacturer sponsoring a pop concert.

Corporate image linkage: The image created by the organization is related to the sponsored activity. For example, a bank providing support for a Chair in Financial Services Marketing or funding a student business game.

By ensuring these linkages are present, target audiences can more easily understand and accept the relationship between sponsor and sponsee.

Tutors may also wish to discuss with students the moral arguments relating to sponsorship of sport by tobacco companies and brewers. Some of these issues are aired in Meerabeau *et al.* (1991).

In the context of Tetley Bitter the brand values related to quality and tradition. Cricket also has strong traditions both nationally and in Yorkshire where the brand is produced. Bitter drinking is associated with a 'macho image' which is similar to that characterized by sportsmen. The profile of bitter drinkers is very similar to that of many cricket followers and, critically, the media coverage of cricket through television, radio, and newspapers is compatible with the media interests of the target audience.

3. What are the major stages in an effective sponsorship programme?

By developing a systematic framework for sponsorship management, organizations will increase their effectiveness and derive greater benefit from this adaptable medium. While there are many activities which contribute to an effective sponsorship programme, the following stages are of particular importance.

Stage 1 Review of corporate objectives and marketing plan

At an early stage it is important to determine corporate objectives and assess the marketing contribution to these. The various elements of the marketing mix can then be combined to achieve competitive advantages. The role of sponsorship activity within the communication mix can then be established. Integration of these elements is an important precursor to the development of an effective sponsorship programme. It is also necessary at an early stage to establish where functional responsibility for sponsorship lies.

Stage 2 Setting and prioritizing sponsorship objectives

Sponsorship provides a mechanism for achieving a range of objectives at both corporate and brand level. Figure 5 summarizes the general pattern which emerges from the literature. In the context of the case it is clear that Tetley's have developed their programme at the brand level. The provision of quantitative objectives will facilitate evaluation at a later stage.

Brand	Corporate
Characteristics	
Short term	Longer term
Market led	Corporate affairs led
Decided at brand level	Decided at board level
Payback tightly quantified	More speculative
Aimed at brand users and potential users	Aimed at opinion followers
Objectives	
Media coverage	Community involvement
Sales leads	Public awareness
Sales/market share	Increase/change public perception/image
Target market awareness	Build goodwill among opinion formers/trade relations
Guest hospitality	Staff relations/recruitment

Figure 5 Characteristics and objectives of brand and corporate sponsorship.
(Source: Thwaites, 1995.)

Stage 3 Evaluation and selection of sponsorship proposals

This stage seeks to assess the benefits of each proposal in terms of predetermined criteria such as cost, impact, image, and fit with the organization's values. Weighting scales can be used to give priority to particular features. For example, Irwin and Asimakopoulos (1992) provide a comprehensive list of marketing and management dimensions grouped under seven headings:

- Budget considerations
- Event management
- Positioning/Image
- Targeting of market
- Integrated communications
- Competition considerations
- Strategies

For illustration, budget considerations can be broken down into affordability, cost effectiveness, and tax benefits. Each of these are then weighted to reflect their importance (1 = extremely insignificant; 10 = extremely significant). Proposals received from potential sponsees can then be considered and scores allocated. (Irwin and Asimakopoulos suggest a range of –4 to +4, representing extremely weak to extremely strong.) By weighting each of the marketing and management dimensions and then rating each proposal on each dimension it is possible to produce a summation of all dimension scores and thereby prioritize different sponsorship proposals.

Stage 4 Implementation

Following the evaluation and selection of the particular event or activity, attention focuses on implementation. Good communication between sponsor and sponsee are important, as is the need to integrate the various elements of the programme through a variety of media. The sponsorship must also complement other marketing activities which are being undertaken. Leverage of the sponsorship through additional advertising and promotional expenditure is a critical success factor at this stage. The case highlights the broad range of media which Tetley have used to exploit the sponsorship. While the degree of leverage will depend upon the inclusive nature of the contract, figures at least equal to the sponsorship fee are commonly cited in the literature.

Stage 5 Evaluation

This is an area of debate in so far as it has been suggested that the effects of sponsorship are not capable of measurement. Several reasons for this are advanced (Meenaghan, 1983):

- The simultaneous use of ingredients within both the communication and marketing mix
- The carry-over effect of earlier activities
- Synergy derived from marketing communication variables
- Exogenous environmental factors
- Creative management issues
- The pursuit of multiple objectives
- The discretionary nature of media cover

Despite these genuine concerns, there is strong support for a range of evaluation techniques which provide useful insights into the effectiveness of sponsorship programmes. These mechanisms broadly consist of measures of exposure, awareness, image, sales effectiveness, and guest feedback. A range of tracking and *ad hoc* dipstick approaches, e.g. before, during, and after the event, are advocated.

REFERENCES

Irwin, R. L. and Asimakopoulos, M. K. (1992) An approach to the evaluation and selection of sport sponsorship proposals, *Sport Marketing Quarterly*, **1**(2), pp. 43–51.

Marshall, D. (1993) Does sponsorship always talk the same language? In *Sponsorship Europe*, Esomar, Monte Carlo, pp. 23–25.

Meenaghan, J. A. (1983) Commercial sponsorship, *European Journal of Marketing*, Special Issue, pp. 5–73.

Meerabeau, E. *et al.* (1991) Sponsorship and the drinks industry, *European Journal of Marketing*, **25**(11), pp. 39–56.

Otker, T. (1988) Exploitation: the key to sponsorship success, *European Research,* May, pp. 77–86.

Parker, K. (1991) Sponsorship: the research contribution theory: the case of professional football, *European Journal of Marketing*, **25**(11), pp. 22–30.

Thwaites, D. (1994) Practical applications of sponsorship theory: the case of professional football, *European Marketing Academy Conference*, May, Maastricht.

Thwaites, D. (1995) Corporate sponsorship by the financial services industry, *Journal of Marketing Management*, in press.

Case 14

Nestlé, General Foods and the Multiples

Synopsis

In the late 1980s, although the UK in terms of consumption of 'coffee per capita/kg' was ranked no. 17 in the world (a rate some 6 times less than the world leader, Finland), the market itself was £50m larger than that for tea. (1988 UK coffee market £621m vs. UK tea market £570m.) In the second half of the 1980s particularly, some growth had been experienced in total market sales, especially in the premium freeze-dried sector. With health concerns causing less sugar and full-fat milk to be consumed with hot beverages, consumers were for the first time tasting the true flavour of what they were drinking. As a consequence demand for powders and fillers declined as tastes became more sophisticated.

Since the abolition of Retail Price Maintenance (RPM) in the UK in 1965 on, *inter alia*, grocery products, the power that national manufacturers and suppliers once possessed had shifted significantly in favour of the retailers. In the late 1980s, the UK retail grocery industry was a classic oligopoly with the top four or five companies accounting for 80 per cent of coffee sales. The manufacturing industry, on the other hand, was a duopoly with the two main companies, Nestlé and Kraft, supplying 70 per cent of the total coffee market.

The fundamental problem of the case is how should the increasingly emasculated suppliers respond to what appears to be the ever increasing power of the retailers?

Teaching Objectives

This case can be used to meet four specific teaching objectives:

1. To identify and track the reasons for a shift in power within a given channel of distribution.
2. To provide students with an opportunity to appreciate the implications of a shift from a conventional (CMS) to a vertical marketing system (VMS).
3. To understand and evaluate the scenario of possible manufacturer responses to a highly concentrated retail industry.
4. To consider how retailers can achieve a long term sustainable competitive advantage.

This teaching note was prepared by David Cook, Lecturer in Marketing, University of Bradford Management Centre, UK.

Suggested Teaching Approach

1. Conventional and vertical marketing systems (CMS/VMS)

A useful introductory device, before drawing out the configuration of and distinction between CMS and VMS, is to ask students to describe how channels of distribution bridge the gap between the points of production and consumption. The essential conundrum can be highlighted by the point that whereas a manufacturer would ideally like to produce long runs of limited variety/choice in the factory, in the retail store a typical consumer is looking for the opposite, namely small quantity purchases of a large variety/choice.

Typical activities that channels of distribution became involved in include:

- Holding stock
- Assembling variety/choice
- Breaking bulk
- Facilitating purchase and valuation
- Shifting time zones, e.g. seasonal produce/gifts (Christmas and Easter)
- Overcoming consumer ignorance, e.g. in-store demonstrations, tastings, etc.

For these functions distributors earn a return on their time and investment.

A typical CMS comprises an independent manufacturer, wholesaler, and retailer. When asked for any comment, students will readily identify the duplication of activity sequentially within the traditional channel. After the abolition of RPM in the UK, a systems view of channels of distribution was increasingly developed, with the exception being a desire to cut out duplication. Any consequent lost saving could then either:

- be retained within the channel and shared among channel members according to their respective power, and/or
- passed on to the ultimate consumer as lower prices.

With VMS, one channel member owns the others, holds franchises, or has the power to make them co-operate.

One implication of the emergence of the VMS is that traditional functions/responsibilities were assumed by other members of the channels, as for example:

- Manufacturers moved forwards in the channel, perhaps to the point of opening retail outlets.
- Retailers moved backwards in the channel, possibly to establish manufacturing plant.

In this process it is not that the function of wholesaling has disappeared, but that it has shifted forwards/backwards in the channel (functional shiftability) and been assumed by the manufacturer or retailer. The traditional wholesaler in many trade sectors has been squeezed.

It is useful here to ask students to ponder under what conditions CMS and VMS channels apply:

- CMS—applies where there is a reasonably low degree of concentration at either the manufacturer/supplier and/or retailer end of the channel, e.g. cut flowers.
- VMS—applies where there is a reasonably high degree of concentration at either the manufacturer/supplier and/or retailer end of the channel, e.g. grocery products.

Within the VMS classification it is worthwhile also requesting students to identify examples from the grocery and allied trade sectors, namely:

Corporate	Brewer-tied house, e.g. Bass, Scottish & Newcastle	
Administered	Birds Eye (Unilever), Heinz, Marks & Spencer	
Contractual	Wholesaler sponsored	Spar, Mace, VG
	Retailer sponsored	Nisa (National Independent Supermarkets' Association)
	Franchise	McDonald's

2. Power shift within the grocery channel

Whereas historically the power in the grocery channel of distribution lay within the national brand manufacturer, e.g. Heinz 57 Varieties, Cadbury Milk Chocolate, etc., with the high level of concentration now in the hands of oligopolist grocery retailers, the locus of power has dramatically shifted. Manufacturers appreciate that they cannot afford not to be listed in all the big four or five grocery multiples otherwise they lose exposure to a large part of the national market.

This shift in power can be illustrated by the simple diagram shown in Figure 6. The precise location profile of present power is for illustrative purposes only.

3. Manufacturer response

The following points identify a range of possible manufacturers' responses to increasing retailer power. Clearly, the possible courses of action are not mutually exclusive, nor is the list itself exhaustive. In each instance a coffee-related example has been added.

NPD/Innovation

A steady flow of new products/innovation will add interest for the retail buyer, e.g.:

- Maxwell House Espresso
- Maxwell House Cappuccino supplied with a sachet of Suchard milk chocolate flakes
- Decaffeinated brands
- Aromitization—a process whereby extra aroma is added to the product

Stress brand names

Nestlé lay great stress on Nescafé Gold Blend with the following copy being printed on a 200 g jar label:

> NESCAFE GOLD BLEND, GOLDEN ROASTED RICH AND SMOOTH, FREEZE DRIED INSTANT COFFEE.

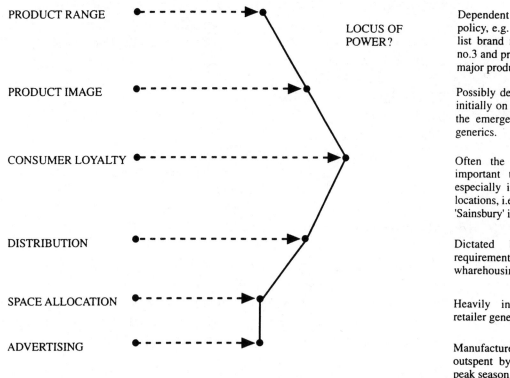

PREVIOUS NATIONAL MANUFACTURER CONTROL	PRESENT MULTIPLE RETAILER CONTROL	APPLICATION
PRODUCT RANGE	LOCUS OF POWER?	Dependent on retailer stocking policy, e.g. a multiple will typically list brand no.1 and no.2, possibly no.3 and probably an own label in a major product group.
PRODUCT IMAGE		Possibly devalued by retailer stress initially on price and challenged by the emergence of own labels and generics.
CONSUMER LOYALTY		Often the store image is more important than the brand image especially in out-of-town one stop locations, i.e. if it is good enough for 'Sainsbury' it is good enough for me!
DISTRIBUTION		Dictated by retailer delivery requirements by day/time to central wharehousing or direct to store.
SPACE ALLOCATION		Heavily influenced by ES/DPP retailer generated data
ADVERTISING		Manufacturers frequently being outspent by retailers especially at peak season, e.g. Christmas.

Figure 6 Marketing mix—transfer of control.

NESCAFE GOLD BLEND IS MADE FROM A SELECTION OF THE FINEST COFFEE BEANS IN THE WORLD, INCLUDING SUPERB ARABICAS FROM LATIN AMERICA AND KENYA. THESE SELECT BEANS ARE CAREFULLY BLENDED AND GOLDEN ROASTED TO CAPTURE THE RICH, SMOOTH TASTE AND AROMA OF THE PERFECT CUP OF COFFEE.

Emphasize quality

As the UK market moved towards a preference for 'better' flavour and taste, manufacturers are placing increased emphasis on quality selected both in advertising copy ('real coffee flavour') and the introduction of more up-market brands. For example:

Nestlé	Arabice
	Cap Colombie
Kraft/Lyons	Costa Rican—'A dark strong coffee with a rich flavour'
	Kenyan—'A bright lively coffee with a fresh flavour'
	Colombian—'A smooth nutty coffee with a rich aroma'

Pull strategy

By heavy advertising via highly visible media, especially television, manufacturers can encourage consumers to pull their brand through the channel of distribution. For example:

- Nescafé Gold Blend ran a series of sequential TV advertisements which achieved almost cult popularity regarding how a relationship between two executives of the opposite sex would develop.
- Kenco positioned against ground coffee 'all we know about coffee in an instant'

EDI (Electronic Data Interchange)/squeeze supplier

- Either by directly linking into IT data flows and reordering mechanisms or attempting to achieve negotiating advantage over suppliers, e.g. EF Man—commodity broker, manufacturers can seek to 'lock in' customers and enhance potential margins by astute buying
- Or by partnership marketing

Furthermore appropriate value chain analysis could be discussed around these issues.

Redesign the channel of distribution

There seems to be little chance of redesigning the retailer end of the channel, but two possible courses of action for manufacturers are:

- Buy beans direct from estates, i.e. cut out any brokerage activity.
- Place greater emphasis on alternative channels, e.g. vending machines, catering outlets, and restaurants.

Trade marketing/key account management

Recognizing the oligopolistic structure of the UK grocery multiples, manufacturers are laying increasing emphasis on trade marketing, with often designated executives/teams being delegated the responsibility of looking after key accounts. The historic role of the salesperson has declined.

Restructure the supply industry

To enhance their negotiating position *vis-à-vis* the grocery multiples, manufacturers have:

- acquired other manufacturers in the same product group (coffee), e.g. Kraft General Foods acquired Lyons), and/or
- acquired manufacturers of other product groups (non-coffee) often with a strong global brand name presence, e.g.
  - Nestlé acquired Rowntree Macintosh (Smarties, Polo, Yorkie Bar, etc.)
  - Kraft General Goods acquired Terry's of York, (Spartan Chocolates, 1797, Chocolate Orange, etc.).

4. Sources of power and conflict resolution

Ultimately real power in a channel of distribution lies with the channel member who possesses greatest power over the market. Various classifications of power are available but one of the more well known is the following:

Coercive
the ability to force a channel member to do something they do not necessarily want to do
e.g.   supply own label
       withhold supplies

Reward
one channel member has the ability to reward another because of the latter's behaviour
e.g.   allowances for returned merchandise
       manufacturer in-store promotional support

Expert
one channel member possesses power over another because of actual or assumed expertise/knowledge
e.g.   space allocation paradigms
       deploying DPP analysis

Legitimate
one channel member possesses the ability to stipulate another's behaviour because of a legal/legitimate agreement/contract
e.g.   the operation of a franchise
       own label product technical specification

Referent
possessed by a channel member because another wishes to be associated with a brand name or store image
e.g.   power of a national brand such as Nescafé, Kenco
       power of a store image such as Sainsbury's, Tesco

Persuasive
the ability to ensure one channel member behaves in a given way because of skilled presentation/persuasion, charisma, persistence, etc.
e.g.   professional negotiation

Economic scale
the power of the big buy/sell especially if it is a large proportion of that company's purchases/sales
e.g.   Porter's ubiquitous five forces model regarding power of buyers and power of suppliers.

Potential sources of conflict in grocery retailing would include:

- Deliveries
- Availability of own label
- Margins/DPP
- Rebates/overriders
- Staffing allowances
- Price discounting
- Space allocation
- Returned stock

86

- In-store demonstrations/displays/promotions
- Co-operative advertising

A meaningful discussion can be generated by asking students how these potential problems might be avoided/overcome in the UK coffee market. For example:

- Partnership marketing
- Conflict handling
- Market partitioning
- Performance improvement
- Channel ownership
- Coercion

5. Sustainable competitive advantage for retailers

Students can be asked in their experience as customers what they think are the key factors for success in the grocery retailing business. Using the two or three stores in which they would ordinarily purchase their grocery requirement, they can then be asked 3 questions:

- Does your preferred/most frequently used store possess that key factor for success?
- Does your preferred/most frequently used store possess that key factor for success in super abundance when compared to other stores that you might use?
- Is it likely to be difficult for the other stores you might use to catch up/equal your preferred store on each of the key factors for success?

If answers are restricted to yes or no, only in the instance where three 'yes's' are registered can it be argued there is a sustainable competitive advantage.

Normally the identified competitive advantages can be classified under one of five headings:

- Location, i.e. localized monopoly
- Image/customer loyalty
- IT/distribution systems
- Low-cost operations
- Vendor relations/buying skills.

End of Module Case

Kodak Photo-CD

Synopsis

Large parts of Kodak's revenues and profits are generated by the imaging division. Traditionally, this division has sold film, cameras, and processing equipment. In recent years, some competitors have made inroads into fully digitized photography. With this product, film is obsolete since images are both captured and stored electronically. This development is a significant long-term threat to Kodak. A strategic alliance of Philips and Kodak which sought to leverage Philips's strength in electronic technology and Kodak's strength in photographic processing and distribution led to the development of the Photo-CD. With this product, Kodak has attempted to preserve the use of conventional film in the face of digital competition.

The present case describes the process, features, and benefits of Photo-CD (the Photo-CD system), the complex infrastructure for the Photo-CD, and makes a beginning with an inventory of possible competing products. How Kodak should launch this new hybrid high-tech product into the market is the major question of this case. Segmenting the industrial market, positioning in the consumer market, and developing the marketing mix are just a few examples of the questions that are touched upon.

Teaching Objectives

The teaching objectives of this case are threefold. First, this case shows the problems of introducing a new, high-tech product into the fascinating market of multimedia. In this market, where different systems and solutions exist for the same kind of problems (without any definite standards), students are urged to identify and analyse competing solutions in the market. Secondly, this case deals with a hybrid product. This means that the product can have applications in the consumer as well as in the industrial market. What are the implications for the positioning of the product when the applications in both major markets differ?

Thirdly, the case attempts to explain that new product development comprises far more than just *developing* a new product. Some of the most important decisions contributing to the (commercial) success of a new product are made in the launch stage. This case focuses on those decisions. Because most of these decisions have been investigated recently (see Suggested Teaching Approach), students' decisions can be compared with the results of these studies. This hopefully will lead to even more fruitful classroom discussions.

This teaching note was prepared by Erik Jan Hultink, Assistant Professor of Marketing, and Walle Oppedijk van Veen, Professor of Marketing and Market Research, Delft University of Technology, The Netherlands.

Suggested Teaching Approach

In our view, the most rewarding approach is to have student-teams of four or five students each prepare a market introduction plan for the Photo-CD. A classroom presentation of about 20 minutes should answer the questions raised in the case. The procedure will be as follows: firstly, an introduction to the case will be given by the teacher. Then, students have about a week to collect data (e.g. through a CD-ROM search or by telephone interviews), which should lead to the formulation of an introduction plan for the Photo-CD. A 3–4 page abstract with the major decisions in the plan should be handed in.

	Hours
Introduction to the case by the teacher and reading of the case	2
Information gathering (e.g. CD-ROM search)	8
Preparing introduction plan (team discussion)	8
Writing 3–4 page abstract	1
Preparing presentation	4
Class discussion	2
Total	25 hours

Of course, it is also possible to spend less time on the case. We had pleasant experiences running the case in just 2–3 hours. In our course (the MarkStrat game), we ran the case just before students launched their first new product into the market.

An introduction of about 20–30 minutes was given, after which two major launch decisions were presented. The student groups had 30 minutes to prepare their solution to the launch problem. Because many groups were dealing with the same questions, the different views on the issue could be contrasted fruitfully.

For your convenience, and to stimulate discussions in the classroom, we have added the results of four empirical studies which the lecturer can use in the class discussion. These studies deal with the major decision issues for Kodak's management in launching the Photo-CD. We have also included the references to those studies.

1. Which business market segments to target?

The Photo-CD may solve many commercial problems. Whether it is used to display an image frequently, archive photographs for occasional reference, distribute high-quality duplicates, or as a bridge to transfer photographs into a computer for further manipulation, the Photo-CD can serve a clear and immediate purpose. For business users, the Photo-CD can be the most cost-effective method of all digital imaging systems. In order to investigate whether or not different industrial customer segments agree on this statement, telephone interviews were held with 18 managers within four segments (Buta *et al.*, 1993). The segments included in this study were: studio photographers, journalists, medical, and real estate. *There are many other segments which may be interested in the Photo-CD, however.*

Studio photographers (*n* = 5)

The interviews with the studio photographers made clear that they have several potential uses for the Photo-CD. It is likely to be used as a medium for distributing pictures. For example, wedding photographers could mail disks containing proofs to family members for easy viewing (assuming that they already own a Photo-CD player). Similarly, photographs taken for catalogues could be quickly and inexpensively sent to printers for publication.

As one photographer noted, 'When you have a quarter of a million pictures, you can't afford to send duplicates to people.' As technology improves and portrait photographers become more comfortable with the idea of using computers to do their own digital retouching, the Photo-CD will provide an inexpensive method for transferring high-resolution images to computer. Currently, high-resolution scanning to a digital computer file can cost over $50 per image. However, the Photo-CD would enable photographers to put dozens of images on a computer for the same price. Additionally, the standardization of the reproduction capabilities (i.e. consistency in shading, contrast, etc.) on Photo-CDs makes them an attractive alternative to scanners, which tend to record colours inconsistently.

Photojournalists (*n* = 5)

Photojournalists, especially at newspapers, have a strong interest in digital image capture and transmission, but apparently not in Photo-CD. Many newspapers already use a fully computerized system, not only for typesetting, but also for most aspects of managing photographs for printing. Pictures taken with 35mm cameras are scanned (using a flat-bed scanner) into a computer for cropping, cleaning up, colour separation, and placement. In addition, most major newspapers own at least one digital camera system. The professional-level digital cameras provide more than adequate resolution for newspaper prints, and the images can be transferred via telephone to the news room.

Most journalists dismissed the Photo-CD technology as irrelevant to their industry. It is not ideal for an environment that is focused on minimizing time to publication. In addition to that, many journalists can easily afford such capital-intensive, fully electronic equipment. While Photo-CD can be useful for archival purposes, newspapers are better served by conventional computer hard disk storage and tape backup systems. They will not see a value in the Photo-CD until the equipment to read and write disks is inexpensive and integrated with their current imaging workstations.

Medical applications (*n* = 4)

Since Photo-CD is capable of storing and reproducing diagnostic-quality images, the medical market may be a promising market segment. For example, a hospital might be able to take X-rays but lack the equipment necessary to analyse them. Thus, Photo-CDs containing duplicates can be sent elsewhere for analysis. However, the interviews made clear that the medical community is not yet ready for this technology. Radiologists and medical record keepers had either not heard of the Photo-CD or took a 'wait and see' position. Potential risks they see include loss of images, inability of the

Photo-CD to integrate with their current environment, and the lack of personnel trained to use the technology. Because costs of failure are extremely high in this sector, Photo-CD will have to develop more of a track record before it is adopted in this market. Some respondents indicated, however, a more promising near-term medical application for the Photo-CD, which does not require immediate processing: Photo-CD as an archival record of medical images. No longer would physicians have to thumb through medical textbooks for images that provide examples of rare ailments. Rather, they could use the extensive search and retrieval Photo-CD software to quickly locate and display large images that would assist in diagnosing rare conditions.

Real estate (*n* = 4)

The real estate industry is another market that holds some potential for the Photo-CD. Photo-CD images could help buyers screen homes before they commit to seeing them in person, thus saving both them and the real estate agent time and money. The interviews made clear that most agencies are small, prefer to have very low overhead costs, and do not invest heavily in office equipment. They are reluctant to make the modest investment required to use a Photo-CD system. Also, the timeliness of processing is an issue. Disks would need to be updated fairly frequently to reflect sales and new listings.

2. What hardware channels to use?

This section identifies which hardware channels may be used to distribute the Photo-CD. The information was collected through interviews with managers and sales people from audio/video, camera, and computer stores, as well as photo-processing outlets and mass-merchandisers (1).

Hardware channels

One key success factor for hardware distributors will be the ability to provide extensive training to their sales staff. The Photo-CD is not a product that 'sells itself'. The Photo-CD will only be viable if knowledgeable sales people are able to help customers to understand the product and its potential uses. The interviews suggest that camera stores are probably the primary channel for the player hardware. Some mass-merchandisers were also planning to carry the product in their electronic department. Computer stores which were contacted do not intend to sell the players. The main reason was that they already sell external CD-ROM players (e.g. NEC, Toshiba, Sony, Apple) that are compatible with Photo-CD.

3. How to position the Photo-CD in the consumer market?

Kodak's management had some doubts about the most appropriate positioning of the Photo-CD in the consumer market. It was felt that input from consumers could simplify the decision. For this reason, five consumer research issues were raised:

1. Which products are competitors to the Photo-CD, according to consumers?
2. What are the advantages and disadvantages of the Photo-CD in comparison with those competing products?
3. What is the purchase intention of consumers for the Photo-CD?
4. What are consumers' perceived product applications?
5. Do experts have a different opinion on the Photo-CD than non-experts?

In a qualitative market research project (Hultink and Loosschilder, 1993), 16 well-educated men and women aged 18 years or older participated in two group discussions and five in-depth interviews. The group of respondents consisted of *expert consumers* (EC) (operationalized as owners of CD-players, computers, cameras, televisions, video, and film equipment, and working in the computer, imaging, or graphical design industry) and of *naive consumers* (NC) (operationalized as not possessing all of the above-mentioned characteristics).

The procedure was as follows:

1. An introduction of 4–5 minutes was given, in which the purpose and goals of the research were explained.
2. The Photo-CD player and its features were introduced and explained by the discussion leader (some pictures were shown on TV).
3. The process from picture capturing through watching the pictures on TV was discussed.

Results

According to the respondents, the Photo-CD will compete with at least six products: slide projectors, pictures, video cameras, audio CD players, digital cameras, and CD-I. Table 3 summarizes the advantages and disadvantages of the Photo-CD in comparison with these products according to the sample of respondents.

About 30 per cent of the respondents discarded the Photo-CD as an unnecessary gadget. The other respondents consider the possibilities of the player to be interesting. Most of them would not buy the player until their audio CD player breaks down, however. Price plays a crucial role. The price cannot be too high in comparison with a CD-I and an audio CD player. The price cannot be too low or respondents develop doubts about the quality of the audio and picture options. The possibility of watching pictures with other people at the same time is seen as the unique selling point of the Photo-CD.

Most respondents think that the major applications of the Photo-CD are in the business market. Among the applications mentioned are: demonstrations by salespeople, advertising, presentations/lectures, recipes/dinner preparation guidelines on a small television in the kitchen, a disk with houses-for-sale for real estate agents; and an overview of the holiday destinations of travel agencies.

Interestingly enough, hardly any differences were found between the expert consumers and the naive consumers in their responses to the four questions. However, as might be expected, the experts knew more about the product and had already heard about its development. They also saw more possible applications for the Photo-CD and they mentioned several additional features that the Photo-CD should possess in the near future. Among these features were, for example, the possibility of playing background music, interactivity, colouring in of the pictures, adding text, and the possibility of producing a direct print out of the player.

Table 3 Advantages and disadvantages of the Photo-CD compared with competing products

Advantages of the Photo-CD	Disadvantages of the Photo-CD
Slide projectors	
• Photo-CD is quieter	• None
• You do not have to sit in the dark	
• Easier selection and better storage of images	
• Most people already own a television	
• Less time needed for preparing a show	
• Slide equipment needs too much space	
• Features of Photo-CD (zooming in/out and flipping) more interesting	
Pictures	
• Easier to watch the images with other people	• Only interesting when someone takes many pictures
• at the same time	• Costs are relatively high
• Option of adding text and colours—ideal for presentations	
• Images more conveniently arranged	• Not suitable for portrait photos
	• Pictures are a nice present
	• Pictures can be enlarged and put on the wall
	• To make a picture album is a pleasant
	• activity
	• Collecting pictures has emotional value
Video-camera	
• More suitable for showing details during presentations	• Video-camera more convenient for education purposes
• Easier method for manipulating pictures	• Video-camera leaves more room for creativity
	• Full-motion is more direct than still-picture
Audio CD player	
• Additional feature for watching pictures on TV	• Is the quality of the audio part good enough?
• If one does not own a CD-audio yet, one gets two-in-one	• Price for extra feature too high, maximum $80
Digital camera	
• None	• You do not have to put the pictures on film first
	• Immediate storage of picture information on disk
CD-I	
• None	• Fewer possibilities
	• No interactivity
	• No moving pictures

4. What launch strategy to use?

In order to find out how product and marketing managers evaluate various launch strategies, 28 product and marketing managers were asked to evaluate eight launch strategies in a conjoint measurement design (Hultink *et al.*, 1993; Hultink and Schoormans, 1995). The participants all had experience in launching new high-technology products. The managers had to imagine that they advised a mid-size Dutch consumer electronics company, which was the third entrant on the market for photo-CD players, on these launch strategies. The eight strategies were characterized by a combination of four launch variables, namely pricing strategy (skimming versus penetration pricing), product assortment (small versus large), promotion strategy (push versus pull promotion), and the product's competitive advantage as the communication theme (higher quality, better design, and being more innovative). To simplify the participants' task, they only responded to one-third of the 24 possible launch strategies. For each of these strategies, the managers rated the chances of success on a nine-point rating scale. Besides these data, they provided information on the background characteristics of the firm .

The results of the conjoint measurement analysis led to an additional cluster analysis that revealed two conceptually meaningful clusters. A summary of the results is shown in Table 4. The part-worths of the launch strategy attribute levels in both clusters are shown in the second and fourth columns of Table 4. A positive part-worth indicates that respondents perceive this attribute level to be positively correlated to new product success. The relative importance of a launch attribute for new-product success (the sensitivity) is determined by calculating the largest absolute difference in the part-worths of the attribute. The sensitivities are shown in the third and fifth columns of Table 4. The first cluster was characterized by an emphasis on a penetration pricing strategy, the second one by an emphasis on a skimming price strategy. Members of the first cluster emphasized penetration pricing, pull promotion, and a small assortment. In the second cluster, a skimming price strategy and a small product assortment were chosen. The major difference between both strategies is the choice of the pricing strategy.

From the information obtained in qualitative follow-up interviews, a tentative interpretation with respect to the managers' pricing preferences was made. Managers in the *penetration* cluster rated the different strategies more according to market share and sales objectives, while managers in the *skimming* cluster were more interested in financial success objectives, like return on sales and profitability. Consequently, both pricing strategies can be successful.

When cross-tabulating company characteristics like the firm's core industry and geographical location of the firm's headquarters with the derived clusters, no statistically significant effects were found. However, some of the findings are conceptually relevant for investigating new product launches. First, there is a trend that managers in the non-consumer electronics industry are more likely to belong to the penetration cluster. Secondly, the findings suggest a weak relationship between membership of the penetration cluster and the company's location of the headquarters in America. The last set of findings suggests that firm characteristics are in one way or another associated with managers' evaluations of the possible success of hypothetical launch strategies (see Table 4).

Table 4 Part-worths and sensitivities of strategy attributes

Strategy attribute	Cluster 1 (n=14) Part-worths	Sensitivities	Cluster 2 (n=13) Part-worths	Sensitivities
Pricing				
penetration	1.18*	2.36	−0.70*	1.40
skimming	−1.18*		70*	
Promotion				
push (trade)	−0.96*	1.92	−0.22	0.44
pull (customer)	0.96*		0.22	
Product Assortment				
small (3)	0.18*	0.36	0.41*	0.82
large	−0.18*		−0.41*	
Competitive Advantage				
quality	−0.02	0.22	−0.26	0.69
design	0.12		−0.17	
innovative	−0.10		0.43	

* $p < 0.05$.

Table 5 Company characteristics and launch strategy clusters

Company characteristics		Cluster I Penetration	Cluster 2 Skimming	Total
Core industry*	Consumer electronics	7	11	18
	Non-consumer electronics	7	2	9
Region headquarters**				
	Japan	5	7	12
	USA	6	1	7
	Europe	3	5	8
		14	13	27

*$\chi 2 = 3.63$, df = 1, $p = 0.057$ (before Yates's-correction), Fisher's exact test $p = 0.066$.
**$\chi 2 = 4.39$, df = 2, $p = 0.111$.

The opinions of these product and marketing managers, summarized by the above analysis, can be compared to the launch strategies described in the student presentations. Students should be asked to justify the launch strategies they propose. The above analysis emphasizes the point that there is no one 'right' answer to this question.

REFERENCES

Buta, P., Hultink, E.J., Vrba, J. and Wise, S. (1993) Kodak's launch of the Photo-CD in the USA: a case in high tech marketing, Internal Report, Delft University of Technology.

Hultink, E. J. and Loosschilder, G. (1993) Qualitative research into the adoption of the Photo-CD in the consumer market, Internal Report, Delft University of Technology (in Dutch).

Hultink, E. J. Oppedijk van Veen, W. M. and Schoormans, J.P.L. (1993) Launching a high tech consumer product: an analysis of marketing managers' strategy choices. In Chias, J. and Sureda, J. (eds), EMAC *Annual Conference Proceedings,* Barcelona, Vol. 1, pp. 579–592.

Hultink, E. J. and Schoormans, J.P.L. (1995) How to launch a high-tech product successfully: an analysis of marketing managers' strategy choices, *Journal of High Technology Management Research*, in press.

Case 15

Optimeyes

Synopsis

One of the strengths of this case is the breadth of the business and marketing issues it encompasses, while still allowing the opportunity for a rigorous analysis of one or two key issues. The key issues facing Optimeyes are how can it successfully alter its marketing strategy in the absence of good market information, and what its new strategy should be. However, the case can also be used in discussions of issues such as the marketing concept, the regulatory environment of marketing, promotional strategy, the role of publicity, and customer service.

Teaching Objectives

1. To provide students with the task of producing a marketing strategy based on limited market information.
2. To give students some exposure to the challenges faced by very small companies in competitive markets.
3. To emphasize to students the importance of strategic change and to show them that past sources of success may not be sufficient in a new situation.
4. To give students some experience in using competitive analysis and strategy development tools such as SWOT analysis and Porter's generic strategies.

Suggested Teaching Approach

The case is designed for a 1.5–2 hour session. The following format is recommended. Begin by ensuring that students understand the structure of the industry and the position of Optimeyes in it, as this will impact on the strategic alternatives which can be considered. From this point the discussion should move to assessing Optimeyes's marketing strategy to date, the strengths and weaknesses of this strategy, and how the company has got to the position it is in today. The next step is to analyse the present market situation, identifying the emerging opportunities and the competitive threats. Using this information a strategy for 1993 or for the next three years can be developed.

1. Marketing strategy

As Optimeyes plans its marketing strategy for 1993 and future years it needs to address a range of strategic issues that are beginning to emerge. The following are some of the most important questions facing the company:

This teaching note was prepared by John Fahy, Lecturer in Strategic Marketing, Trinity College, University of Dublin, Ireland.

1. The company's strengths of innovativeness, variety of product, price, and quality of service have served them very well against the traditional optometrist. But will these strengths sustain the company in the face of stronger and better capitalized international competition?
2. There are indications in the case that the price of ophthalmic products will continue to be driven down. What are the implications of this trend for a small company like Optimeyes?
3. In the light of both of the above points, how has the Irish market changed? Is the desire for variety as strong as it was when Optimeyes started, or is it now being met by the new competitors? Is price now the key issue? In other words, can Optimeyes still maintain its positioning as the 'Marks & Spencer' of ophthalmics retailing or must it change?
4. The company has geographically diversified to reduce its dependence on the highly competitive Dublin market. Should the company continue to move away from Dublin or should it reinvest in Dublin. Are its customers more likely to be in Dublin or the country towns and cities, and indeed who are its customers?
5. The absence of market information continues to impede the company's efforts to develop a marketing strategy. Should the company conduct marketing research? Can it afford to do so, and if yes, what questions should it ask?

2. Market analysis

The case is ideally suited to conducting a SWOT analysis of the company in advance of the development of a new strategy. The findings of such an analysis would reveal the following:

Strengths	*Weaknesses*
Innovativeness	Small market share
Product range	Lack of capital for investment
Low prices	Limited promotion budget
Quality of service	High level of current liabilities
Fully integrated operations	Very little market information
Geographically diversified	
Optimeyes brand name	

Opportunities	*Threats*
Growth in spectacles as fashion	Market penetration by bigger chains
Growth in repeat purchases	Aggressive discounting by bigger chains

3. Making use of limited market information

The case affords students the opportunity to try to draw some conclusions about the market based on very limited information.

Market size

Estimates of market size in volume terms are presented in the case. Alternative estimates in value terms can be gauged by combining the information in the case from the Household Budget Survey with that from the Census of Population. The total population in 1991 was 3,523,401 persons and the average household expenditure per week on optician's fees was IR£0.102. The calculation proceeds as follows:

100

1. Annual expenditure on optician's fees/household: IR£0.102 × 52 = 5.304
2. Average household size = 3.53 persons
3. Total number of households = 3,523,401/3.53 = 998,130.6
4. Annual market for optician's fees = (1) × (3) = IR£5.29 million
5. As optician's fees generally represent up to 20 per cent of industry sales, the market can be estimated to be worth at least IR£26.45 million

Market share

Whichever estimate of the market size is used, it can be concluded that Optimeyes has a very small share of market. To get an estimate of share in volume terms, it is necessary to know the number of spectacles that Optimeyes sells in one year. Total turnover for 1992 had increased by 51 per cent to IR£471,502 (IR£312,253 × 51 per cent). Spectacle frames account for 36 per cent of Optimeyes's turnover, thus IR£169,704 for 1992. Assuming an average selling price of IR£40.00, we can estimate that Optimeyes sold 4,243 spectacles in 1992. As the total market is estimated to be one million units, this represents less than 1 per cent of the market.

A similar picture emerges from our estimates in value terms. Optimeyes's total turnover of IR£471,502 in 1992 in a business estimated to be worth IR£26.45 million represents a share of just under 2 per cent of the market.

Therefore we must conclude that the market figures are grossly inflated or that we are looking at a company which has a very limited share of the market.

4. Strategic options

The findings of the analysis to date suggest that Optimeyes is a unique company in terms of its products, with a very small share of the Irish market. The important questions are what strengths should it build on and what opportunities should it attempt to exploit? Answering these questions requires the students to use his/her knowledge of competitive strategy, segmentation, and market targeting.

Competitive strategy

The Porter model of competitive strategy is appropriate in this case. It is immediately clear that Optimeyes is a small niche player in the business. Its strategic choices are focus low-cost and focus differentiation. The low-cost option can be discounted as the company does not have the requisite scale to drive the price down to levels that even the superopticals cannot match. In any event the company has been competing on the basis of both higher perceived value, in terms of range, and lower delivered cost than the traditional optometrist and should attempt to continue to compete on both these bases.

Thus, the company must attempt to maintain this lower delivered cost and find suitable ways of differentiating itself from both Specsavers and Vision Express. The question then becomes: what should be the basis for differentiation? The two qualities that seem to be still unique to Optimeyes are its range of French frames and the quality of its customer service. It might be recommended that the company leverage these two strengths to exploit one of the few opportunities for growth in this business in Ireland, which the case tells us is in the increasing use of spectacles as fashion items, and the fact that Irish consumers generally own only one pair of spectacles compared with a European average of three or four.

Segmentation

In terms of implementing the above strategy, the case affords students the opportunity to conduct a segmentation analysis on three bases, namely demographic, psychographic, and geographic. In terms of demographics, the data show the level of usage by age group and the relevant size of those age groups in Ireland. Similarly, data are available for level of usage classified by socio-economic groups along with details of the size of the socio-economic groups in Ireland. Geographic segmentation raises the issue of whether the company should continue its strategy of expanding throughout the country.

Market targeting

Given its limited resources and its strategy of focusing on the fashion conscious consumer, the student should then nominate on which segments of the market the company should concentrate its marketing effort. Fashion leaders are more likely to be young, urban, female, and from the higher socio-economic groups. Using the data in the tables, the size of this target market can be estimated and the analysis could include recommendations on the most suitable media and message to reach this market.

Case 16

Amstrad 1512

Synopsis

The case concerns the successful entry of Amstrad to the IBM-compatible personal computer ('clone') market in 1986. Amstrad's success can be attributed to the skilful identification of an opportunity in latent market segments, the formulation of a consistent and focused offer, the bold use of Amstrad's marketing assets, and the resolute use of Porter's Overall Cost Leadership strategy.

Teaching Objectives

This case illustrates a number of different things, and can be slanted several different ways, according to the needs of the course and the knowledge of the student. It can be taken as a case in market segmentation, targeting, and positioning, an approach that is useful for the early stages of a general introductory marketing course. The market segmentation discussion illustrates the difference between existing and latent markets, and the potential to be found in targeting the latter, i.e. growing the market rather than merely winning competitor's customers.

Under positioning, the case illustrates how the various elements of a marketing mix should work together to send a cohesive and consistent message about the offer to the consumer, i.e. the differential advantage. Asset-based marketing is also illustrated, i.e. how a good marketing strategy not only addresses a consumer demand, but also capitalizes on the company's strengths and sidesteps its weaknesses, allowing it to satisfy that demand better than competitors.

The case can be used to discuss Porter's Overall Cost Leadership generic strategy and quite neatly shows that the core ideas of marketing and the ideas of Porter can be seen as different ways of looking at the same thing.

Suggested Teaching Approach

Market segmentation and targeting: students should be asked to segment the IBM PC-compatible market in 1986, and briefly profile the segments.

One possible outcome will be the identification of four segments. The existing market of larger corporation users is less price sensitive, demands customization and backup, is likely to buy through value-added resellers or direct, and represents heavy users. The three latent, or largely latent, segments are education, home, and small business users. These segments are latent because they are unable or unwilling to pay the high prices demanded for IBM-compatible PCs, and are making do with cheaper 'home' computers (like the then ubiquitous BBC 'B') or doing without. They are generally more likely to use consumer goods channels, represent light or occasional users, be less

---

This teaching note was prepared by Robert Duke, Lecturer in Marketing, University of Leeds, UK.

computer literate, have limited access to backup and support, and limited willingness to pay extra for it. Some may already have Amstrad PCW word processing systems.

Positioning and competitive strategy: the best approach to this part of the discussion is to use the '4-Ps' as a framework to analyse Amstrad's offer, both from a 'marketing' point of view, and from Porter's Overall Cost Leadership perspective.

Product: Minimal intrinsic innovation from the consumer's point of view, although having an IBM-compatible PC that works 'straight from the box' without need for expert setting up or customization is a significant novelty, as is the 'bundling' of some software with the computer. The basic design of the computer offers nothing to the customer that is not already available elsewhere. However, the design is innovative, the innovation being aimed squarely at making the machines less costly to manufacture, in line with an Overall Cost Leadership strategy. Note the use of cheaper materials (plastic instead of metal), and more straightforward design (all major functions incorporated onto one 'motherboard', for example).

The design aim of producing adequate rather than (more costly) excellent quality is worthy of discussion. Clearly a cost leader will seek to add cost only where it adds more value in the view of the target customer. The paragraph that describes the shortcomings of screen and keyboard highlights this: it appears to be critical, but on closer analysis, makes it clear that only heavy users had major difficulties. Are the target market segments for the 1512 likely to contain heavy users? Low cost, adequate quality will be acceptable for the occasional/light user, which appears to be the target.

Further discussions here could embrace the question of why PCs were designed the way they were in the first place. Why were the cases made of metal? A discussion paralleling the development of jug kettles is possible.

Note also the use of the 'hollow corporation' approach, the buying in of production capacity from the cheapest source rather than owning it oneself. This not only reduces manufacturing cost, it also negates economy of scale and experience curve entry barriers (as described in Porter's Framework for Industry Analysis) that might otherwise have presented a problem to a new entrant utilizing an Overall Cost Leadership strategy. This approach has come to be widely used in the PC market, giving rise to the slang term 'badge engineering'.

Also worthy of note is the presence of complementary products (hardware and software), each useless without the other. Amstrad was careful to offer reasonably priced software along with the hardware.

Place: Porter indicates that, in the interests of cutting costs, low-cost channels should be used. High street consumer electrical stores are low-cost channels compared to the added-value resellers who supplied most PCs at this time; resellers who set up and customized machines and took a hefty margin for doing so.

As well as being a low-cost channel, place illustrates very neatly both asset-based marketing and the consistency of the marketing mix. Amstrad already had strength in high street consumer electrical durables distribution, and a power base derived from the other products (televisions, videos, etc.) it supplied to the same retailers. This explains the bold and innovative step of distributing IBM-compatible PCs through these channels: Amstrad used a marketing strength, as

104

well as avoiding potential difficulty with the conventional outlets, the added-value resellers, where it had no power base or distribution synergies; Amstrad machines might have been rejected by such resellers (since such computers would damage their lucrative 'setting up and customizing' business), or had a higher selling price imposed, thus negating Amstrad's differential advantage. However, since most high street electrical shops would not have the expertise to offer setting up, customization, or support services to customers, the fact that the Amstrad 1512 worked 'straight from the box' became all the more important. Notice the consistency between product and place elements of the marketing mix.

It is interesting to note that price-cutting PC suppliers in the UK used an even lower cost distribution method. Companies like Dell, Compuadd, and Elonex used mail order.

The tutor might encourage students to carry out a SWOT analysis at some stage. When they do, Amstrad strengths should include consumer durables distribution; weaknesses should include industrial/commercial distribution.

Price: It is worth stressing, as ever, that Porter's Overall Cost Leadership strategy does not necessarily mean offering the lowest price. However, in practice, it is very often the case that the cost leader uses price as the differential advantage. The fact that the product is probably not innovative from the consumer's point of view, not intrinsically differentiated, is one possible explanation. Another is the likely use by the overall cost leader of penetration pricing strategy— seizing large market share and thus making cost gains through economies of scale and the experience curve effect. Amstrad Marketing Director, Simon Miller, interviewed in September 1986, stated that Amstrad were aiming for a 40 per cent market share by the end of 1987.

The main target market segments include the hitherto largely latent segments of home, small business, and educational users, all of which are likely to be more price sensitive than the major corporate segment that dominated the market up to this point. The price differential advantage is therefore important.

Promotion: Porter says that promotion costs, like all other costs, are kept to a minimum by cost leaders. However, he also says that even cost leaders are prepared to spend heavily where there will be a long-run cost benefit.

Promotion for the 1512 clearly emphasized two things: it was IBM compatible, and was very cheap. 'Compatible with you know who, priced as only we know how' was the catch phrase.

Those of us who followed the launch of the 1512 closely will also remember Amstrad's heavy use of publicity, a marketing communications technique that is both cheap and highly effective during the early stages of a new product launch. Note again the neat overlap between good marketing strategy and Porter's Overall Cost Leadership.

The outcome: The 1512 was a great success, outselling IBM in the UK, and so we can regard the above strategy as effective. The 1512 was followed up by the marginally improved 1640. However, Amstrad were not able to keep up this momentum. It has been sagely observed that the act of consumption changes the consumer, and this is what happened in this case. Amstrad drew many new users into IBM-compatible PC computing, opening up previously latent market segments. However, users soon began to demand more than the 1512 and 1640 could deliver: they wanted better PCs based on the more powerful 80286 processor chip. To their credit, Amstrad was not caught napping:

the company tried to deliver a more advanced machine, but for various reasons, including memory chip shortages and unreliable components from third-party suppliers, lost momentum and the initiative to other cost-cutting new entrants like Dell, Compuadd, and Elonex.

End of Module Case

Gadan

Synopsis

A small company, managed by the founder and owner, manufactures machines for dairies. Buyers are reduced in numbers but are growing bigger, and demand is growing still more complex. At the same time, tailor-made process lines for the production of cheese are increasingly being demanded. The company takes up the challenge and takes several significant initiatives within a few years: acquisitions, licenses, opening of new markets, product development projects, and changes in the international distribution channels.

Teaching Objectives

1. To identify and rank the strategic issues of a relatively small export-oriented company.
2. To assess the different actions taken by management through the time period described in the case.
3. To discuss the overall problem of structural rationalization taking place in most of the markets and the implications for a single company.
4. To formulate an overall strategic plan for the company on the premises set out by the management.
5. To consider alternative strategies for the company in question.

Suggested Teaching Approach

This case can be used in many different ways. However, it has proven very successful with respect to the following elements of strategic analysis and assessment: international distribution channels, acquisitions and their organizational and market implications, and strategies aimed at dramatically changing markets. The case gives the opportunity to train students in making assumptions in order to come up with reasonable issues, discussions, assessments, and suggestions for actions, despite the fact that the information in the case is scarce. The suggested questions below have proven productive in the discussions of the case.

1. Describe the market served by Gadan, the changes over the years, and the implications for Gadan.

This question is a natural entry to the discussion of the competitive environment of Gadan. The structural rationalization of the dairies can be analysed. What are the likely forces causing this development? What is the impact on suppliers to and buyers from the dairies? Which strategic

This teaching note was prepared by Dr Klaus Møller Hansen, Visiting Lecturer, Copenhagen School of Economics and Business Administration, Denmark.

alternatives are the dairies facing? Is it possible to identify any factors that would stop the development and/or reduce the process of structural rationalization? What kinds of alternative strategies exist for suppliers to the dairies?

Consumers are demanding ecological products and quality as well as low prices. Structural rationalization has meant dramatically rising transport costs to the dairies. At least in Europe, there is a trend to make transporters pay the real socio-economic costs of establishing and maintaining highways, and, not least, the pollution of the environment. When producers pay more for these services, structural rationalization provides a very distinct barrier for further rationalizations.

Dairies are squeezed between retail chains pressing for lower prices and the farmers' co-operative movement, which traditionally has been very powerful. This leaves the dairies with a number of alternatives: (i) to grow very big in order to exploit economies of scale and scope; (ii) to change the production completely and start producing ecological/'green' products since this strategy, at least initially, does not require large-scale production.

2. Assess the core skills and capabilities of Gadan.

This question typically involves a relevant assessment of the changes in the capabilities in Gadan that the changes in the market call for. From being a producer of single machines used in dairies, Gadan is now facing the problem of producing and installing parts of and even whole process lines. Students must be able to discuss all the implications of these needed changes.

The implications are that the people in Gadan generally have no expertise in developing, producing, marketing, selling, financing, and servicing entire process systems or parts of systems. From being experts in producing machines—in a rather standardized way—the organization now must face customers expecting 'tailor-made solutions'. The most important questions Gadan must ask itself are: How do we start some kind of continuing education? How do we start organizational processes aimed at changing behaviour and the thinking of the whole company? To put it another way: the most important barrier to exports is found within the company. Additionally, Gadan fights the traditional problems derived from integrating companies that have merged.

3. Rank the main strategic problems and challenges that Gadan is facing in 1988.

Based on the discussion above, students must be motivated to rank the different issues faced by the management in Gadan. No doubt the external issue of exportation is of importance. The international sale is spread over many countries: what are the challenges of cross-licensing with the Americans; how to market, sell, and service process lines (turnkey projects) internationally; and agents versus distributors. However, internally shaping the whole company after the two acquisitions seems even more important. Very little information is given in the text on this subject, but students must be motivated to suggest possible barriers for the functioning of the whole organization and for international sales. Examples are the co-ordination of international marketing, the actual exploitation of economies of scale and scope after the acquisitions, and sharing knowledge and technology between the differently located manufacturing units.

4. Which generic strategy should Gaden choose in 1988?

Students are requested to suggest an overall strategy for Gadan and the implications of this strategy for international marketing and sales. Good points of departure may be the size of Gadan and its position in the international industry for equipment to dairies, the culture of the company (the owner is the manager), and the question of Gadan being able to transform its capabilities in accordance with the on-going changes in the market. Important points of departure for students to formulate the overall strategy must be explicitly formulated, where information is absent. Emphasis is typically laid on a careful analysis and assessment of the implications of the overall strategy on the international marketing and sales strategy. Among strategies worth considering are to re-establish the position of a highly recognized manufacturer of single machines, to concentrate efforts on a considerably smaller amount of markets, to be acquired by one of the giants in the industry, and to diversify into other industries such as breweries, wineries, slaughter-houses, etc.

The company is 'playing with too many balls at the same time'. The management in Gadan must realize the time-consuming tasks of making the merged organization work and turning the people of the organization towards 'tailor-made solutions'. This leaves only room for very few initiatives in the market. The company must concentrate its efforts.

5. What is the main implication for Gadan's marketing channel?

The most important task is to build up trust and confidence with the agents in the foreign markets. Without any international sales, Gadan management must invest much time in this task. Apart from building up personal relationships, it is important to implement a new system of managing and controlling the relationships. Help, assistance, resources, money for marketing, etc., from Gadan to the individual agent should be considered. Also, action plans, budgets, reporting systems on realized sales, customers, competitors, market trends, etc., must be developed and implemented.

Case 17

Hansen Bathrooms (B)

Synopsis

Susan Clements had convinced Rob Vincent about the need for a premium price for the new bathroom furniture but Vincent still faced the task of convincing the board. Despite his enthusiasm, Karl Hansen and the other board members were sceptical.

Teaching Objectives

1. To illustrate the parallels between marketing to external customers and internal marketing.
2. To understand the issues that need to be faced when marketing proposals internally.
3. To provide an opportunity to develop an internal marketing strategy.

Suggested Teaching Approach

Having decided upon a premium pricing strategy when analysing Hansen Bathrooms (A), students can forget that marketing managers may have to convince other people in the organization before the strategy is accepted for implementation. This case, then, naturally follows on from the earlier case and illustrates many of the internal marketing issues discussed in Chapter 17.

1. What do you think of Rob Vincent as a manager?

When presenting their answers to this question, students are invariably critical of Vincent in his dealings with the board. During discussion, however, they can be asked what the board thinks of Vincent and what Vincent thinks of himself. This usually elicits lists such as:

The board on Vincent	*Vincent on Vincent*
Brash	Dynamic
Aggressive	Enthusiastic
Mr Right	Intelligent
Inexperienced	Professional

They are then asked 'who is right?' The answer is that both are right: it is the same person from two different viewpoints. The telling point can then be made that this happens to all of us. The way we perceive ourselves is often very different from the way other people perceive us. People need to be conscious of this and manage the process so as not to make matters worse. For example, the innocent act of leaving a folder on a desk labelled 'Executive Development Course' or 'MBA'

This teaching note was prepared by David Jobber.

upon returning to work may provoke adverse reaction from colleagues. People need to think about how they market themselves and their ideas internally within organizations.

This discussion leads into an analysis of Rob Vincent's actions—an opportunity to learn from his mistakes.

2. How well has he marketed his pricing proposals internally?

Vincent has clearly failed to assess the culture of Hansen Bathrooms. Karl Hansen and his board appear conservative in their approach to decision-making, and being older and more senior than him will want to feel involved in the pricing decision rather than being asked to act as a 'rubber stamp' for a decision taken by marketing. Just as marketing managers need to understand and respond to external customers' psychological needs, so must Vincent recognize the needs of his *internal customers*—the board. In the event, he *overpowered* using strong language which was inappropriate given his standing in the organization.

3. Can you suggest a better internal marketing approach?

Rob Vincent should have implemented the following:

(i) Gain affinity.

He should have attempted to build bridges between himself and the board. He told Susan Clements that the only time he visited the executive dining room was when he was appointed. Instead he preferred to go jogging at lunchtime. This may have been construed by the board as aloofness.

(ii) Share his ideas.

Three weeks had elapsed between the meetings. This gave Vincent ample opportunity to talk to each board member privately about their views on the proposal. Had he done this, France's idea of a test would undoubtedly have surfaced. This would have allowed Vincent to have evaluated it (and other suggestions) before the second meeting.

(iii) Adapt proposal and set negotiating objectives.

Vincent could have adapted his proposal to include France's suggestion. This could have taken the form of proposing the test (this would have immediately given him one ally on the board). This might have made sense given that his earlier proposal was rejected at the first meeting. Or he could have incorporated it into his negotiating objectives, thus:

Would like objective: immediate acceptance of premium price
Must have objective: test two price levels

(iv) Provide the evidence.

As discussed in Chapter 17, providing evidence of propositions aids their acceptance. Hence, he should have:

112

- Presented statements from 'delighted customers' taken from the marketing research report.
- Shown how the 'bottom-line profit figures' changed through adopting the premium price.
- Given examples of other products that have sold well despite having a premium price (reference sell).

(v) Use appropriate language and behaviour.

As the youngest person at the meeting the board probably perceived him as their junior. Vincent needed to adapt his communicational strategy to this reality. Therefore, he should have used softer language and less aggressive behaviour. Language such as the following could have been used:

'I have a proposal that I should like the board to *consider*.'

'I should like to *suggest* the following pricing strategy.'

This would have reflected the board's desire to feel part of the decision-making process. Another approach would have been to present the board with several options (a premium price and testing could have been two of them) for debate.

Case 18

Schur Group

Synopsis

This Danish corporation, producing packaging materials and machinery, is already highly internationalized, but the process of sustaining its international position is continuing. From being oriented towards Europe through production subsidiaries in Germany and companies in Denmark, the corporation is expanding in other European countries and in the United States. Partly due to these expansions the management is increasingly met with issues related to organizing the whole corporation. Should the corporation follow its well-known strategy of customization? Or should management define a new strategy, emphasizing the fruits of sharing knowledge, technology and market reputation through standardization of various functional areas in the corporation? What does it actually take to implement new philosophies in an international corporation if this is decided?

Teaching Objectives

1. To identify and discuss the strategic choice of following the principle of national responsiveness versus standardization in international marketing.
2. To assess the strategic assets of the company in question and identify the theoretical implications for organizing and managing the international business activities.
3. To identify and assess the organizational issues of the Schur Group and evaluate the initiatives hitherto taken at the corporate level in the corporation.
4. To work out a specific plan that in detail describes the strategic and organizational objectives for each of the key functional areas in the corporation.

Suggested Teaching Approach

This case has the potential to be used in isolation from lectures. A lot of assumptions may be needed in order to clarify the internationalization stage of the corporation, its strategic assets, its organizational structure, the informal organizational processes the corporate management is relying on, etc. In focus is the external organization of marketing and sales. As said in the case, no formal sales organization at present exists in the corporation. Among other interesting discussion themes are the changing policies regarding recruitment, the discussion of which functions to centralize and which functions to decentralize, the understanding (or disagreement?) between corporate management and managers in the subsidiaries, and how to market goods and services to European customers.

Schur has been highly concentrated on expansion and lots of initiatives have been taken in order to grow and 'learn internationalization'. The next phase in the international life of the organization may be consolidation, meaning how do we manage international business in the most

This teaching note was prepared by Klaus Møller Hansen, Visiting Lecturer, Copenhagen School of Economics and Business Administration, Denmark.

efficient way. This assumption concerning the internationalization stage of the company is the most important one. An important assumption is that the business concept shall not change. Another is that management is seriously engaged in its efforts to find new resource allocations mechanisms in the corporate structure—what to decentralize and what to centralize. In all different parts of the company there is a feeling of transformation: new ways of managing the corporation are under way and new initiatives that have already been implemented are discussed.

Discussion of the case can revolve around the following five questions:

1. Describe and assess the basic business concept of the Schur Group and the way the corporate management are taking care of the core strategic assets of the group.

Turnkey export from Denmark of the packing machines—which are not sold but leased—combined with traditional export from Denmark or Germany of the packing material has been the basic building block for the group in Europe. Other ways of internationalization have been implemented in distant markets.

Schur has developed a very powerful business concept: (i) Schur is capable of producing highly tailor-made packing machinery to individual producers—especially within the food industry; (ii) typically Schur additionally delivers the packing material—plastics, carton, paper or whatever—developed, produced and delivered in time for the producer of tobacco, frozen food, fresh food or whatever it might be. The buyer faces high switching costs.

2. Discuss the issue of decentralization and centralization.

Within some fields the Schur Group is very decentralized: marketing and sales in Europe is the prime example. In other fields—product and technology development—the approach is very centralized. Discussion of the pros and cons of the two principles should take place before a specific analysis of the Schur Group's activities.

The following fields ought to be considered as candidates for centralization:

- Product development—tailor-making of packing machinery—keep that in Denmark.
- The 'new' Human Resource Development must be supervised and followed very closely by corporate management—centralization to a very high degree is a solid proposal.
- Financial management naturally must be centralized to take full advantage of different cash-flows in the different subsidiaries and units of the corporation.
- New international market entries must be a centralized, corporate decision.
- Strategies for distant markets—implying alternative ways of selling the expertise of the company—is at the corporate level in Denmark.
- Information management systems and financial control systems are anchored in Denmark.
- Internal continuing education, etc., is co-ordinated in Denmark.

Fields that might be considered as candidates for a predominantly decentralized approach are:

- Marketing and sales must still be very locally oriented so that the company can understand the specific needs of buyers.
- On the other hand some kind of overall co-ordination of the decentralized marketing and sales is needed.

116

- On the other hand some kind of overall co-ordination of the decentralized marketing and sales is needed.
- If economically viable, the service of installed machinery must be decentralized in the sense that customers can contact local Schur people, e.g. representatives. Danes, afterwards, can be sent out from Denmark but the decisive element is the local responsiveness initially.
- Some mechanism for sharing knowledge and experience among the board of directors in the different subsidiaries and units without the participation of the corporate management in Denmark seems productive.

4. Draw a relevant organigram of Schur's international activities.

Co-ordination of international sales in Europe is very much needed. A proposed organigram is shown in Figure 7. The most striking feature of this suggestion is that the four German subsidiaries are given the competence and responsibility to sell all products from the Schur Group but each subsidiary is only given market access to precisely defined territories. For example, Germany 1 could cover the former state planned countries; Germany 2 the German market; Germany 3 the Mediterranean countries; and Germany 4 the rest of Europe.

These subsidiaries must be given direct access to important departments like product development, finance and HRM in Denmark. A matrix structure is proposed and area managers in Denmark are essential to make this structure work.

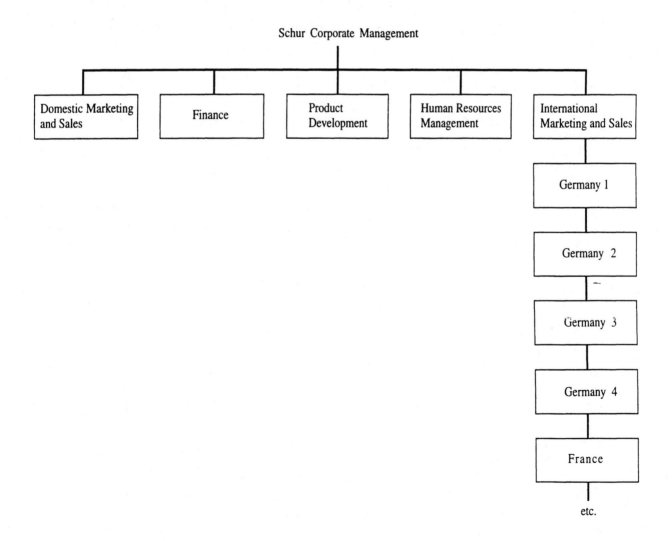

5. Discuss the implementation issues needed to make the new organizational structure work.

Currently the German subsidiaries have one very important success criterion: production effectiveness. In the new structure these companies are expected still to be effective producers but also very targeted sellers in predetermined markets, and also sellers of all products from the Schur Group. This was not the case in the old structure, where they only sold their own varieties in all European markets.

New incentives must be developed and implemented for the managers and employees. Mechanisms for the sharing of experience and knowledge must be developed and implemented. These mechanisms should include those that work without members the top management group in Denmark. A change of attitude must be implemented: 'We are all members of a large family. If the customer does not like this type of packing material, could I then persuade him/her to try some of the other types produced in the Schur Group.'

Transferrals of employees from different levels in the organization to the different units of the corporation is a very powerful tool. Top management must be the first to show the way. Openness and willingness to discuss with and listen to employees in the corporation seems to be a prerequisite to achieve the full-hearted back-up from most of the employees. Experimentation is needed, but after a while firmness is required and clear decisions and direction from top management will be essential.

End of Module Case

Ford Motor Company

Synopsis

Set around 1992/93, the case sketches the contemporary trends and issues facing car manufacturers as they battle for share of the European car market. It paints a picture of intensive competition, overcapacity, stagnant growth, deregulation, price wars, growing import penetration, currency fluctuations, poor productivity, and the need for new models which offer customers greater value and quality—in short, a cameo of the difficult problems facing many European firms as they attempt to compete on a global basis.

Against this background, the case focuses on the situation facing Ford Europe and the various strategic steps it has taken to deal specifically with the problems of its product range. It looks in some detail at the central plank of its European marketing strategy for the mid-to-late 1990s: the launch of the Mondeo. The case then throws into the foreground the local execution of this strategy in one national market, that of the Republic of Ireland, where annual car sales are around IR£750m.

The key point to be made is that marketing strategies need to be translated into action through effective implementation. Careful analysis is not enough. The face that customers see in the real world is marketing in action, so that managing this implementation has an important bearing on success. For Ford Ireland (FI) this is further complicated by the fact that it also has to manage its relationships with dealers as customers too, since there is a limited supply of dealerships available and many manufacturers chasing after them.

The case thus relates in many ways to the discussions of *implementation* and *organization* presented in Chapters 17 and 18 of the text. Many important concepts are to be found in those chapters and the case provides students with the opportunity to make use of those concepts.

Teaching Objectives

1. To introduce participants to the kinds of issues that arise when a global marketing strategy is to be executed at the level of a local market by an operating company.
2. To allow them to explore the relationship between the organization of marketing activities and the implementation of marketing strategy.
3. To examine the specific implementation considerations that arise where third parties have an active role to play in realizing marketing strategy.

This teaching note was prepared by Douglas Brownlie, Reader in Marketing, University of Stirling, UK.

Suggested Teaching Approach

This is not a case that can easily be read and analysed in a single session. Ideally, it should be distributed to students prior to class discussion.

The case has been used successfully at undergraduate and postgraduate levels to provide a context within which to discuss the various elements of the marketing mix and how they might be integrated given the situation that FI faces. It has also been used with executive students to focus on the managerial issues, specifically those regarding channel strategy and the management and control of the dealership network.

Early discussion should focus on the marketing objectives and priorities for FI (perhaps through asking students about FI's various SWOTs) and how the marketing mix can be mobilized towards the attainment of those objectives. Having done this, it is then possible to move on to a consideration of how to manage and develop the relationships with dealers.

Legislative framework

The instructor should be aware that the discussion of the dealership network should also be set in the context of recently amended (5/10/94) EC legislation governing the distribution of cars. No information on this matter is provided in the case. But, since dealership issues are an important element of the case, the instructor may care to bring the following information to the attention of the class at a suitable point, or to set students the task of finding out about the legislative arrangements governing the distribution of cars in the EU countries.

In a recent proposal, the EC decided to renew the block exemption of motor industry practices from EU competition law. The central principles of this exemption recognize that manufacturers will continue to be able to choose which dealers to supply and to limit those dealers to selling only one brand at one location, thus permitting exclusive franchises within designated territories. It also formally recognizes the right of dealers to stock competing brands at separate outlets and to advertise outside their franchise territories.

The new EC proposal dismayed consumer groups, while bringing relief to car makers by allowing them to keep their selective and exclusive distribution networks for another 10 years. The EC cited the complex nature of cars and their safety implications as major reasons for continuing to exempt car makers from normal EU competition rules governing the sale of goods.

A number of changes have been made which allow dealer organizations to distribute and sell more than one make of vehicle, subject to conditions such as separate premises, even if on the same site, with separate management and no possible confusion between the makes. Manufacturers will be able to terminate a dealer's contract if the dealer wishes to distribute other makes, but only if the termination is based on objective criteria, with arbitration being available in trade disputes. This should allow large multi-dealer groups to emerge. They already exist in the UK, but not in France.

Sales targets have now to be set by mutual agreement between manufacturers and dealers. This represents a small but significant shift in the balance of power between the two. At present car makers have the power effectively to impose those targets. Often dealers have regarded those targets as unrealistic, and as placing them under excessive pressure to move metal. Again arbitration is now available.

120

Now dealers can also obtain spare parts other than those of the manufacturer, provided they are of equivalent quality. There is an intensely competitive market for spare parts, with many independent suppliers undercutting original equipment prices.

As part of the new proposals, there is a measure allowing independent garage owners access to the technical knowledge required for repairing vehicles. This is an attempt to stimulate competition in after sales service, even if manufacturers will hand over knowledge very reluctantly. Dealers will also now have the freedom to advertise outside their own sales territories.

The minimum duration of agreements between manufacturers and dealers has been extended from four to five years; the minimum notice of termination has also been increased from one to two years. A ban has been put on all anti-competitive clauses in dealer contracts, on pain of the manufacturer forfeiting its own exemption from competition rules. Practices designed to discourage consumers of one country from buying a new car in another EU state have also been outlawed.

Some changes were made to tackle the limitations of the regime, e.g. to loosen manufacturers' monopoly over the supply of spare parts and to reduce obstacles to cross-border car purchases—this is repeatedly blamed by consumer organizations for creating gaping differentials in prices across the EU. Some of these obstacles are already seen to be illegal and the EC's failure to correct them inspires, for some, little confidence that the new rules will be enforced rigorously. Consumer groups argue that price convergence is one of the crucial tests of a unified market and that only when producers are compelled by strong cross-border competition to treat Europe as one market will there be effective pressure to abolish regulatory and fiscal obstacles to distribution. On the other hand, car makers have long argued that price convergence has not been achieved because of currency fluctuations and differences in national taxes and costs.

Exemption was originally granted on the grounds that cars are complex products that require big investments in after-sales service facilities. But by continuing the restrictions on multi-brand dealerships, some argue that innovation in car retailing will be deterred, denying car-buyers the convenience of comparing a wide range of competing models in one showroom. It is not clear whether abolishing these curbs will necessarily affect manufacturers' power to discipline wayward dealers, or lead to an unhealthy concentration of distribution.

Some facts and figures

Some facts and figures to bear in mind about the Irish market at the time of the case are as follows:

Dublin City and County	30% of population	Cork	4%
Limerick	1.5%	Galway	1.5%
Waterford	1%	Dundalk	1%
Bray	0.7%	Drogheda	0.7%
Sligo	0.5%	Tralee	0.5%

With around 1.1m households, and a population of 3.5m, it is clear that outside the Dublin conurbation and the other main towns, there exists a very large rural community, reflected in a population density per sq. km of 50, compared to 235 for the UK.

Of the estimated 1.1m motor vehicles on the road in Ireland, around 77 per cent are private cars, giving a figure of 210 cars per thousand inhabitants, compared to 400 in the UK. Sixty-five per cent of Irish households own a car, compared to 70 per cent in the UK and there are around 1.3m holders of a driving licence in Ireland.

Around IR£16m is spent annually on advertising, allocated among television, press, radio and posters as 13 per cent, 75 per cent, 8 per cent, and 4 per cent, respectively. The main fleet buyers in Ireland operate from Dublin-based headquarters, although some are located outside Dublin in Waterford, Galway, Limerick, and Cork.

There are around 1350 garages and filling stations in the Republic of Ireland, a 30 per cent decline since 1988. In the Dublin City and County area there are about 120; 360 in the rest of Leinster; 530 in Munster; and 360 in the areas of Connaught and part of Ulster.

The following set of questions have been used to structure group discussion.

1. What should Ford Ireland's priorities be?

This is a good way to open up a broad discussion of the various issues facing FI. In a freewheeling discussion, students will tend towards quick-fix solutions rather than a more thoughtful account of FI's situation. The idea here is to build an exhaustive inventory of signs and symptoms before attempting to connect them in any way in a fixed and final diagnosis. A useful device to encourage a more careful mapping-out of the issues is to ask students to comment on the wisdom of each others' ideas and to trace possible connections between symptoms, before elaborating on them.

Early discussion is likely to focus on advertising and direct marketing as key issues for FI. And while this discussion is worth pursuing, you can divert attention to more fundamental concerns through asking students to discuss when they last bought a car; where they bought it; what kind of car it was; how many cars they looked at before coming to a decision to purchase; how did they use advertising in their purchasing; and what sources of information were important to them? If they bought from a dealer, how many dealers they visited; how were they treated; what services were available; what do they use dealers for after they have bought the car; how this dealer could have improved its service, etc.?

A car is by any standards a big-ticket item and the reputations of the car manufacturers are probably just as important as the reputations of dealers in influencing purchasing behaviour.

Where the structure of the class permits, the instructor can also ask students to collect further background information on the Mondeo: for instance, where it is available locally; what services are provided by the dealer; what brochures and marketing materials are available; prices; competing models, etc.?

In this way the students can gather useful insights into the realization of the marketing strategy. They can also begin to consider the various factors that influence the purchasing behaviour of those who buy through a dealer, and those who buy through some other means, e.g. auctions, classified adverts, etc. The instructor can then ask the class to consider what information FI might need about car buyers and their purchasing behaviour to help it in its planning for the implementation of its strategy.

At this stage it is also useful to differentiate between the motives and needs of buyers on such bases as:

- First time versus repeat buyers
- Buyers of new cars versus buyers of second-hand cars
- Out-of-town buyers versus local buyers
- Buyers of second cars versus buyers of first, or sole cars
- Domestic buyers versus company (fleet) buyers
- Loyal buyers versus switchers

Through this discussion the various roles of different sources of influence in the purchasing process should emerge and you can ask students to consider the relative importance of those sources in different market segments. This should draw attention to the pivotal role played by the car salesperson in the purchasing process. And if the class are not already aware of it, the instructor can remind them that the salesperson is not employed directly by FI, but rather by the dealer. This raises the spectre of how to exercise any kind of control over the activities and approaches of a salesforce that is not in your direct employ.

2. What information does Ford Ireland need in order to construct a sound plan for the implementation of its markting strategy?

At this point in the discussion you can move on to consider what other information FI might need to assemble in order to begin to construct a reasonable plan. A brainstorming approach is helpful here. Typically the following information needs are suggested:

- Ford Europe's volume and revenue targets for FI by model and type
- Marketing resources provided by Ford Europe in terms of media ads and sales promotional schemes
- Available marketing spend for years 1–3
- Audience data for the various media—television, radio, press, poster
- Data on customer base of existing owners of Sierra and other Ford models:
  — address
  — date of purchase
  — type of purchase
  — financing arrangements
  — service/repair history
  — demographics
- Data on customer base of past/lapsed Ford owners
- Data on customer base of fleet buyers:
  — address of key contacts
  — sector, size, prospects
  — number/type of vehicles purchased
  — financing
  — servicing/livery arrangements
  — other suppliers being considered
  — insurance arrangements
- Location of dealerships
- Reputation of dealers and the type of clientele they attract
- Quality of sales staff and customer service of dealers
- Growth, profit, and solvency record of dealers

- Quality of merchandising effort
- Dealerships coming up for renegotiation in different areas
- Competitor information about models, dealerships, marketing activities
- Profit margins required by dealerships
- Potential size of new-model and second-hand model markets
- Opportunities for new dealership sites

3. Do the same set of priorities apply across the Republic of Ireland?

If it has not already arisen in the previous discussion, at this point it is helpful to begin to unpack some of the issues that seem to be specific to the important Dublin market, as against those that might apply to the other key urban sales areas in Ireland.

The point of raising the question is for students to consider the different marketing problems that FI faces in the Dublin conurbation (city and council) compared to the other major towns, and to the rural areas.

The scale of importance of the Dublin market is clear from the tables provided in the case. But it is also useful to explore the possible differences and similarities of car-purchasing behaviour between the main population areas and the rural areas. It should be obvious that it is uneconomic for dealers to operate outside the main population centres and that this has implications for the services available as well as the purchasing behaviour of customers.

In the light of the discussion of the first three questions, the class can then move back to reconsider FI's priorities and to outline a headline marketing strategy in terms of broad target market segments and appropriate marketing mixes. The instructor can easily provoke debate about the feasibility of the various objectives set for marketing effort, for instance, in terms of market share in the different markets; building awareness of the new model; testing consumer reactions to it; exciting press and media coverage of the new model; developing suitable direct marketing instruments; building interest in the new models through various incentive schemes and below-the-line promotional devices, etc.

Students can then go on to consider what all these measures should mean in terms of building vehicle sales. You can ask students to consider what factors might facilitate or impede the take-off of sales of the new model and which of them are within the control or influence of FI. And at this point you should arrive at the issues of selecting, recruiting, motivating and supervising dealers.

4. What role could the dealers play in developing the marketing strategy?

At this stage students must begin to separate strategic issues from implementation issues and to decide if the key problems facing FI are rooted in strategy or implementation. In this case the grand strategy imperatives are broadly dictated by Ford Europe, set within the legislative framework. But, at the local level, FI is able to exercise some discretion over its marketing strategy and implementation activities within the general framework of corporate expectations.

Students need to be given the chance to think through how the marketing strategy they have outlined is to be carried out, i.e. who is responsible for what, where and when, and how will their performance be measured. You can usefully stress that implementation is a consequence of strategy, an outcome, and that their strategy is likely to fail, no matter how well conceived, if people are incapable of carrying out the necessary tasks to make the strategy work in the market place. Thus,
124

implementation then affects the choice of marketing strategy at a local level: you have to factor-in the capabilities of the local staff—in this case the dealerships and especially their sales and service staff.

It is possible to ask students to consider why FI has suffered in the Dublin market. Various explanations will be offered in terms of: weaknesses in the model range; poor market coverage from the dealerships; inappropriate locations of dealerships; intense price and product competition from other manufacturers; poor service levels from dealerships; inadequately trained sales staff; poor delivery; poor display areas, etc. You might ask students to talk about what reasons there may be for underperformance in each of those factors and what steps FI could have taken to overcome them.

At this stage the instructor can build the argument for saying that FI may previously have had a good strategy for the Dublin area, but that it was poorly implemented; and that if this was so, it clearly points to the importance of the dealers in making product available; in providing the vital sales and merchandising effort; in dealing with customer complaints; in providing important information about customers; and in delivering the service required. It also throws up issues of record keeping, service, and training, as well as the technical, sales, and marketing support provided by Ford to help dealers achieve desired service levels.

This discussion should explore the various elements of service in purchasing and running a car. The instructor can easily start this discussion by asking students to reflect on their own experience of buying and running a car, where they have any. This should very quickly lead to a list of the main elements of service. At this juncture the instructor can ask the students to consider what weaknesses there may be in FI's dealership network and what changes might be needed in the light of their broad marketing strategy.

5. In the light of your priorities, what should FI's key objectives be for the implementation of its local strategy, and how should it approach the setting of those objectives?

Discussion here should be nudged towards the following:

Gaining support from key decision makers in specific dealers

In terms of the communications component of its marketing strategy, FI not only has to persuade end-consumers towards its strategy, it also has to persuade its distributors—FI not only sells through its dealers, it must also sell to them. So, if FI is to overcome the concerns of dealers about the new marketing strategy, it must attempt to anticipate them, for some of its ideas may mean significant changes in terms of jobs, responsibilities, systems, and procedures. The first step in forging a partnership with dealers is to understand their needs and concerns.

FI must then have a plan to sell to the dealers that makes clear what operational changes are required and how FI are going to help with specific problems, such as the provision of resources for training and development; for setting up new systems and procedures for order processing, arranging financial deals, invoicing, customer care, complaints handling, and others that support the front-line sales and service staff. FI will have to sell the concept of its marketing strategy to the dealers and explain the support available, the rewards, and how dealer efforts and activities link into the overall marketing activities of FI nationally. Otherwise FI is unlikely to attract dealers with the necessary commitment, competence, and resources. A number of motivators should be appreciated, such as margins; special deals; the provision of co-operative advertising and display allowances; sales contests, etc.

Anticipating resistance

FI should anticipate resistance in terms of: criticisms of the basic plan; slow response to requests for ideas about how to implement the changes; and arguments that proposals are too ambitious and call for too much change.

The level of resistance will depend on how much change is being suggested, the proposed speed of its introduction, and how much it is expected to disrupt the existing culture of the dealer. Students should think through what could be done to ameliorate those concerns. For instance, where the sales job has to change, perhaps with staff moving out of direct sales and into telemarketing, what can be done to help staff become accustomed to new ways? Those kind of ideas have to be considered before dealership staff will reach the point of accepting the new regime and becoming committed to it. FI has to cultivate a positive attitude towards change in the dealers.

One step that FI could take is to set up a separate unit to manage dealer relationships and to work with them in planning marketing effort. The unit would take charge of arrangements for merchandising, sales training, co-ordinating advertising and promotional activities, and the collection of information needed by FI to monitor dealer activities and customer requirements. It could also set up a dealership council in which representatives of the various dealers meet at regular intervals to discuss their various problems and activities, providing a management report to FI.

Students also need to be clear about the enthusiasm and commitment needed at different levels of the dealership organization, as well as from their own organization. They must also bear in mind the importance of working out low-cost solutions to meeting the needs of end-customers as well as those of their dealers.

Meeting customer needs may come into conflict with other objectives of the dealers, such as in the area of delivery and inventory which have serious working capital implications for the dealers. A compromise may have to be found in terms of the desired speed of response to problems about vehicle delivery and parts availability and the financing of working capital.

Measuring performance towards targets

Students should be asked to consider how they might quantify the various measures they think would be appropriate in terms of monitoring dealer activity towards its marketing targets. The benefits of what students believe FI should be offering the dealers must also be quantifiable, so that both FI and its dealers can measure the increase in revenues and costs attributed to the new way of doing things.

Those measures must also be linked into the personal ambitions of the dealer and his/her staff. So FI must also think of reward and incentive systems for dealers and individual sales staff: are they to be rewarded on the basis of short-term sales, and if they are, what can be done to compensate for the fact that sales staff are likely not to pay heed to market factors such as building the long-term customer satisfaction that underpins repeat sales? And if the sales payment system is to be increasingly incentivized, FI must anticipate dealer worries about how sales targets are going to be achieved. It is also important to monitor post-sale activity and targets may also have to be set here. Typically corporate support is available for this sort of activity in terms of database management, newsletters, magazines, promotional offers, etc.

FI must be prepared to support its fine words with corresponding action, i.e. if it stresses customer service, it must follow this up with a system for measuring it and rewarding good efforts,

126

and training people in the FI approach. But in doing so it must allow for some local control over details, otherwise the important sense of ownership and empowerment may be jeopardized.

FI could approach the task of setting objectives through developing:

Concession objectives

In terms of what we would like to achieve and what we must achieve, i.e. minimum requirements, there will be room for negotiation between the two extremes. And thinking about where this room might lie will clarify the scope for bargaining with dealers who might be resistant, say, to a new payment system for sales staff based on higher commission on sales and lower basic salary component. FI may have to recognize that dealers are in a position of some strength in the negotiations and it may not get everything its own way. Students can be asked to consider the sort of concessions that might be appropriate in the short and medium term.

Internal marketing objectives

FI will have to help dealers with the internal marketing of the new approach if they are to gain support and commitment. FI needs to understand the situation from the dealer's point of view and from that of their various staff: FI may stand to gain from the new approach, and end-customers may too if it is successfully executed, but what about distributors and their staff? How will FI's plan benefit its dealers and their staff—and what evidence is there for those claims. It must make clear what it expects from dealers in terms of account development, services, the delivery of market information, etc.

If the goal is to forge a long-term partnership ethos between manufacturer and dealers, FI must help dealers to articulate a shared vision of the destination sought and the desired results of change to the key staff in their organizations. FI then has to help dealers see the wider picture and this may involve a significant communications effort where a large number of dealers are involved. But only through this process can FI hope to eliminate misconceptions of the vision, the pace of change, its direction, and its consequences. Students can be asked to think about what form the communication effort might take.

Dealership processes and systems

Dealers are unlikely to possess or to be able to afford a formal marketing department with direct responsibility for developing customer relations. It is likely to be conducted by someone who already has responsibility for other functions. Students can be asked to think about the allocation of responsibilities to staff for the various tasks they think dealers will need to conduct. They should be encouraged to locate responsibility in terms of a person, or a job. A category management structure may be relevant here, i.e. managers dedicated to customers types—e.g. the fleet market versus the domestic buyer.

This leads on to a discussion of controlling the activities of dealers. Students can be asked to think about the components of a system for monitoring marketing performance at various levels. Clearly this discussion will consider controlling dealer activity as well as FI's own marketing activity, since FI are likely to be heavily involved in selling to fleet buyers.

The discussion might begin by deciding marketing objectives leading to the setting of performance standards. For instance in terms of widening the customer base, a target might lead to

127

the performance standard of generating so many new accounts in a set period of time, which is then thought to lead to the attainment of FI's market share objectives.

Students can be directed to consider two types of control systems: are dealers doing the right things—i.e. company strengths and weaknesses and the marketing audit; and are they doing things right—i.e. day-to-day marketing activities through measuring customer satisfaction? They can also explore different ways of analysing variance from targets and the kinds of information required for those analyses to be conducted at national, regional, and local level.

Case   19

Olsen Watch Repairs

Synopsis

A customer calls on a watch repairer to collect a watch. A difference of interests causes a clash that results in an aggrieved customer.

Teaching Objectives

1. To emphasize that technical competence alone is insufficient to provide customer satisfaction in a service encounter.
2. To illustrate the importance of the intangible aspects of service quality.

Suggested Teaching Approaches

The case describes a real-life service encounter and provides the opportunity to discuss eight of the ten criteria discussed in Chapter 19 which can be used to evaluate service quality, namely: access; credibility; security; understanding the customer; responsiveness; courtesy; competence; tangibles.

The background to the case is that John Nielsen had brought only enough money to make a number of purchases, assuming the watch could be paid for by cheque. By the time he arrived at the watch repairers the banks had closed and he did not have his cash card with him. Therefore to pay by cash was a great inconvenience, meaning that he would not be able to make all his planned purchases that day.

Analysis of the case can begin by evaluating each element of the service encounter as it happened. First, the opening was cold and unwelcoming. It immediately made the customer feel ill-at-ease and on the defensive. Olsen seemed to be suggesting that Nielsen should have known that the shop was normally closed on a Saturday. Even if he had left the watch (rather than his wife leaving it), it is unreasonable to expect customers to remember times of opening.

The times of opening displayed a complete disregard of customer expectations. Customers require the shop to be open when it is most convenient for them. Saturdays and lunchtimes are two of the most convenient periods for many people to visit the shop. Furthermore, the inconsistent opening and closing times is bound to confuse customers.

When Olsen gave Nielsen the watch, the customer had to rely on Olsen's word that it was now keeping the correct time. Olsen should have ensured that the watch was wound up since repair so that Nielsen could see for himself that it had been satisfactorily repaired.

This teaching note was prepared by David Jobber.

The dispute over the method of payment showed an all-too-frequent event: the service provider putting his/her interests before that of the customer. Whether the benefit to Olsen was convenience or tax evasion is irrelevant. By insisting on cash payment he alienated Nielsen, and by insulting him he ensured that Nielsen would never use his services again.

The evaluation of service quality can thus be summed up by reference to eight criteria:

- *Access:* by closing at inconvenient times (Saturdays and lunchtimes) and through inconsistent opening and closing times, access was poor.
- *Credibility:* Nielsen was not provided with the evidence that the watch was working properly. Confidence about the service provider's technical quality was, therefore, low.
- *Security:* if Nielsen had brought in another watch to be repaired, because of low credibility, he would have had to accept a high level of risk if he had left it with Olsen.
- *Understanding the customer:* Olsen's failure was to believe that technical competence was enough. To succeed in a service business all facets of customer service expectancies need to be met.
- *Responsiveness:* Olsen failed to respond positively to Nielsen's cash problem.
- *Courtesy:* Olsen began by being unfriendly and finished by being rude.
- *Competence:* the irony of this case is that the watch kept excellent time following the repair. Olsen clearly had the necessary skills and knowledge to perform well technically.
- *Tangibility:* the shop was dimly lit, accentuating the unfriendly atmosphere.

Nine months after this experience Nielsen happened to pass Olsen Watch Repairs. The shop was closed with a large 'Premises for Sale' sign fixed to the window.

Case 20

Dandy

Synopsis

Dandy is a Danish company that markets chewing gum internationally. Its main consumer brand is Stimorol. In Europe, Dandy faces stiff competition from the Wrigley brand, which is the market leader. Dandy management face the task of developing an international marketing strategy in the face of strong global competition.

Teaching Objectives

1. To develop an international marketing strategy working with limited marketing data.
2. To understand the characteristics of the chewing gum market in foreign countries.
3. To develop target marketing strategies for different submarkets (children, medical care).

Specifically:

Q1   To consider the appropriateness of product/market strategies
Q2   To design medium/long-range international market strategy
Q3   To analyse the pros and cons of standardized marketing
Q4   To evaluate the marketing organization
Q5   To develop a marketing strategy in France
Q6   To analyse the pros and cons of starting a licence operation in Poland.

Suggested Teaching Approach

The questions at the end of the case can provide a structure for case analysis.

1. Make an evaluation of Dandy's product/market strategy.

Dandy's strategy is primarily concerned with consolidating the current markets with the existing product line. The primary market areas are Western Europe, where Dandy is attempting to increase their market share with their flagship brand, Stimorol—especially in Germany where they have a subsidiary.

This teaching note was prepared by Marcus Schmidt and Svend Hollensen, Business School of Southern Denmark, and Lynn A Kahle, Engineering College of Copenhagen, Denmark.

2. Make a proposal for Dandy's international product/market strategy from now to year 2000.

In order to avoid excessive investments in marketing for the development of new brands, the new chewing gum product types will be launched under the existing umbrella brands, primarily Stimorol. Dandy should attempt to cultivate their core competence and base their international marketing on this core competence. Dandy is considered a champion in production technology within dragée products. Therefore Dandy should continue to develop and maintain their leading position within this product area, which is primarily Stimorol.

The health aspect will also continue to be a priority. Therefore product development in the Fertin Lab must not be allowed to come to a standstill. The primary geographical market will continue to be West Europe, and Dandy must, before the year 2000, provide for market development and establish some distribution channels for Stimorol in the Central and Eastern European markets, where there is expected to be an increasing consumption of 'western' chewing gum in connection with the implementation of market economies.

If Dandy were to prioritize its resources and choose either product or market development, there are still great market opportunities within the dragée-product market. Although Dandy has a relatively large market share within this area, a large portion of chewing gum consumption will be attributed to consumers switching from sticks to dragée. Considering the market opportunities in the dragée products, market development would still be preferable.

Therefore the optimal strategy would be: not launching completely new brands, but new product variations under the existing brand-name umbrella, combined with market development; first in Central and Eastern Europe (due to the relative short geographic distance) and then the rest of the world.

3. Which international branded good strategy would you recommend to Dandy—high or low standardization?

Clearly the general trend for many companies is toward international or global branding due to the 'borderless world' of today. Dandy must be able to weigh the advantages and disadvantages of this strategy.

- *Advantages:* Economies of scale in standard packaging, promotions, advertising, greater acceptance in trade channels, etc.
- *Disadvantages:* Changing a recognized local brand name to a global one can be very costly, resistance from local managers and possible lost creative input, global standardization can ignore the great differences between countries, etc.

In general, the company must look at opportunities for economies of scale by having a global brand, and localize those variables that would help them to gain competitive advantage.

4. Estimate the impact of your proposals in questions 2 and 3 on Dandy's international organization.

The suggestion from question 2 concerning internationalization of core competencies (primarily production technology) with respect to dragée products suggests a market-development strategy, where the international marketing organization would eventually be divided up into regions rather

132

than product groups. This is an obvious solution since Dandy only produces chewing gum. It would seem inappropriate to divide up the market into production divisions instead of one, geographic market division.

One could imagine that the external as well as internal sales and marketing organization could eventually be divided up into the following seven regions: countries in mainland EU, Northern Europe (the Nordic countries and the UK), Central and Eastern Europe, Middle East and Africa, the Far East, the Pacific Rim, North and South America. The importers and subsidiaries in each region could refer to their respective regional directors, who would have the overall sales and marketing responsibilities in the region for chewing gum products in addition to the sale of know-how. One could also establish a central marketing department to build up a marketing information system (MIS), which could function as a back-up for marketing in each region.

5. Taking relevant strategies for distribution in France into consideration, make a considered choice.

As in any type of co-operation, both parties are interested in taking advantage of each other's strengths, and feeling that they are getting something in return for their invested resources. KGFF has a salient strength in their 'downstream' function (sales and marketing) through their established distribution system, as they enjoy 80 per cent of the French chewing gum market. Dandy, on the other hand, has a strength in the French market because of their 'upstream' function, which is their competitive strength in the production technology of dragée. Obviously, KGFF could offer Dandy access to better distribution channels, which could be the basis for a larger market share in France and perhaps other French-speaking countries (Belgium and Switzerland).

Why, then, should KGFF be interested in distributing Stimorol when they have their own brands of chewing gum? Isn't there a risk of Stimorol cannibalizing KGFF brands? This depends on how much chewing gum manufacturers are able to differentiate their brands. Chewing gum is not just chewing gum. Actually, Stimorol appeals to a slightly older target group compared to the Hollywood brands, which have a milder taste. Therefore, Stimorol could actually supplement KGFF's product line. On the other hand, Dandy could offer their production technology for dragée. As it happens, KGFF chose to invest approximately 40m Danish kroner in new production technology in a run-down dragée factory in Italy.

The following are two alternative strategies for the French market:

- Establish a French subsidiary of Dandy, keeping the independent Dandy profile in marketing and distribution:

    Advantages
    Dandy choose their own marketing strategies for the French market.
    Dandy ensures that Stimorol has the desired position and profile in the retail stores.

    Disadvantages
    Dandy has large overhead tied up in the subsidiary, leading to financial problems.
    Dandy only has chewing gum to bear these costs.
    Dandy will have to spend a great deal of money to be 'listed' so that the product will be put on the retailers' shelves.

- Closing the French subsidiary of Dandy and allowing KGFF to distribute Stimorol:

Advantages
Dandy can save on overhead expenses.
Dandy can save the 'listing' cost.
KGFF has good market coverage and a good distribution network. It would be expensive for Dandy to establish comparable distribution and coverage of the market.
The co-operation could lead to other areas of co-operation (Dandy's dragée technology).

Disadvantages
Dandy should be wary of KGFF's salesforce who would favour Hollywood chewing gum rather than Stimorol, their former competitor.
Dandy could also risk that the conglomerate Kraft General Foods would 'smother' them, as Dandy is a small company in an international context.

It seems as if the advantages of a co-operation outweigh the disadvantages, so this option would be recommended. Table 5 shows the outcome of this decision.

Table 5 Market share for chewing gum in France

Brand (Company)	1987	1990	1992
Stimorol (Dandy)	5.3	6.1	7.2
Hollywood (KGFF)	87.2	82.0	78.8
Freedent (Wrigley)	3.2	8.5	11.3
Others	1.8	3.4	2.7
All	100.0	100.0	100.0

The development for Stimorol looks very positive, so the decision to let KGFF distribute Stimorol seems to be the right one. For KGFF, however, the figures do not look that positive, and Dandy might have reason to fear that KGFF will give Stimorol's success some of the blame for KGFF's decline in market share. This, in the long run, could be a threat to the distribution co-operation in France.

6. **Discuss the advantages and disadvantages of starting license production of chewing gum in Poland.**

Advantages

- Increase in total turnover for the selected, already developed, products if the alternative is no export through the usual channels.
- Licence option can (together with establishing production facilities or in joint-venture agreement) the only way of avoiding high import tariffs, etc.
- If the Polish market has a strong nationalistic attitude it could be an advantage to let the local market manufacture one's products.
- Quicker market penetration compared to Dandy trying to establish themselves in the Polish market.
- Less expensive than Dandy starting their own manufacturing in Poland.

Disadvantages

- There is a risk that a new competitor will be born. There is also the danger that the market in Western Europe could be flooded with cheap dragée products, which, of course, have another name, but are a cheap imitation of Stimorol. There are, of course, elements that a company can attempt to control through a contract, but this can present problems. It is very difficult to control a licensee by long distance, in the physical and cultural sense.
- The resources required by Dandy to start-up licensing agreement and the marketing of Stimorol in Poland could be just as expensive as establishing a joint venture (stated in the case).
- Due to the political and economic instability in the country, there is the risk that the licensee will not be able to pay royalties. If the licensee's company is not doing well, perhaps Dandy would be able to take over a portion of the company's shares, which could mean a joint-venture situation.

Dandy's opinion of licensing is actually rather negative as, contrary to popular belief, starting-up a licensee is very resource demanding; sometimes even to the extent that the start-up costs can easily devour profit potential.

End of Module Case

Halifax Building Society

Synopsis

Despite their position as the main suppliers of finance for owner-occupation in the UK, building societies were traditionally prohibited from operating overseas. This situation changed with the passing of the 1986 Building Societies Act and several societies have now established a presence in Western Europe. This case relates to the activities of the largest UK building society, the Halifax.

Teaching Objectives

This case is best used to highlight the positive and negative features of a range of international market entry strategies. Consideration focuses on agents, greenfield start, acquisition, and joint ventures. Important project management issues such as the type of advisory services, location of development work, and cultural implications are also addressed.

Suggested Teaching Approach

An effective way of analysing this case is to follow the questions that appear at the end of the case.

1. **The Halifax Building Society decided to enter the Spanish market by developing a wholly owned subsidiary. What are the positive and negative features on this mode of entry?**

The benefit of the greenfield start approach for a new entrant is that it allows the organization to retain control of the pace and direction of the business and the scale of operations. It is also in a position to develop its corporate philosophy from scratch rather than seeking to remove existing impediments. While the greenfield start can prove too slow where a strong and immediate market presence is needed, for example in relation to distribution channels, this can also be seen as a positive feature because it allows time for thorough preparation of all facets of the business and limits risk.

These first steps allow the new entrant to gain practical experience of a new market and assess future expansion strategy prior to making more significant commitments. Initially the presence can be seen as practical research—in order to allow expansion, again at a rate and scale of the entrant's choosing to be based on greater practical knowledge. Balanced against these positive features is the fact that a retail focus to the funding of the business ideally requires a larger network and that it is more difficult to become established as a familiar 'brand' in the minds of customers when the number of outlets is limited.

This teaching note was prepared by Des Thwaites, Senior Lecturer in Marketing, University of Leeds, and Chris Toole, European Operations Controller, Halifax Building Society, UK.

2. What alternative entry modes could have been chosen? What are the positive and negative features of each?

The nature of retail financial services are such that some of the strategies associated with manufacturing companies are inappropriate, namely exporting, licensing, and foreign direct investment.

Accordingly, the most appropriate alternative foreign market entry methods are agents, acquisitions and joint ventures.

Agents

Agents earn commission by selling products on behalf of the supplier. They do not take title to the products nor can they accept deposits from host-country customers. Although the capital investment in this type of operation is low, given the extensive market coverage which can be secured, this is often outweighed by the lack of control over activities. This approach offers little scope for creating a significant presence in the market and is not generally adopted by UK financial institutions.

Acquisitions

This may be the only viable option to becoming a meaningful player in certain markets, but it does not usually make sense as a first step. The ability to secure access to assets or distribution systems very quickly is attractive, although there are more often than not two reasons why something is for sale. Either it is good quality and a forced sale of part of the crown jewels, in which case it is very expensive; or it is of dubious quality and unsuccessful. Either way this can present problems. The acquisition of foreign institutions may also lead to less than cordial relationships with host governments.

Further positive features include:

- Name awareness amongst the target market
- Goodwill in terms of trading record (at a price)
- Infrastructure—staff and premises
- An existing customer base with cross-selling opportunities
- An existing income stream

On the other hand, the negatives would include:

- Unknown inherent problems (despite due diligence)
- Staff resignations (i.e. goodwill value is diluted)
- Customer resistance to name change (e.g. Deutsche Bank in Italy and Spain retained the old, known trading name for a transitional period)
- Higher risk
- Lack of approval by the foreign regulatory authorities

Joint Ventures

Corporate linkages incorporate a number of forms of agreement, including both equity and non-equity joint ventures, franchising, licensing, etc. Several motives for joint ventures are suggested in the literature, for example:

- Circumvent trade and foreign investment restrictions and satisfy nationalistic demands
- Secure access to resources, e.g. raw materials, local knowledge, distribution channels
- Pooling of risk
- Gain synergies, e.g. manufacturing, distribution, technology
- Reduce cost of R&D, production, etc.
- Secure scale economies
- Utilize idle resources
- Achieve product differentiation
- Where the business fit is correct, the outcome is greater than the sum of the parts

Despite these potential advantages there is evidence in the literature to suggest that benefits are not always achieved. Particular problems occur in relation to the following:

- Partner identification and selection
- Differing strategic motivations
- Time spent on management and administrative issues
- Cultural impediments
- Hidden agendas
- Acceptance of a minority position
- Concerns over how long the relationship will survive
- Profit sharing
- Image confusion
- Dissolution issues

3. **Consider some of the project management issues which faced the Halifax Building Society once a decision to enter the Spanish market was taken.**

Important project management issues that need to be addressed by the new entrant include the type of advisory services to be used and the location of the development work. Cultural dimensions must also be examined and managed. There may be legitimate differences in relation to personnel management approaches, systems requirements, premises layout, marketing design and control, product differentiation, security, company formation and regulatory styles, all of which need to be understood and accommodated. In each case the solution has to meet both local business needs and the overall philosophy of the parent company. Attention will also focus on the relationship of the subsidiary with the parent—the degree of autonomy, the management information flow, and the level of operational support. The following section relates these issues specifically to the Halifax.

The route taken by the Halifax was to develop a project team from all parts of the organization to contribute specialist expertise in a wide variety of disciplines, e.g. legal, treasury, finance, personnel, marketing, and information technology. The role of co-ordinating these contributions fell on the society's European Operations Department. Subsequently, to provide advice and guidance on the Spanish market, e.g. regulation and culture, a panel of professional contacts was recruited in Spain. Information generated both internally and externally allowed a co-ordinated response to a number of key issues.

- Staffing: often said to be the most important resource and, in this case, the area where a challenge of mixing UK Halifax culture and local market practice is the most real. The Halifax view is that UK staff are needed to become expatriates in other markets, to be the living presence of Halifax's approach, but also as a long-term investment in broadening their scope and increasing their contribution on returning to the UK after a 3- or 4-year secondment. It is also considered that the ratio of UK staff to locals should be quite low, but that the UK individuals need to be senior and of the highest possible calibre.
- General policies were drafted following advice taken from local human resource consultants and input received from the Head Office Group Personnel function;
- Premises: distribution is the key to the success of financial services, whether retail or wholesale. The Halifax decided to export its well-proven Branch 2000 concept to create the right image of openness and a modern feel to the network right from the beginning. This area involved liaison with property advisers and through them architects, quantity surveyors, office fitters, and security firms.
- IT systems: perhaps the lifeblood of the operation and the one that can cause the most headaches in an operating environment. In order to maximize flexibility and minimize disruption to the UK data systems, a stand-alone retail banking package was introduced.
- Marketing: the IT system is also seen as an integral part of the marketing campaign, as it will deliver a modern, efficient point-of-sale information base for customer enquiries or quotations. Again, this is a large and complex area, but as well as product advertising, there is clearly a need for substantial corporate promotion.
- Product development: another area where the needs of the target market must be researched and their characteristics identified. Products that are successful in the UK may need adapting to accommodate regulatory, social, or cultural conventions.
- Autonomy: the extent of control exhibited by the parent will influence the development of the subsidiary. While close supervision is to be expected in the initial stages, this will reduce over time. Nevertheless close liaison and skills transfer between the two units will be ongoing.

Particular skills required of the project management team are as follows:

- Careful planning: even the best-laid plans will not always run smoothly, but in a new situation, foresight and clear planning are essential. Proper project management, timetabling, and monitoring are needed to maintain progress and commitment, and although the planning documents may change in the light of experience, it would be foolhardy to dispense with them altogether.
- Communication skills: the need for clear and constantly updated information is also paramount. Internal project teams, external advisers, locally recruited management, senior executives, and other interested parties all require information in different forms and at different times. Since it is a job that cannot be done by one area alone because it covers the whole of a building society's operations, effective management of all these areas through communication is available.
- Allied to this is the need to be able to think creatively and approach things in a new way. The unproven nature of such a project can lead to either scepticism or die-hard stubbornness to do things as they have always been done, but the skill is to adapt and amend where appropriate without missing the crucial points which will not submit to alteration.
- Linking back to the long-term perspective at all times is also helpful, even when involved in the minutiae of a system's specification or a job description for the opening headcount—because it is the first step only, in a dynamic process towards a goal that may be many years away. The balance between conscientious detail checking and ensuring that long-term objectives are not blocked also offers a constant challenge.

140

- Finally, patience is also required to believe that the long-term aims will be met, however circuitous the route!

REFERENCES

Buckley, P.J., Pass, C. and Prescott, K. (1992) Foreign market servicing strategies of UK retail financial service firms in continental Europe, in *Europe and the Multinationals*, Young, S. and Hamill, J. (eds), Edward Elgar, Aldershot.

Glaister, K. and Thwaites, D. (1995) International joint venture formation. The financial services sector, *Service Industries Journal*, in press.

Ohlsen, J. and Markgraf, K. (1991) European market entry and expansion: case study of an international mortgage bank, *European Management Journal*, vol. 9, no. 3, pp. 317–320.

Reid, K. (1992) Opportunities and challenges for building societies in Europe, *Journal of the Chartered Building Societies Institute*, January, pp. 2–7.

Toole, C. (1993) First steps into Europe, *Banking World*, August, pp. 25–27.

Whitelock, J. and Jobber, D. (1993) An evaluation of the factors affecting the selection of market entry method in non-domestic markets, North West Centre for European Marketing, University of Salford, Working Paper no. 9302.

PART TWO

STUDY QUESTIONS

Chapter 1 Study Questions

Marketing in the Modern Firm

---

1. What are the essential characteristics of a marketing- oriented company?

The answer to this question will be based on a discussion of the following characteristics:

- Focus on creating customer satisfaction (even delight!)
- Building strong customer relationships
- Creation of new customers and the retention of current ones by providing added value
- Focus on customer needs: getting close to the customer by personal contact and/or marketing research
- Acceptance that change is the Darwinian condition for survival
- Adaptation to current and latent markets: seeking new opportunities that match company strengths
- Eagerness to innovate: being first into new markets and the desire to reward innovation
- A desire to understand competitors and their strengths while seeking a competitive advantage over them
- Customer concern permeates all areas of business
- Provision of incentives to those who create customer satisfaction

2. Are there any situations where marketing orientation is not the most appropriate business philosophy?

While customer needs can never be ignored or neglected, it has to be recognized that creating customer satisfaction may come at a price. For example, giving all customers exactly what they want may conflict with such efficiency concerns as economies of scale and continuous production runs if many product variants have to be made. Profits, therefore, may be maximized at a point prior to the realization of complete customer satisfaction.

This is one reason why market segmentation (to be discussed in more depth in later chapters) is a useful tool of analysis. By grouping customers with similar needs and providing products that match those needs a high (though not total) degree of customer satisfaction may be realized, while the firm can still benefit from long production runs and economies of scale.

A second situation where marketing orientation may not be applicable is when customers demand a standardized product (and accompanying service) in a highly competitive market. A production orientation focusing on cost cutting and control may be desirable, indeed necessary, to achieve profitability. Note that the study by Narver and Slater cited in the chapter showed that high profitability could be achieved with both high and *low* levels of marketing-orientation. They suggested that the high performance of low marketing orientated companies may have been achieved through a low-cost strategy.

However, even when such a strategy is employed, there is still a need to be aware of changing customer needs and new opportunities—characteristics that are associated with a marketing approach to business.

3.   Explain how the desire to become efficient may conflict with being effective.

A sensible starting point would be to define both concepts:

- *Efficiency:* concerned with input and output—'doing things right'.
- *Effectiveness:* concerned with 'doing the right things', e.g. marketing products that customers want in attractive markets.

There can be a conflict because efficiency is essentially cost-focused (achieving a given output at low cost). Effectiveness, however, is customer- and market-focused. The problem is that improving the quality of customer satisfaction often necessitates higher costs. For example, improving service by employing extra staff, manufacturing a better product by using better quality ingredients or components, and widening the product range may all raise customer satisfaction while lowering efficiency through raising costs per unit of output. Management may therefore ask 'are the extra costs going to be recouped through higher sales revenue?'

Effective companies do not seek to satisfy the needs of any potential customer: they seek attractive markets (groups of customers) in which to operate. Outstanding business success follows a combination of high effectiveness and high efficiency (see Figure 1.4). A key skill is the understanding of where it is necessary to lower maximum achievable levels of efficiency in order to create added value to the customer.

4.   What barriers may a marketing manager face when trying to convince other people within an organization that they should adopt the marketing concept?

The answer to this question is not directly covered in this chapter but the question may be used to stimulate considerable thought about why companies resist the implementation of the marketing concept. This issue is covered in Chapter 17, Managing Marketing Implementation and Change, but it may be beneficial to raise the issue at the start of a marketing course to create an awareness of potential problems.

Some barriers that need to be addressed are:

- High cost solutions: as discussed when considering question 2, giving customers what they want may involve extra costs. This can give rise to resistance.
- Unquantifiable benefits: the benefits of raising service levels or improving product quality may be difficult to quantify in terms of extra sales revenue.
- Personal ambitions: not all individuals in companies are motivated solely by organizational objectives. For example, an R&D manager may prefer working on a complex technical problem to solving a less challenging problem, even though the latter may be more important from a customer point of view.

- Reward systems: these may cause managers to focus on short-term cost cutting rather than long-term customer satisfaction.
- Saying versus doing: people may give 'lip-service' to the marketing concept yet their actions may conflict with what they are saying (e.g. saying 'be customer oriented' then cutting back on marketing research funds).

5. **To what extent do you agree with the criticisms of the marketing concept and the 4-Ps approach to marketing decision-making?**

The answer to this question may provide a range of opinions. Relevant points include:

- The marketing concept is only one business philosophy; others such as cost minimization are equally legitimate and may predominate in certain situations.
- The concept focuses on individual rather than societal welfare. These do not always equate since the individual may not take into account the social costs associated with a purchase (e.g. non-biodegradable packaging, pollutants from washing powders).
- Some companies are responding to societal concerns by providing new products (e.g. reusable packaging, eco-friendly washing powders).
- Customers are a poor source of new product ideas—but is this really central to the definition of the marketing concept?
- The 4-Ps approach simplifies reality neglecting people, process and physical evidence.
- The extra 3-Ps can comfortably be discussed within the 4-P framework (e.g. people as part of the product in a restaurant.
- Relationship building is more important than manipulation of the 4-Ps.
- Relationship building activities can be accommodated within the 4-P framework (e.g. as part of the personal setting function.)

Chapter 2 Study Questions

Marketing Planning: An Overview of Marketing

---

1. **Is a company that forecasts future sales and develops a budget on the basis of these forecasts conducting marketing planning?**

Marketing planning is part of the strategic planning process that has the function of shaping and reshaping a company so that its business and products succeed in the market place.

The aim is to be aware of the environment and the changes that may impinge on company performance, and to be conscious of internal corporate strengths and weaknesses. By analysing these factors, strategies can be designed to take advantage of opportunities while minimizing the impact of environmental threats.

Forecasting sales and budgeting is clearly very different from this process. Essentially, it is a closed-loop system in that its focus is the marketing of the same products in the same markets. Marketing planning is an attempt to break out of this closed loop by considering other opportunities. The Ansoff matrix is useful here.

In summary, forecasting and budgeting systems are about what a company is doing today; marketing planning concerns the strategic changes that are necessary to compete effectively tomorrow.

2. **Explain how each stage of the marketing planning process links with the fundamental planning questions identified in Table 2.1.**

This question can be answered using Table 2.2.

- Where are we now and how did we get there?

The business mission states the purpose of the business in terms of what business is the company in (and what business does the company want to be in). It explains why the business exists and for whose benefit.

The marketing audit is a systematic examination of a business's marketing environment, objectives, strategies, and activities with a view to identifying key strategic issues problem areas, and opportunities. Many of the conclusions of the marketing audit can be summarized in a SWOT analysis.

The business mission, marketing audit and SWOT analysis all have a role to play in answering the questions where are we now and how did we get there.

- Where are we heading?

Part of the marketing audit will focus on where the company is heading if no action is taken. Perhaps a key market is in decline meaning that future sales and profits are likely to be unsatisfactory. This finding from the audit could be summarized in a SWOT analysis under the 'threats' heading since it is an external trend that has implications for performance.

- Where would we like to be?

Strategic option analysis and the setting of marketing objectives contribute to answering this question.

Strategic option analysis concerns the generation and evaluation of strategic options. This involves deep strategic thinking about issues. Figures 2.4 and 2.5 in this chapter are helpful in highlighting methods of increasing sales and improving profitability. Not only may ways of improving performance of existing products be identified, but also opportunities for new product development and entry into new segments and markets be revealed. Strategic option analysis, thus, provides the foundation for the future direction of the business.

The setting of marketing objectives will be based on strategic option analysis. Two types of objective need to be considered: (i) strategic thrust which determines which products should be sold in which markets, and (ii) strategic objectives which concern the role of each product in the product portfolio—to build, hold, harvest, or divest. These define where we would like to be, e.g. building product x in market y.

- How do we get there?

Having defined our marketing objectives we need to decide how to accomplish them. For example, what marketing activities are needed to build product x in market y? Determining core strategy, designing an appropriate marketing mix, and creating an organization capable of implementing the plan are required. Core strategy focuses on target market selection; competitor targets and the establishment of a competitive advantage; marketing mix design requires the blending of product, price, promotion, and place decisions into a coherent mix that matches (and exceeds) customer requirements; and organization and implementation concern the transformation of core strategy and marketing mix decisions into actions.

- Are we on course?

Control systems are required to monitor performance so that corrective action can be taken if required. Short-term control focuses on results versus objectives on a weekly, monthly, quarterly and/or annual basis. Long-term control checks whether marketing plans still retain strategic credibility.

3. **Under what circumstances may *incremental* planning be preferable to *synoptic* marketing planning and vice versa?**

Incremental planning is a problem-focused approach to planning. Solutions to problems give rise to strategy which emerges as a loosely-linked group of decisions that are made individually.

Synoptic planning is the so-called logical step-by-step process exemplified in Figure 2.1.

Incremental planning may better fit the culture of some organisations whose members may feel uncomfortable proceeding through a predetermined set of questions perhaps as a group over a weekend. Synoptic planning, however, is more comprehensive since its framework ensures that key planning issues such as strategic option evaluation and consideration of marketing objectives are discussed.

However, there are a number of contextual difficulties with 'synoptic' planning such as politics, opportunity costs, reward systems, lack of information, personality clashes, and lack of managerial knowledge and skills that can make the process hazardous.

4. Why is a clear business mission statement a help to marketing planners?

A business mission is a broadly defined, enduring statement of purpose that distinguishes a business from others of its type. Two fundamental questions are: what business are we in? And what business do we want to be in? The answers to these questions define the scope and activities of the organization.

A business mission can also incorporate a 'sense of mission', that reflects managers' views of what they are doing and their enthusiasm for company goals. This can be described by the Ashridge Mission Model that defines the company's purpose (why the company exists), strategy (the commercial rationale), company values (what senior management believes in) and standards and behaviour (the policies and behaviour patterns that guide how the organization operates).

A clear business mission statement is helpful to marketing planners by defining boundaries within which new opportunities are sought, and by motivating staff to overcome the difficulties associated with the marketing planning process, and to succeed in the implementation of the resulting plans.

5. What is meant by core strategy? What role does it play in the process of marketing planning?

Core strategy focuses on how objectives can be achieved (the 'how do we get there?' question). It consists of target market selection, competitor targets, and the creation of a competitive advantage. The choice of target market not only defines the group of customers to serve but also the group of competitors against which we must compete. In order to succeed a company must create a competitive advantage by establishing a differential advantage, or by achieving the lowest cost position while marketing products that are acceptable to customers.

Core strategy is a critical element in the marketing planning process since it concerns how marketing objectives can be achieved. By selecting a target market, the needs of those customers can be understood and a differential advantage created to better serve those needs than the competition, and/or operations managed in such a way that their needs can be satisfied more efficiently (lowest cost) than the competition.

6. Distinguish between 'strategic thrust' and 'strategic objectives'

Both strategic thrust and strategic objectives from part of the process of setting marketing objectives. As such they define where in strategic terms the company should be heading.

Strategic thrust concerns which products to sell in which markets. The Ansoff Matrix shown in Figure 2.6 gives the alternatives.

Strategic objectives need to be agreed for each product. An essential point to grasp is that not all products should be built. Other valid objectives are to hold, harvest or divest. Chapter 16 entitled 'Competitive Marketing Strategy' gives the situations where each strategic objective makes sense.

Together strategic thrust and strategic objectives define where the business and its products intend to go in the future. Decisions regarding strategic thrust may have implications for business mission redefinition.

Chapter 3 Study Questions

Understanding Consumer Behaviour

1. **Choose a recent purchase that included not only yourself but also other people in making the decision. What role(s) did you play in the buying centre? What roles did these other people play and how did they influence your choice?**

The answer to this question will obviously depend on the chosen purchase situation. Often students choose a consumer durable purchase such as an audio-system to describe how the purchase was made.

The question provides an opportunity for students to relate the theory of the buying centre to their real-life experiences.

Influences on choice may be based on social acceptability ('my friend owns product x'), personal experiences ('I tried/listened to product x on holiday/in a store and liked it') or factual information ('I read in a magazine that product x has the best performance'). Other people may provide information to help make a judgement on choice criteria already perceived by the purchaser (decision-maker), or bring new choice criteria to bear on the decision ('it's very important that product x is portable').

2. **What decision-making process did you go through? At each stage—need recognition, information search, etc.—try to remember what you were thinking about and what activities took place.**

This question focuses on how purchases are made—the decision-making process. Like question 1, the answer will depend on the purchase situation but if a consumer durable is chosen all of the stages in the consumer decision-making process given in Figure 3.2 will be evident in the answers given.

The answer to the question can also provide a framework for discussing the marketing stimuli that were operating and how companies can use marketing tools to influence consumers at every stage of the decision-making process.

If this question is used as part of classroom discussion and a variety of products are chosen, the contrast between the evaluation and purchase of products in low and high involvement situations can be highlighted. Students can be asked the extent to which the high involvement (Fishbein–Azjen) and low involvement (Ehrenberg–Goodhart) models shown in Figure 3.3 reflect their experiences.

3. **What choice criteria did you use? Did they change between drawing up a short-list and making the final choice?**

Choice criteria can be organized under the headings of technical, economic, social, and personal criteria. The question can illustrate that even with expensive purchases social and personal criteria can sometimes outweigh more 'rational' technical and economic factors.

Relating the question to the consumer decision-making process can show that the short-list of brands/models that were evaluated (stage 3 in Figure 3.2) may have been chosen using different criteria than those used when the final decision is made. Reputation of manufacturer/service provider may be important at stage 3, but price may be key consideration ultimately.

4. **Think of the last time you made an impulse purchase. What stimulated you to buy? Have you bought the brand again? Why or why not? Did your thoughts and actions resemble those suggested by the Ehrenberg–Goodhart model?**

The Ehrenberg–Goodhart model suggests the purchase of goods in low involvement situations will follow the very simple process of awareness–trial–repeat purchase. If trial is satisfactory, repeat purchase may occur with very little conscious evaluation of alternatives.

An impulse purchase is an example of a low involvement purchase situation. The purchaser decides to buy a brand (perhaps the brand name is recognized from a television commercial) to try it. The purchase price is low, so the cost of not liking the brand is negligible. If the brand is liked it will probably be bought again but other factors such as availability and the desire for change may mean that it is only one of an array of brands in the product category that is bought.

The marketing implications of the A–T–R model should be discussed.

5. **Can you think of a brand that has used the principles of classical conditioning in its advertising?**

Classical conditioning is the process of using an established relationship between a stimulus and a response to cause the learning of the same response to a different stimulus. It is a form of learning by association, and is an important method of establishing a brand image.

A brand is shown in an advertisement in a situation for which there is a known response. The same (or similar) response is gradually associated with the brand. For example, Martini was shown being drunk in socially desirable situations. The objective was to persuade people that Martini was a socially acceptable drink. Other examples are given in the text of this chapter.

6. **Are there any brands that you buy (e.g. beer, perfume) that have personalities that match your own?**

Personality is the inner psychological characteristics of people that lead to consistent responses to their environment. There has been considerable debate about the matching of human and brand personalities. Some studies have found no relationship between the two, while others have found a link. The situation is by no means clear-cut but there appears to be a stronger link with products that are worn 'as a badge', that is as a statement to say 'who I am' to other people. Thus for products like beer and clothing there is a stronger link than for toilet soap or shampoo.

154

7. **To what kind of lifestyle do you aspire? How does this affect the types of products (particularly visible ones) you buy now and in the future?**

Lifestyle refers to the patterns of living as expressed in a person's activities, interests and opinions.

As with personality, lifestyles have been found to correlate to some degree with purchasing behaviour. This is not surprising in that people may wish to display their lifestyle through the clothes they wear and the cars they drive. The relationship may be weakened because of intervening variables. For example, a student may aspire to a sophisticated lifestyle, and desire products that reflect that, but be unable to afford them. The marketing implications of lifestyle analysis are discussed on page 83 of the textbook.

8. **Are you influenced by any reference groups? How does this influence what you buy?**

Some people may be reluctant to admit they are influenced by reference groups, but most of us are. A reference group is a group of people that influence an individual's attitudes or behaviour. Purchases may be influenced by what people regard as likely to be well thought of by their reference group. The more conspicuous the choice as to the reference group, the stronger is its influence.

The question allows the student to consider social influences on purchasing, and how companies can use this knowledge when marketing their products (see page 88 of the textbook).

Chapter 4 Study Questions

Understanding Organizational Buying Behaviour

1. **What are the six roles that form the decision-making unit (DMU) for an organizational purchase? What are the marketing implications of the DMU?**

The answer to this question is clearly given in the text. It serves as a revision question to test knowledge and understanding. The six roles are:

*   Initiators
*   Users
*   Deciders
*   Influencers
*   Buyers
*   Gatekeepers

The marketing implications are that the composition of the decision-making unit needs to be identified, the roles played by each member defined, and appropriate communication strategies devised to reach them. When DMU members prove to be inaccessible or are too numerous for a salesperson to contact, other media such as advertising or direct mail may be considered as alternatives. Salespeople need to avoid working in their 'comfort zone': contacting only those people in organizations with whom they have established links.

2. **Why do the choice criteria used by different members of the DMU often change with the varying roles?**

Choice criteria are the criteria used by DMU members to evaluate suppliers and/or products. The Winters case study shows that choice criteria often differ between members of the DMU because they are related to the performance criteria used to judge how well members of the DMU are doing their jobs.

For example, a purchasing manager may be more concerned about cost considerations than a technical person because the former is judged on cost savings while the latter is evaluated on technical matters.

Even in organizations, personal criteria such as how well the purchase of a product from a particular supplier may affect promotional prospects can be important. However, because purchases have to be justified to other people in the organization technical and economic criteria are often key factors.

3. What are creeping commitment and lock-out criteria? Why are they important factors in the choice of a supplier?

Both of these terms are related to the organizational decision-making process. Creeping commitment refers to the process by which a purchaser becomes increasingly dependent on one supplier through the latter's early involvement in the decision-making process and the technical assistance (goodwill) it provides.

A key stage in the decision-making process is the determination of specifications. A supplier may become involved in this decision and recommend specifications that only its products meet. In so doing, the specifications would contain 'lock-out' criteria which effectively would lock-out the competition (or most of it) from winning the order.

By working with purchasers early in the process suppliers can gain significant marketing advantages in the ways described above.

4. Explain the difference between a straight re-buy, a modified re-buy, and a new task purchasing situation. What implications do these concepts have for the marketing of industrial products?

A straight re-buy occurs when an organization buys previously purchased items from suppliers already judged acceptable.

A new task purchase is found when the need for the product has not arisen previously, so purchasing experience and information is usually lacking.

A modified re-buy falls between these two situations. Buying alternatives are known but something has happened to cause an alteration to the normal supply situation.

There are a number of marketing implications:

- For an in-supplier the task is to maintain the situation as a straight re-buy. Automatic re-ordering systems help to achieve this but ultimately it requires the continuance of a differential advantage through such factors as outstanding product performance and high-quality service
- For an out-supplier the task is to change a straight re-buy to a modified re-buy situation. Communications should be channelled when the buyer is most likely to be interested in hearing new proposals (e.g. when considering the renewal of a contract). Offering superior product performance, better service levels, lower price, lower lifecycle costs, etc. may be important but recognizing that changing supplier incurs risk on the part of the buyer means that the following tactics may be necessary:
  — offering free or low cost trial
  — accepting an unprofitable initial order
  — reference selling
  — offering guarantees with penalty clauses
  — acquiring a total quality management standard
- For new task purchases big gains can be expected for potential suppliers entering the decision-making process early and helping the buying organization to solve problems. This can lead to 'creeping commitment'.
- Heavy sales and marketing investments may be needed in new task situations since the decision-making process may be long with many people in the decision-making unit.

5. Why is relationship management important in many supplier–customer interactions? How can suppliers build up close relationships with organizational customers?

Organizational buyers are not passive recipients of marketing programmes designed by suppliers: they are active members of a network of relationships between themselves and many organizations. Successful organizational marketing, then, is much more than the traditional manipulation of the 4-Ps—product, place, promotion and price. Relationship management is a key ingredient in holding onto customers. This requires the skilful handling of interpersonal relationships and the recognition that buyers may wish to be proactive in their dealings with suppliers.

Buyers and sellers are increasingly forming strategic partnerships where information is shared and joint teams work on projects for mutual benefit. The appointment of customer relationships managers and the growth in key account management within the selling function reflect the importance given to the handling of customer relationships. When 80 per cent of business is in the hands of 20 per cent of customers, suppliers cannot afford to neglect key customers.

Close relationships can be built up by:

- Providing technical support.
- Offering expertise, for example in design and selling.
- Giving resource support, such as extending credit facilities.
- Improving service levels.
- Reducing risk, e.g. by offering delivery guarantees.

The aim is to build trust so that buyers are confident that their suppliers will meet their obligations and place a high priority on their interests.

6. Explain the meaning of reverse marketing. What implications does it have for suppliers?

The contrast between the traditional view of marketing and reverse marketing is clearly shown in Figure 4.3. With traditional marketing, the initiative is placed with the supplier, with purchasers viewed as passive recipients of marketing research studies, and the 4-Ps.

Reverse marketing, however, emphasizes the proactive role of purchasers. It is the process whereby the purchaser attempts to persuade the supplier to provide exactly what the buying organization wants. Vignette 4.1 describes reverse marketing in action.

The market implications for suppliers are:

- Suppliers need to be receptive to purchasers' ideas.
- Lack of co-operation may damage relationships
- Co-operation may develop stronger, longer-lasting relationships
- The ideas may be a source of new product opportunities on a wider scale.

Chapter 5 Study Questions

The Marketing Environment

1. **Choose an organization (if you are in paid employment use your own organization) and identify the major forces in the environment that are likely to affect its prospects in the next five to ten years.**

The answer to this question will depend upon which organization is chosen but should contain an analysis of the following environmental forces:

- Economic
- Social
- Legal
- Physical
- Technological

   Although Chapter 5 focuses on these macro-environmental forces, the answer to this question could also include micro-environmental factors such as competition, customers, distributors, and suppliers.

   By extending the question to include internal strengths and weaknesses, the answer could form a marketing audit of the chosen organization.

2. **Assess the impact of the Single European Market on the prospects for a motor car manufacturer such as the Rover Group.**

Vignette 5.1 discussed the impact of the Single European Market on Fiat. It showed how fierce competition stimulated Fiat into an £18 billion investment programme to update its tired product line and outdated production facilities.

   For other companies competition is also likely to be more intense with Japan investing heavily in European-based car manufacturing facilities (see Table 15.3), and the barriers that protected their home market gradually falling.

   Other factors which are affecting the car industry are:

- Lower physical barriers—freer movement of cars between countries
- Reduced technical barriers—differences in technical standards, testing and certification procedures are falling, but slowly
- Less freedom to support ailing car manufacturers through state aid
- Scale building and strategic alliances to compete internationally

3. **What are the major opportunities and threats to EU businesses arising from the move to market-driven economies of Eastern bloc countries?**

Opportunities:

- Greater marketing access to cover 400 million people
- For distributors, access to new suppliers (e.g. EU supermarkets buying Hungarian and Bulgarian wine)
- Low cost manufacturing

Threats:

- Cut-price competition (e.g. commodities)
- Greater general competition as Eastern bloc companies acquire skills and technologies to compete internationally.

4. **Generate two lists of physical products and services. The first list will identify those physical products and services that are likely to be associated with falling demand as a result of changes in the age structure in Europe. The second list will consist of those that are likely to increase in demand. What are the marketing implications for their providers?**

The age structure in the EU is given in Figure 5.4. It shows that between 1995 and 2010 the proportion of people younger than 44 years of age will fall, while that for people older than 45 will rise. This is likely to be mirrored across the whole of Europe. Demand for products bought by younger people is likely to fall while that for products bought by older people is likely to rise.

Two suggestive (but not exhaustive) lists are:

Falling demand	*Rising demand*
Jeans	Weekend and winter holidays
Trainers	Personal pension plans
Personal stereo systems	Health care
CDs	Holiday homes
Nightclubs	
New homes	

One marketing implication is that companies marketing products such as jeans and trainers need to position them as 'ageless' rather than focused on younger age groups. A second implication is that companies should be aware of the long-term opportunities provided by the growth markets associated with the increasing numbers of people over 45 years old.

5. **Discuss how you would approach the task of selling to German buyers.**

Vignette 5.4 discusses the essentials of doing business in Germany. The selling implications are:

- Be precise, e.g. try to be as exact as possible regarding delivery (not 'next month' but January 20th)
- Visit German customers personally
- Be polite and discrete

- Do not use humour, particularly at first meetings
- Use formal titles, e.g. Herr Schmidt or Frau Strauss
- Dress soberly
- Recognize the importance of purchasing departments
- Use trade fairs and advertising to communicate to otherwise inaccessible technical specialists

6. Evaluate the marketing opportunities and threats posed by the growing importance of the socially conscious consumer.

Opportunities:

- New products using environmentally friendly ingredients (e.g. biodegradable, disposable diapers)
- Recyclable packaging and materials. Some companies advertise the recyclability of their materials (e.g. BMW)
- Marketing to new market segments (e.g. Bodyshop)
- Favourable publicity resulting from taking positive steps to become socially/ environmentally friendly (e.g. Norsk Hydro)

Threats:

- Decline of previously successful products (e.g. CFCs)
- Fragmentation of demand in product/markets reducing average market segment size and therefore economies of scale. This threat may be offset by the use of flexible manufacturing systems
- Unfavourable publicity resulting from not responding to social/environmental issues

---

Chapter 6 Study Questions

Marketing Research and Information Systems

---

1. **What are the essential differences between a marketing information system and marketing research?**

A marketing information system is a system in which marketing information is formally gathered, stored, analysed, and distributed to managers in accord with their informational needs on a regular planned basis.

This consists of four subsystems:

- Internal continuous data
- Internal *ad hoc* data
- Environmental scanning
- Marketing research

Each of these subsystems is discussed in-depth in this chapter.

Marketing research is, therefore, a part of the overall marketing information system and is primarily concerned with the provision of information about markets and the reaction of these to various product, price, distribution, and promotion actions. A major distinction is between:

- Continuous research
- *Ad hoc* research

Continuous studies focus on the same sample of respondents repeatedly. Three types of continuous studies are consumer panels, retail audits, and television viewership surveys.

Ad hoc research focuses on a specific marketing problem and collects data at one point in time from one sample of respondents.

Marketing research for many companies is the major component of their marketing information system providing essential information about their markets.

2. **What are secondary and primary data? Why should secondary data be collected before primary data?**

Secondary data comes to the researcher 'second-hand': it has been gathered/compiled by other people who publish the information for dissemination. Examples include government statistics, market reports (e.g. Mintel), and directories.

Primary data comes to the researcher 'first-hand': it has been gathered by the researcher (or his/her agent) not by a third-party. Often this will require field research (e.g. interviewing respondents) and as such is expensive.

Since secondary data is either published as a public service (e.g. government statistics) or for a wide audience (e.g. Mintel reports) it is much cheaper than conducting primary research. In practice, it is often free through the use of libraries.

Researchers should inspect secondary data first to see what information is readily available. This may remove the need to conduct expensive primary research, or help in focusing the research on topics that are not covered by published information. It is also, usually, quicker to collect secondary information than to brief an agency, consider proposals and execute a primary research study.

3. **What is the difference between a research brief and proposal? What advice would you give a marketing research agency when making a research proposal?**

A research brief explains what the client wants from a given research study. It explains the marketing problems and outlines the research objectives. It will include:

- Background information
- Sources of information that the client is aware of
- Scale of the project
- The timetable

Each of these points is discussed in more detail in the chapter.

A research proposal tells the client what the research agency will do to satisfy the client's needs. It will include:

- Statement of objectives
- The research design
- The timetable
- Costs

Good proposals should:

- Clearly define terms
- Focus on the client's problem not favourite techniques
- Avoid the use of jargon
- Be specific—clearly define what is being offered and when so that no misunderstandings occur.

4. **Mail surveys should only be used as a last resort. Do you agree?**

The mail survey suffers from a number of disadvantages (see Table 6.3) including low response rates, and lack of flexibility (e.g. there is no opportunity to probe). Note, however, that response rates can be improved with the use of various techniques (see Table 6.4).

However, all survey methods have their disadvantages. Face-to-face interviews are expensive unless the sample is very conveniently located, and telephone surveys are limited in the time that can reasonably be expected for a respondent to spend being interviewed.

Mail surveys are attractive when information of a fairly simple nature (e.g. agree–disagree statements) is required from widely dispersed respondents. If the questionnaire is carefully designed with the use of closed questions in an attractive format, some of the techniques outlined in Table 6.4 are used, and the topic is of some interest and/or benefit to the recipient, response rates should not be too low. The average response to industrial mail surveys published in the marketing literature is around 30 per cent.

Mail surveys should not be used as a 'last resort' but when the research situation suggests that they will meet research objectives better than face-to-face or telephone interviews.

5. Discuss the problems of conducting a multi-country market research survey in the EU. How can these problems be minimized?

The major problems are:

- Question wording: there is a danger that a translation may alter the nuance of a question, resulting in different interpretations and answers between countries.
- Classifying respondents: different EU countries use different criteria for placing respondents in a social grade. In the UK a single criterion (occupation of the chief wage earner is the traditional method) is used, but in France, Germany, and Italy multiple criteria are used (see Vignette 6.3). Foreign agency personnel and interviewers may not be used to a 'foreign' method of classifying respondents and mistakes may be made.
- Sampling: the method of choosing a sample may differ between countries. For example, the criteria used to choose a quota sample may differ because of differences in classifying respondents (see above).
- Co-ordination: with large distances involved communication problems may lead to misunderstandings and errors.
- Varying uses of qualitative research: some countries use qualitative research without quantitative backup; others usually follow up with a quantitative survey. This can affect how the qualitative research is conducted and the way each report in each country is written up, thus leading to inconsistencies (see Vignette 6.2).

Minimization of these problems is by checking and double checking for mistakes and difficulties and by personally communicating wherever feasible. Employing experienced multinational agencies who can plan centrally while using foreign nationals in overseas offices can be an advantage.

6. Why are marketing research reports more likely to be used if they conform to the prior beliefs of the client? Does this raise any ethical questions regarding the interpretation and presentation of findings?

Research by Deshpande and Jeffries reported in Chapter 6 suggests that one of the factors influencing the use of marketing research information is that the results conform to the client's prior beliefs.

One reason for this is that the client is more likely to accept that the results are valid (truly reflect the market situation) if they confirm what they believed to be true. For example, if the research results confirm that there is a delivery problem, then that information is more likely to be used than if it is contrary to the client's previously held beliefs.

When there is a discrepancy a challenge to the competence of the research is more likely. The researcher may be asked to justify exactly who was interviewed, how many and what questions were asked. Given that no research is perfect, weaknesses may give the client the opportunity to throw doubt on the findings. The alternative is to simply ignore the findings and proceed on the basis of unaltered prior beliefs.

A temptation for a marketing research agency that wants to get its research results accepted and thereby receive praise from its clients is to interpret findings in accord with what it thinks its clients believe. The results are more likely to be used and there is less chance of their research methodology being challenged. The fallacy in this argument is that it would soon get a reputation of producing bland, uninteresting research reports. It is probably true, however, that a mixture of results that conform to prior prejudices, and new original insights is probably a good combination. In the final analysis, market research agencies need to maintain their integrity by presenting information to their clients in an unbiased way no matter how unpalatable the findings are to the client.

Chapter 7 Study Questions

Market Segmentation and Positioning

---

1. **What are the advantages of market segmentation? Can you see any advantages of mass marketing, i.e. treating a market as homogeneous and marketing to the whole market with one marketing mix?**

Market segmentation is the identification of individuals or organizations with characteristics in common that have significant implications for the determination of marketing strategy.

Its benefits are in:

- The identification of a target market
- The tailoring of a marketing mix to target market requirements
- The development of differential marketing strategies between segments
- The creation of a differential advantage within the chosen target market

Treating a market as homogeneous and marketing to the whole market with one marketing mix is called undifferentiated marketing. It can make sense when there are no strong differences in customer characteristics that have implications for marketing strategy. The advantage is that a single marketing mix can reap large economies of scale. For example, a single product design or advertising campaign may lead to lower production costs.

In reality few markets are homogeneous. Offering only one marketing mix leaves opportunities for competitors to segment the market and serve target customers better.

2. **Choose a market that you are familiar with and use benefit segmentation to identify market segments. What are the likely profiles of the resulting segments?**

This question allows students to see how the principles of market segmentation appear to have been used by companies when designing marketing strategies in real-life.

The answer obviously depends on the chosen market and a tutorial discussion is a good way of generating ideas. For example, if the chosen market was for cars an analysis might include:

Benefits sought	Profile
Economy	Lower income; thrifty minded
Status	Company drivers; higher income
Performance	Company drivers; young males; aggressive-minded
Space; large boot	Families
Compactness, small boot	Single/retired couples

Environmental friendliness	The socially/environmentally concerned
Distinctiveness	Higher income individualists

Students could then be asked to discuss the types of car that fit each benefit segment:

Economy:	Small cars (e.g. Fiat Punto)
Status:	BMW, Mercedes-Benz
Performance:	Any car with the suffix XRi, sports cars
Space; large boot:	Ford Mondeo, Vauxhall Cavalier
Compactness; small boot:	Vauxhall Nova, Ford Fiesta
Environmental friendliness:	Electric cars; cars fitted with catalytic converters as standard, e.g. Volvo range
Distinctiveness:	Sports cars; 'off-road' vehicles

3. In what kind of markets is psychographic segmentation likely to prove useful? Why?

Psychographic segmentation involves grouping people according to their lifestyle and personality characteristics. Lifestyle segmentation attempts to group people according to their way of living as reflected in their activities, interests and opinions. For example, Europeans with similar lifestyles have been grouped under such headings as trendsetter, avantgarde, and socially-concerned (see Vignette 7.1). The question that arises, however, is the extent to which general measures of lifestyle predict buyer behaviour in specific markets. Lifestyle segmentation is likely to be useful when brand choice is a public statement about the purchaser—and hence his/her lifestyle.

Personality segmentation is also likely to be more useful when brand choice is a reflection of self-expression. The brand makes public an aspect of personality. The brand is used as a badge stating how the buyer would like to be regarded by others. Successful personality segmentation has been found in the cosmetics, alcoholic drinks and cigarettes product groups where brands act as badges (with cosmetics people are often asked 'what perfume are you wearing?').

4. How might segmentation be of use when marketing in Europe?

Segmenting across national boundaries in Europe opens up the possibility of meeting target customers' needs while reaping economies of scale. If people can be segmented by benefits sought, lifestyle, personality, lifecycle, etc., or a combination of these, pan-European branding can be based on consumer commonalities.

Vignette 7.2 shows how geodemographic segmentation can be used to locate distinct 'Euro-regions' or customer groups that span country boundaries. Although this is only the starting point for European segmentation, it is this kind of analysis that will allow marketing managers to tap large cross-national Euro-segments.

Segmentation across Europe is possible because large sections of the population share common values, experiences and consumption patterns: young adults buy international brands such as Levi jeans and Nike trainers; wealthy adults buy Gucci shoes and Chanel perfume. In organizational markets, companies throughout Europe buy international brands such as Microsoft Windows software, Compaq computers and Bosch electrical products.

5. **One way of segmenting organizational markets is to begin with macrosegmentation variables and then develop subsegments using microsegmentation criteria. Does this seem sensible to you? Are there any circumstances where the process should be reversed?**

Macrosegmentation is based on broad characteristics of buying organizations such as size, geographic location, and industry.

Microsegmentation requires a more detailed analysis of the characteristics of decision-making such as choice criteria, decision-making unit composition, and decision-making processes. Usually organizational markets are subjected to macrosegmentation and then finer subsegments are identified through microsegmentation (see Figure 7.4).

However, this does not have to be the case. Logically an organizational market could be segmented on the basis of a microsegmentation variable first. For example, two segments may be based on those who buy on the basis of price, and those who are more concerned with service. The segments could then be profiled using macrosegmentation variables such as size or industry. Or macrosegmentation could be omitted in favour of individual identification of companies falling into each segment.

6. **Why is *buy class* a potentially useful method of segmenting organizational markets? (Use both this chapter and Chapter 4 when answering this question.)**

Chapter 4 provides definitions of the three buy classes:

* Straight re-buy: a previously purchased item is repurchased from suppliers already judged acceptable
* New task: the purchase has not occurred before so purchasing experience and information is lacking
* Modified re-buy: the buying options are known but something has happened to alter the normal supply situation

Segmentation can be based on the buy class situation as there are different implications for marketing in each case.

For example, a company which is purchasing in a straight re-buy situation will need to be convinced that the risk of change is low (for an out-supplier) to move to a modified re-buy. Communications need to be focused on the period prior to contract renewal.

In the new task situation much more marketing investment may be needed as the decision making process is likely to be long. The aim should be to enter the process early (be first) and provide advice and guidance to build up 'creeping commitment'.

7. **What is the majority fallacy? Why should it be taken into account when evaluating market segments?**

When evaluating the attractiveness of market segments, large size is generally thought to be advantageous since sales potential is greater. This is true, *ceteris paribus*. However, large segment size is often associated with high levels of competition: many companies are attracted by high sales potential.

The largest segment (the one that forms the majority of the market in terms of potential customers and sales) may, therefore, not be the most attractive. This is called the 'majority fallacy'. Companies should guard against blindly chasing large market segments; smaller less competitive segments may actually yield better results.

8. **What is the difference between positioning and repositioning? Choose three products and services and describe how they are positioned in the marketplace, i.e. what is their target market and differential advantage?**

Positioning a product in the marketplace involves the choice of:

- Target market
- Differential advantage

This defines where and how the product competes. The objective is to maintain a distinctive place in the market. Marketers are involved in a battle for the minds of target customers.

Figure 7.8 shows some key factors in successful positioning.

Repositioning concerns changing the target market, the differential advantage or both.

The answer to the second part of the question allows students to crystallize their thoughts on positioning. Using the car market, a student might contrast the position of the Fiat Punto, the Ford Mondeo and the BMW to show their different target markets and differential advantages.

Chapter 8 Study Questions

Managing Products

---

1. Why do companies develop core products into brands?

A core product is anything that is capable of satisfying customer needs. For example, a car satisfies the need for transport, toothpaste satisfies the need for clean teeth and a meal satisfies the need for energy.

Core products are developed to create individual identities that can offer added values to customers. These augmented products are called brands. For example, all cars satisfy the need for transportation but each car model (brand) has its own distinctive features that confer different benefits to customers. Certain models are regarded as symbols of success (e.g. BMW, Mercedes-Benz) whereas others offer high levels of reliability at lower prices (e.g. Volkswagen).

Branding aids consumer decision-making because consumers associate functional and emotional characteristics with individual brands. Manufacturers have to be extremely careful to maintain high quality standards otherwise brand image may be tarnished. The BMW 300 series was criticized for a period in the early 1990s for lower standards of quality than customers had been used to. This led to a concerted effort on BMW's part to improve quality standards.

Unsuccessful brands offer no added values over the competition. Without this added value (differential advantage) they provide no reason for customers to buy them rather than competitor brands.

2. Suppose you were the marketing director of a medium-sized bank. How would you tackle the job of building the company brand?

Figure 8.2 'Building successful brands' provides a useful framework for tackling this question:

- Building quality into the core product: the bank should ensure that the basic functional requirements (i.e. banking) of its customers are provided well. The bank should ensure that transactions are carried out speedily and efficiently. Marketing research should be used to understand the essential requirements of customers (e.g. short queues, friendly staff) and the bank organized to provide them.
- Brand positioning: by analysing customer needs and competitor strengths and weaknesses, the marketing director should attempt to create a unique position for the bank in the marketplace. This might be based on (a combination of) superior services, location, image, product offerings or bank design.
- Brand repositioning: the marketing director should be aware of the need to change the positioning of the bank if customer requirements, technology and computer activities render the old brand position redundant. For example, bank design may need to be updated as more modern forms of banking emerge.

- Well-blended communications: messages regarding brand position should be clear, consistent, competitive and credible. The same message (and desired response) should be disseminated through advertising, in-store posters, staff, public relations and promotional materials.
- Being first: the marketing director should be aware of first-mover advantages. For example, being first to offer a new product to customers creates the opportunity to establish a clear position in the minds of target customers before competition enters the market. A problem, however, is that many financial services are very easy to copy (e.g. a higher interest rate account). However, many smaller building societies in the UK have gained an advantage over their larger rivals by offering high-interest rate postal accounts. Their larger competitors with more high street branches have generally been slow (reluctant?) to follow.
- Long-term perspective: the marketing director must realize that brand building is a long-term process. Communicating brand values, and building people's perception of the bank as being different from its competitors will not happen quickly. He/she must convince senior management of the need to invest in the brand consistently over time.
- Internal marketing: convincing management colleagues of the need for marketing, and training staff to achieve high service standards are essential requirements for the implemention of a brand building programme.

3. **Think of five brand names. To what extent do they meet the criteria of good brand naming as laid out in Table 8.3? Do any of the names legitimately break these guidelines?**

Table 8.3 provides the following guidelines for brand names:

- Evoke positive associations
- Be easy to pronounce and remember
- Suggest product benefits
- Be distinctive
- Use numerals when emphasizing technology
- Do not infringe on existing registered brand names.

It may not be possible for a given brand name to achieve all six ideals but Head and Shoulders (anti-dandruff shampoo) and "Toys-R-Us" (toy store) are examples of strong brand names. The use of numerals for technological products has been successfully exploited by BMW (300, 500, 700 series), Microsoft Windows 3.1, etc..

Students may suggest the names of brands that successfully break some of the above guidelines. Sometimes a brand has such a strong differential advantage that it succeeds despite having a name that may be difficult to pronounce and remember, e.g. it is not immediately clear how to pronounce Häagen-Dazs. However, the chapter text explains why such a brand name can succeed despite this drawback. Indeed, for some people, the ability to pronounce the name correctly (when others cannot) may have a social cachet.

4. **Do you think there will be a large increase in the number of pan-European brands over the next ten years or not? Justify your answer.**

The arguments for a growth in the number of pan-European brands include:

- Most consumers required good quality products at low prices. This can only be achieved through pan-European economies of scale. Companies that rely on their national market only cannot be cost-competitive.

174

- Fast technological change requires pan-European markets (at the very least) to achieve break-even before product obsolescence.

   Arguments against the growth of pan-European brands include:

- Differences in national taste, culture and buying behaviour will severely limit the capability to standardize a brand across Europe. Note that even such high-profile 'global' brands as Coca Cola and McDonald's make local adaptations to their product offerings.
- People will be increasingly unwilling to buy standardized products in their search for individual identities.

   For many companies the question is not whether brands can be standardized, but which parts of the brand can be standardized and which must be varied to adapt to local preferences.

5. What are the strategic options for pan-European brand building? What are the advantages and disadvantages of each option?

There are three strategic options:

- Geographic extension: taking present brands into new geographic markets. Unless the company is already a major global player this is likely to be the slowest route to pan-European brand building. However, it gives a high degree of control since the company has full authority to plan which brands to globalize.
- Brand acquisition: purchasing brands. This option provides the fastest method of developing pan-European brands. For example Unilever's 1989 acquisition of Fabergé, Elizabeth Arden and Calvin Klein gave it immediate presence in fragrances, cosmetics and skin care. Brand acquisition can be very costly, however, because of the goodwill that existing brands possess.
- Brand alliance: joint venture or partnership to market brands in national or cross-national markets. This can be a relatively low-cost method of pan-European extension since costs and expertise are shared. However, they foster the lowest form of control since strategy and resource allocation need to be negotiated between partners.

6. The product lifecycle is more likely to mislead marketing management than provide useful insights. Discuss.

The product lifecycle conceptualizes the sales and profit changes that take place during the time a product is on the market. It can be applied, with varying degrees of success, to product lines and brands. The four stages—introduction, growth, maturity, and decline—are discussed in the chapter, and the discussion will not be repeated here.

   The PLC may mislead marketing management into believing that all products follow the classic S-shaped curve. The actual shape is dependent on the type of product (e.g. fashion goods may have a short hump-shaped curve), technological change, competitor activity, volatility of consumer tastes, and the marketing activities of the company concerned. A massive rise in marketing investment can give a hitherto stable sales trend a sharp upward progression. The shape of the curve is not, therefore, inevitable but is dependent upon decisions made by marketing management.

   A classic situation when the PLC would be used in an inappropriate way would be the dropping of a product if it appeared to enter the decline stage. A sensible approach would be to discover the reason for the sales decline. Perhaps the reason was lack of marketing support. A good example of this was the cinema industry which was in decline in the UK until Showcase Cinemas made substantial investments in a new cinema concept.

However, used intelligently the PLC can be useful to marketing management by:

- Emphasizing the fact that nothing lasts forever
- Emphasizing the need to review marketing objectives and strategies as products pass through the various stages
- Emphasizing the need for portfolio planning
- Highlighting the dangers of overpowering

Each of these strengths is discussed in detail in Chapter 8.

7. Evaluate the usefulness of the BCG matrix. Do you believe that it has a role to play in portfolio planning?

The Boston Consulting Group Growth-Share matrix allows the positions of products (or strategic business units) to be shown on a 2 × 2 box. Depending on their position, each product is labelled a star, cash cow, problem child, or dog. Broad strategy prescriptions are made depending on this categorization.

The uses of the BCG matrix are:

- It provides guidelines for setting strategic objectives.
- It aids the maintenance of a balanced product portfolio.

As such it stimulates management to think strategically about its products, and analyse them collectively rather than solely on an individual basis.

However, it would be dangerous to base strategic planning totally on the results of this kind of analysis as there are a number of limitations:

- Cash flow is not dependent solely on the position of a product on the matrix.
- The focus on market share and growth rate may distract attention from attaining and maintaining a competitive advantage.
- Other factors besides market share and growth rate affect strategic decisions.
- The emphasis on market share may mislead companies into believing that market share gain is always desirable.
- The analysis ignores product interpendences.
- Star products may decline before they become cash cows, rendering investment unprofitable.
- Competitive reactions are ignored.
- Capital markets are ignored.
- The definition of 'the market' is vague.
- Too much dependency on 'cash flow' rather than 'profitability'.
- Lacks precision regarding which problem children to build, harvest, or drop.

8. What is the difference between product and market development in the Ansoff matrix? Give examples of each form of product growth strategy.

The Ansoff matrix considers four strategies for growth based upon existing and new products and markets: market penetration, product development, market development and diversification.

Product development concerns the development of new products in existing markets while market development is the sale of existing products in new markets. Product development is an essential process given technological change and competitor activities. Examples include the upgrading of computer hardware and software, car model replacements and new formula washing powders.

Market development may involve moving into new geographical markets such as Marks and Spencer's move into Europe and the USA or by moving into new market segments such as Apple's move into the desk-top publishing sector.

Chapter 9 Study Questions

Developing New Products

---

1. **Try to think of an unsatisfied need that you feel could be solved by the introduction of a new product. How would you set about testing your idea to examine its commercial potential?**

This question is to allow students full freedom to use their imagination to identify possible new product ideas. Some ideas are given in the text such as a voice-activated language translator, artificial bone and grass that only grows to one inch. When evaluating a new product idea, potential customer benefits need to be assessed. The automatic language translator would be useful for holiday makers abroad who do not speak the relevant foreign language; artificial bone would be useful in the treatment of bone diseases; and one-inch grass would remove the chore of grass cutting.

Although these benefits sound appealing, each idea would need to be concept tested with potential customers to assess the value they place on the idea and to see if they any associated problems arise. For example, the one-inch grass idea requires a solution to deal with weeds, Application of chemical weed killers would almost certainly be needed. If business analysis suggests that the idea has profit potential expenditure on product development may be authorized.

Once the idea is transformed into a product, testing would follow to evaluate performance. For example, the appearance of the one-inch grass would be assessed, the success of keeping down weeds with chemicals evaluated, and any side-effects that repeated doses of chemical have on the grass identified. Also, measuring customer perceptions of the benefits and costs of the product would be critical. Perhaps the need to apply weed killers regularly offsets the advantages of not cutting the lawn.

Once the product appears to be acceptable, and commercially viable market testing may take place. An area test may be feasible for the grass to gauge distributor take-up, promotional effectiveness, price acceptability and customer response. This, hopefully, would be followed by a national launch.

Such discussion can highlight the need to involve customers in new product development and not rely solely on the 'professionals' at head office whose perceptions and prejudices may be very different.

2. **The Sinclair C5 was soon withdrawn from the market in the UK. The three-wheeled vehicle was designed to provide electric-powered transport over short distances. If you can remember the vehicle try to think of reasons why the product was a failure. Video recorders and fax machines have been huge successes. Why?**

This question permits students to evaluate new products using the five criteria discussed on pages 310–11 that affect their diffusion rate. These are:

- Differential advantage
- Compatibility
- Complexity
- Divisibility
- Communicability

The problem with the Sinclair C5 was that although it possessed the potential differential advantage of cheap transport over short distances, it failed to live up to its promise because of unreliability and the inherent danger of taking to the road in a slow and fragile vehicle.

Its use was incompatible with people's lifestyle and values. They were concerned that they would look foolish travelling in a small, open-topped three-wheel vehicle.

Video recorders and fax machines, on the other hand, pose clear differential advantages with no serious negatives. They are compatible with many people's lifestyles and values and their benefits can be easily communicated to target customers. Although by no means cheap, they are now affordable to many people. Divisibility is therefore not a major problem to most western industrialized markets. The complexity of use of video recorders has hampered diffusion among some sections of the population, although the development of the Video-Plus facility greatly simplifies recording these days. The diffusion of fax machines may also be retarded somewhat by their perceived complexity.

3. **Why is it difficult for a service company such as a bank to develop new products that have lasting success?**

For a manufacturer of physical goods, the distinctive features of a new product, and/or the production processes, often can be patented, giving a barrier against copy-cat alternatives produced by competitors. Also the time needed to develop the necessary technology may slow-down competitive response.

With a service company such as a bank patent protection of new products is less likely to arise since we are talking about intangible product features such as a high-interest account. Occasionally, a new savings concept targeted at a particular sector of the community is launched by a bank, e.g. a guaranteed income bond for the over 60s. The problem is that another bank, if it so wishes, can fairly swiftly launch a similar product aimed at the same target group.

Where the new product is based on technology, their parties such as computer manufacturers may have developed and own the technical rights which are therefore available to other banks. Once more a major barrier to competitive response is removed.

This is not to say that a sustainable competitive advantage is not possible. Size may be important with branches in many locations providing an advantage; service quality and a high profile image (e.g. Leeds Liquid Gold Savings Account) may also be important.

4. **You are the marketing manager for a fast-food restaurant chain. A colleague returns from France with an idea for a new dish that she thinks will be a winner. How would you go about evaluating the idea?**

Any or all of the following stages could be used to evaluate the idea:

- Screening: the idea could be evaluated against chosen criteria, e.g. fit with current menu, profit potential.
- Concept testing: the idea could be presented to a small sample of customers to discuss its potential. The dish could be described verbally and/or pictorially.
- Business analysis: detailed analysis of sales, costs and profits would be made at this stage.
- Product development: the dish or a number of variants could be tested with a small sample of people chosen to be representative of the restaurant's clientele. This stage may be omitted in favour of directly market testing the dish.
- Market testing: the restaurant is in an ideal position to give the dish a trial to gauge market acceptance. A sample of outlets would be chosen for this purpose. The costs of trial are likely to be low and the results more valid than product development tests.
- Commercialization: if acceptance rates are satisfactory the dish would be added to the menu.

5. What are the advantages and disadvantages of test marketing? In what circumstances should you be reluctant to use test marketing?

Test marketing involves the launch of a new product in one or more geographical areas chosen to be representative of its intended market.

It is the acid test of new product development since the product is promoted as it would be in a national launch (or something very similar) and consumers are being asked to choose it over competitor products in a similar fashion to a national launch. From the results national sales predictions can be made and the go/no go decision facilitated.

Alternative marketing strategies (e.g. high price/high promotion vs. low price/low promotion) can be tested if more than one region is chosen. Even in one area a 'feel' for what went well and what should be changed can be made. Furthermore, potential distribution and packaging problems may be revealed in test markets.

The method does have its problems, however. The chosen region(s) may not be representative and so false predictions may result. Competitors may invalidate test market results by blocking distribution and increasing promotional spend in the test market area. Also, the need to go national quickly may mean that the test market is run over a period too short to give valid results. Finally, co-operation from distributors may be denied making the test market an impractical idea. If any of these potential problems are thought to be series test marketing may not be a viable option.

6. Your company has developed a new range of spicy flavoured soups. They are intended to compete against the market leader in curry-flavoured soups. How would you conduct product tests for this new line?

The major two alternatives are paired comparison and monadic placement tests. These are discussed on page 305 of the text.

With a period comparison test the new range of spicy-flavoured soups would be compared to the market leader (and perhaps other major brands) in a series of paired tests. These could take place at home, or in a hall test with people being recruited from the street to take part. After testing they would be asked for their opinion on such measures as taste, colour, smell, richness, and overall preference. A home test is more realistic but a hall test provides more control.

In the monadic placement test only the new soup would be given to people for trial in their home. They would be asked to try the soup and afterwards be asked for their opinion both absolutely and relative to the market leader, other major brands and/or their previously bought brands.

7. What are the particular problems associated with commercializing technology? What are the key factors for success?

The major problem with commercializing technology is that if it is new people may find difficulty articulating their reactions because they are unfamiliar with the new product and its potential benefits. Indeed, the diffusion of innovation curve suggests that most people will only adopt (accept) the product after it has been on the market for some time. Hence using conventional marketing research techniques is likely to underestimate market potential.

A second problem is that market acceptance may be dependent on the price that the new technological product is sold for. Video recorders are very successful in the marketplace but if the technology had been developed such that their price was £2,000+ rather than £200+ their success would have been far more limited.

Extreme care is required to minimize the chances of research and development specialists developing technological toys based upon their own 'pet' projects rather than focusing on new products and technologies that have a high potential for providing distinct customer benefits.

A final problem is the fast replacement of existing technologies and the enormous cost of doing so. This has led (been caused by?) Japanese companies streamlining the product development processes to reduce 'time to market' and to practice product churning where a market is characterized by numerous new product releases based upon incremental product improvements.

The key success features are given on pages 314–15. In summary they are:

- Being faster to market
- Applying technologies to a wide range of markets
- Launching a large number of new products
- Understanding and controlling a wide breadth of technologies

8. Discuss how marketing and R&D can form effective teams to develop new products.

Marketing and R&D need to achieve greater integration of effort so that marketing understand R&D's problems and potential, and R&D understand the need to produce products that possess features that confer customer benefits rather than solve interesting technical problems.

Research into how such integration may be achieved has suggested twelve ways in which marketing and R&D personnel can help the process. These are given on pages 296–8 and require no further elaboration here.

Chapter 10 Study Questions

Pricing Strategy

1. **Accountants are always interested in profit margins; sales managers want low prices to help push sales; and marketing managers are interested in high prices to establish premium positions in the marketplace. To what extent do you agree with this statement in relation to the setting of prices?**

From a scientific viewpoint it is relevant to question the source of the evidence on which the statement is made: it may be intuitively plausible but is unlikely to be based on scientific research.

Logically, it is not untenable that accountants and sales and marketing managers will hold the views expressed in the question. In many companies, accountants may have no procedure for calculating profit margins on individual products or product lines. Where such information exists their interest may focus on gross profit generated (gross profit margin × number of units sold) rather than margin alone.

Although low prices often help salespeople to sell products, they may be evaluated on sales revenue (price × number of units sold) or even profit achievement rather than unit sales alone. Hence, the assumption that sales managers always want low prices may be misplaced.

Finally, marketing managers are concerned about product positioning but this does not automatically imply premium pricing. Marketing-oriented pricing is based on the ten factors described in Figure 10.2 and discussed on pages 332–48. There are specific instances when charging a low price is sensible and these are summarized in Table 10.4.

There is no reason to believe therefore that the statement is true.

2. **You are the marketing manager of a company that is about to launch the first voice-activated language translator. The owner talks into the device, the machine electronically translates into the relevant language and speaks to the listener. What factors should you take into consideration when pricing this product?**

This question provides the opportunity for students to apply the framework for marketing-oriented pricing summarized in Figure 10.2 and discussed in detail on pages 332–48.

Cost will provide a floor to price level for this new-to-the-world product but about this marketing issues will prevail:

Positioning: a key decision will be choice of target market. If the product is aimed at the wealthy middle class, price will be higher than if the product is positioned as more of a mass market good. Whichever is chosen, marketing research is needed to gauge customer response. This will give a feel for the value of the benefits the product provides (extent of differential advantage). Experimentation (possibly a test market) might be used prior to launch to gauge price acceptance.

Price–quality relationships: a low price may confer low quality connotations. A high price may indicate high quality.

Product line pricing: unlikely to be an issue as it is a new-to-the-world product. However, after launch several replacement versions may be developed with different features. Care needs to be taken to price in accord with their extra benefits.

Explicability: if a high price is charged salespeople will need to be versed in the arguments justifying it. High technological development costs would provide a credible justification.

Competition: there is no direct competitor but the cost of taking language courses (including time) needs to be calculated to provide some kind of benchmark.

Negotiating margins: the likely reaction of distributors in demanding concessions from list price needs to be assessed, and appropriate negotiating margin built in.

Effect on distributors/retailers: the requirements of distributors and retailers need to be understood in terms of what profit margin is required to encourage them to stock the product.

Political factors: unlikely to be an issue.

3. **Why is value to the customer a more logical approach to setting prices than cost of production? What role can costs play in the setting of prices?**

People do not evaluate a product in terms of how much it cost to produce. They assess the value of the benefits conferred by the product. They use choice criteria to provide a framework for this assessment. The implication is that price should be decided on the basis of marketing-oriented criteria (value to the customer being a key one) rather than costs. Simply because one product in a product line cost more to make than another does not necessarily mean a higher price should be charged. If the latter product gives higher value then it should have the higher price.

The role costs play in price setting is to provide a check on whether a product launch is worthwhile. If it is believed that a price cannot be charged which covers full costs a decision not to launch the product (or to delete it if it is an existing product) may be made. Exceptions are when experience curve effects may quickly reduce costs so that profitability can be achieved in the future, when the product is important to market for other reasons (e.g. to be seen as a full product line company or because of product interdependencies), and where direct cost pricing is used to fill spare capacity (see pages 329–30).

Costs, therefore, indicate a price floor usually but market considerations dictate where, above this minimum, the actual price will be set. Where value can be measured in cost savings and revenue terms, economic value to the customer analysis can be used (see pages 343-4).

4. **Discuss the advantages and disadvantages of experimentation in assessing customers' willingness to pay.**

Chapter 10 discusses four methods of calculating customers' willingness to pay: the buy-response method, trade-off analysis, economic value to the customer analysis, and experimentation. Each has its own advantages and disadvantages as discussed on pages 339–44.

A key problem with the buy-response method and trade-off analysis is that customers are asked to indicate what they would be willing to pay in an hypothetical situation but they are not required to support their preferences with cash expenditure. There is, therefore, a doubt as to the external validity of these methods.

Experimentation in marketing can also suffer from this limitation if it is in the form of a laboratory experiment but two types of field test—the controlled store experiment and test marketing—provide realism in that customers have to pay for the products they choose rather than simply stating a preference.

These techniques are discussed on pages 341–2. Briefly the major advantage and disadvantages are:

- High external validity because the purchase situation is realistic.
- Controlled store experiments may be difficult to set up because they require the co-operation of distributors.
- They can also be difficult to control.
- Competitors can invalidate test marketing results.
- Test marketing gives competitors advance warning of impending new product launches.
- Choosing a representative test area(s) can be difficult.
- Where more than one area is chosen, alternative marketing mix designs (including different price levels) can be tested.

5. **What is economic value to the customer analysis? Under what conditions can it play an important role in price setting?**

The nature of economic value to the customer analysis is fully discussed on pages 343–4 and so does not need to be repeated here.

It can play an important role in price setting when the customers' major choice criterion is economic (cost savings and/or extra revenue generated) and where it is possible to quantitatively compare competing products in economic terms. Many organizational purchases are motivated by economic value considerations since reducing costs and increasing revenues are prime objectives for most profit-oriented companies. EVC analysis is therefore a tool used more in organizational than consumer marketing.

6. **Under intense cost inflationary pressure you are considering a price increase. What other considerations would you take into account before initiating the price rise?**

Four major factors influencing this decision are the market situation, customer and competitor reactions, and the nature of strategic objectives. A price rise would be more likely if there was excess demand rather than excess supply in the market. It would also be more likely if customers were not particularly price sensitive since this would indicate a tolerance to accept a higher price.

The price rise would also depend upon estimated competitor reactions. The rise would be less harmful to demand for our products if competitors followed it. Since wage cost inflation is likely to be general for domestic-based competitors, the more competition is domestic rather than internationally based, the more likely are all competitors to experience it. If cost inflation is due to raw material price rises, all competition is likely to be under the same pressure, however.

A final key factor is the strategic objective for our product and that for competitors' products. We are more likely to increase our price if we are following a harvest objective than a build objective. Competitors are less likely to follow our price increase if they have adopted a build objective rather than a hold or harvest objective.

A price rise is dependent on an array of factors—not just costs.

7. **You are the marketing manager of a premium-priced industrial chemical. A competitor has launched a cut-price alternative that possesses 90 per cent of the effectiveness of your product. If you do not react you estimate that you will lose 30 per cent of sales. What are your strategic pricing options? What would you do?**

The differential advantage of the rival product is based on price, but we still retain a performance advantage. It may be possible to quantify the economic value to the customer of the 10 per cent performance advantage. The industrial chemical company should do this. Their initial estimate of 30 per cent sales fall may be excessive. The salesforce would need to be trained in selling the chemical on an economic value to the customer basis. Advertising in trade magazines could also be used to communicate the value of their differential advantage.

The first option, then, is to maintain the price differential. This may be viable if the EVC analysis is favourable. It may also be maintained if the strategic objective is to harvest the product.

The second option is to reduce the price. This is likely if the EVC analysis is less favourable indicating extra value for the rival product given its lower price. It is also more likely if we have set a build or hold objective for our product.

The third option is to maintain the price of our product but to introduce a fighter brand (see page 350) at a lower price. This would allow the maintenance of the premium-price position for the original product while offsetting the threat of the cut-price rival. If we wished to attempt to remove the rival from the market we could encircle it by introducing a fighter brand at price parity and a modification (which gives even greater value) at a discount.

The final decision depends upon EVC calculations, our strategic objectives and whether our strategic intention is to remove the rival from the market. However, introducing a lighter brand appears to be more attractive than a simple price reduction which could ruin the price positioning of our original product and lead to a general lowering of profit margins in the product field.

8. **The only reason that companies set low prices is that their products are undifferentiated. Discuss.**

Differentiation (added value to the customer) is a major factor in achieving higher than average prices in a market. Where there are numerous suppliers offering commodity products (perfect competition) prices are likely to be low. However, this does not mean that an undifferentiated product is the sole reason for low prices.

The conditions where companies set low prices are when it is the only feasible alternative, when the strategic objective is market presence or domination, when the company is wishing to be a cost leader through experience curve effects and when there is good reason to believe that high profits can be achieved later. Each of these factors is discussed on pages 336–8.

Chapter 11 Study Questions

Advertising

1. **Compare the situations where advertising and personal selling are more likely to feature strongly in the promotional mix.**

Advertising is more likely to be used in mass markets that are geographically dispersed. In this situation, personal selling to the ultimate customer may not be cost effective although it may still play a part in selling to distributors. Where sales are heavily dependent on brand image building, advertising is invariably used. Personal selling can contribute to building favourable associates but really comes into its own when complex technical arguments are required. The interaction between seller and customer gives the opportunity to demonstrate the product, answer questions, overcome objections, negotiate terms and conditions, and close the sale.

For these reasons personal selling is more often used in business-to-business marketing while consumer goods companies tend to spend more on advertising.

The balance between personal selling and advertising expenditure is also dependent on the use of push versus pull strategies. Push strategies tend to favour the use of personal selling, while pull strategies are usually associated with greater expenditure on advertising (see page 360).

2. **Describe the strong and weak theories of how advertising works. Which theory is more likely to apply to the purchase of a car, and the purchase of a soap powder?**

The strong and weak theories of advertising are fully described on pages 362–4 of the textbook. Also relevant are the models of consumer evaluation processes described in Chapter 3 'Understanding Consumer Behaviour' (pages 70–3). High involvement decisions are characterized by the Fishbein–Ajzen model and low involvement by the Ehrenberg–Goodhart model.

The purchase of a car is likely to be a high involvement situation where the Fishbein–Ajzen model is likely to represent the evaluative process and the strong (AIDA) theory of advertising is relevant. Advertising can help in creating a desire to purchase a car or, at least, to visit a particular showroom.

For the purchase of a soap powder, a low involvement situation is likely, and the Ehrenberg–Goodhart model apply. This weak theory of how advertising works suggest that highly repetitive simple advertising desired to reinforce already held favourable perceptions should be used for existing brands, and to create awareness for new brands.

3. **Within an advertising context, what is 'positioning in the mind of the consumer'?Using examples, discuss the alternative positioning options available to an advertiser.**

Positioning in the minds of the consumer involves the development or reinforcement of an image or set of associations for a brand. Good positioning means that the image or associations should be clear, credible, competitive and consistent.

The positioning options are based on:

- Product characteristics and customer benefits
- Price/quality
- Product use
- Product user
- Product class
- Symbols
- Competition

Each of these positioning bases are fully discussed, with examples, on pages 366–8. Students should provide their own examples rather than rely on those given in the textbook.

4. **Advertising has no place in the industrial marketing communications mix. Discuss.**

The major advantages of advertising are that it can reach a wide audience with simple messages at relatively low cost. However, it is impersonal and lacks the flexibility to respond to the individual needs of customers. It is also restricted in the amount of technical information that can be communicated effectively, and has only a limited capability to close the sale (coupons are sometimes used).

Despite these limitations advertising often has a role in industrial (business-to-business) marketing but it is usually in a supportive role. It can create awareness of industrial products and companies, and can create interest in these products. In so doing, it can help the salesforce to gain access to key decision-making unit members, since they are more likely to be willing to spend time with salespeople from companies they have heard of, and who sell products they may be interested in. In short, advertising can legitimize a company and its products.

Advertising can also support the salesforce by identifying warm prospects through the use of coupon returns. This allows the salesforce to use their time more efficiently. Given that salespeople cannot hope to reach all members of the decision-making unit personally, advertising can be used to reach the too numerous (e.g. secretaries) or the inaccessible (e.g. managing directors).

5. **Media class decisions should always be based on creative considerations, while media vehicle decisions should solely be determined by cost per thousand calculations. Do you agree?**

The media class decision concerns the choice of using television, the press, cinema, posters, and radio. It thus concerns the broad media choice. The media vehicle decision is more specific: it refers to the choice of the particular newspaper, magazine, television spot, poster site, etc.

Creative considerations usually dominate the media class choice since the medium must be capable of allowing the communication objectives to be realized. The creative properties of the media classes are discussed on pages 376–7 of the textbook. However, other candidates do play a part. These are:

- Cost per opportunity to see
- Competitive activity
- Views of the retail trade

Although creative factors influence the media vehicle decision, cost per thousand calculations are more important since having chosen television or the press a critical factor in the choice of which television spot to buy or newspaper to use is how economically they reach the target audience.

The question overstates the case, however. Creative considerations are not the sole determinant of the media class decision, nor are cost per thousand calculations the only factor to bear on media vehicle choice: a media vehicle's ambience may, for example, be important.

6. Discuss the contention that advertising should be based on the skills of the creative team, not the statistics of the research department.

Some creative people argue that advertising researcher's input leads to bland, uninteresting advertising. They support their argument by pointing to top campaigns that would never have run if research results had been slavishly followed. The Heineken campaign 'Refreshes the parts that other beers cannot reach' is a good example.

Nevertheless, allowing creative people unfettered freedom also has its drawbacks. They may place creativity above the need for advertising that helps sell products. Their targets may be their peer group and their objective to win awards for creativity rather than focusing on the target market for the product and the need to stimulate/defend sales.

Research can make the following contributions:

1. Identification of target audience
2. An understanding of their needs, motivations, preferences and dislikes
3. Pre-testing advertising to discover likes, dislikes, comprehension, credibility, etc.
4. Post-testing advertising to check achievement of awareness, belief and attitude change, intention to buy, distribution, sales, etc.

7. Describe the structure of a large advertising agency. Why should an advertiser prefer to use an advertising agency rather than set up a full-service internal advertising department?

A typical structure for a large advertising agency is to organize by function: account management (to manage accounts), creative (to develop advertising concepts, and create copy and artwork), media (to select media and negotiate price), production (to make the advertisements and ensure that advertisements appear in the selected media at the correct time), and planning (to develop advertising strategy, and commission, conduct and interpret research for campaign planning). Figure 11.6 shows a structure based on these divisions.

An advertiser may prefer to use an advertising agency rather than set up a full-service internal advertising department because:

1. An advertising agency can split overhead costs between many clients. An internal advertising department cannot do this and this may be uneconomic.
2. An advertising agency has greater media buying power since it negotiates prices for several clients.
3. The continuous contact with many clients can stimulate new ideas within the advertising agency and provide an outsider's view on the advertising situation. An internal department may lack this variety of work, become too close to the narrower range of products it is advertising, and thereby lack fresh insights.

A client company will still require staff to liaise with agencies and may prefer to hire the specialist skills of creative hot shops or media buyers (see Vignette 11.3).

8. Discuss the advantages and limitations of developing pan-European advertising campaigns.

Pan-European advertising is created, co-ordinated, or directed from one central point, for execution with or without local adaptation in a number of countries. The great advantage is the enormous cost savings that can be achieved. Levi Strauss saved about £1.5 billion by shooting a single advertisement to span six European markets. The more adaptation that is needed, the less opportunity for this kind of efficiency. Most pan-European advertising requires some degree of local adaptation. Vignette 11.1 discussed how Volkswagen, Nestlé, and Philips have employed a common theme with local adaptation strategy.

The limitations of pan-European advertising are that local advertising agency staff may lack commitment for implementing centrally created campaigns (the 'not invented here' syndrome) and attempting to create a single campaign to span many countries may lead to compromise and bland mediocrity. Also, it may not be possible because of national advertising regulations, for example wine cannot be advertised on television in Denmark; similarly beer cannot be advertised on television in France.

Advertising that is based on humour may also be difficult to centralize since humour is notoriously difficult to transfer across borders. Finally, cultural and language differences may also limit the extent of pan-European advertising. Cultural differences in product usage may require local campaigns, and language idiosyncrasies may render brand names unsuitable in foreign countries (e.g. the French drink PSCHITT would require a name change in the UK).

Chapter 12 Study Questions

Personal Selling and Sales Management

---

1. Select a car with which you are familiar. Identify its features and translate them into customer benefits.

The objective of this question is to familiarize students with the process of analysing product features and their derived customer benefits. Taking the Ford Mondeo 1.8LX as an example, the following analysis could be conducted:

Product feature	Customer benefit
Airbag/side-impact bars	Higher safety levels
ABS brakes	Greater car control when emergency breaking
Power steering	Less effort to steer car
Sunroof	In-car comfort on hot days
Deadlocking/immobilizer	Security from thieves
Electric windows	Less effort to open windows
Ten-second delay on interior light going out after closing door	Easier to find ignition key and seat belt sockets in the dark
Small torch light on key	Easier to find door lock in dark

2. Imagine you are face-to-face with a customer for that car. Write down five objections to purchase and prepare convincing responses to these objections?

Some salespeople believe that an ability to 'think on their feet' is all that is required to answer objections. However, thorough preparation can form an invaluable basis for objection handling because it allows salespeople time to carry out the necessary research to have the necessary facts and figures to hand, and to consider the relative merits of alternative responses. Anticipating likely objections and preparing convincing answers is a simple but often neglected art. Here are five objections and possible responses.

Objection	Response
I am concerned that the engine will be underpowered for a car of that size.	Take customer for a test drive. Have information available showing acceleration figures (preferably compared to major competitors where comparisons are favourable). Could use reference sell (if available), e.g. 'a friend of mine has one and towed a caravan around France last year. He had no problems!'

It looks as though it will be heavy on petrol.	Produce miles per gallon figures. Identify favourable comparisons with competition.
I like the car but it is very expensive.	This objection may be partially offset by low depreciation costs (the salesperson needs to research this). Explain that the list price is only the starting point. Explain that we give top part-exchange allowances. Ask 'if we could agree a good deal, might you be interested in buying the car?' to gain commitment (sharp angle question—see page 400). Work out attractive deal. Build up benefits to make cost appear reasonable.
I don't like the colour of the seats.	Explain that the model is available in a range of interior colours. Show brochure illustrating range. Give accurate figures for availability. If near the end of the sales interview the salesperson could attempt a trial close: 'if I could get you the same car in the colour of your choice within a week, would you buy it'. This needs to be handled carefully so that the salesperson does not appear too pushy.
The boot looks a bit small.	Have comparative figures available: 'it is a bit deceptive. In fact it is bigger than a Cavalier boot'. Show the customer the figures. Explain how space can be increased by lowering back seats.

As emphasized in the text the salesperson should also practise methods of responding to objections so that the customer is not antagonized (see pages 401–2).

3. You are the new sales manager for a company selling abrasives to the motor trade. Your salesforce are paid by fixed salary, and you believe them to be suffering from motivational problems. Discuss how you would handle this problem.

The sales manager should begin by talking to the salesforce to check his/her assumption that motivation is a key problem. Correct problem identification is the first step in analysing this new situation. Low motivation may be a symptom of a more fundamental problem (e.g. inferior product design and performance).

Assuming that motivation is a key issue students should discuss the varying approaches to motivation given on pages 416–19. Major points to include are:

- The attitudes, values, problems and needs of salespeople must be identified on an individual basis.
- The salesforce needs to believe that increasing effort will bring results, and that the results will be rewarded in a way that each salesperson will value.

- Consider sales training for its motivational as well as its skill-enhancing potential.
- Link rewards to the performance that requires improvement.
- Give both non-financial (e.g. praise) as well as financial rewards (consider a salary plus commission-based payment system).
- Be prepared to punish negative role models (e.g. lazy, incompetent salespeople).
- Eliminate disincentives (e.g. unfair aspects of the job).

4. Because of its inherent efficiency the only sensible method of organizing a salesforce is by geographically defined territories. Discuss.

This question provides an opportunity for students to analyse the relative merits of geographical vs. product, and customer-based salesforce structures. This discussion is fully covered on pages 409–12 and need not be repeated here. Vignette 12.2 (page 411) provides an international perspective.

Students should be aware that efficiency is not the only criterion for organizing a salesforce. Effectiveness, in terms of meeting customer needs, is equally if not more important. A hybrid structure may be required which combines the efficiency of the geographic structure with the specialization inherent in the product or customer-based systems.

5. Quantitative methods of salesforce organization are superior to qualitative methods because they rely on hard numbers. Evaluate this statement.

A description of quantitative and qualitative methods of salesforce organization is given on pages 420–2 of the text. Many quantitative methods are diagnostic pointing to reasons why a sales target is not being reached (e.g. call rate), others represent achievement levels (e.g. sales and profits generated) which can be compared with targets to assess performance.

Qualitative measures are more subjective relying on the judgement of the sales manager (e.g. assessment of selling skills and the ability to develop close customer relationships). They are also diagnostic. Quantitative and qualitative measures are not alternatives but complement each other in the assessment of salespeople. For example, a poor sales per call ratio may mean a close assessment of selling and customer relations skills and product knowledge. Quantitative methods are not necessarily superior to but are simply part of the complete evaluation exercise.

6. A company wishes to strengthen its relationships with key customers. How might it approach this task?

A common device for strengthening its relationships with key customers is to organize the salesforce by key account management. By creating a dedicated team of salespeople and support staff to service the needs of one (or a small number of) client(s), close personal relationships can be developed, communication and co-ordination improved, after-sales service enhanced, and more in-depth penetration of the decision-making unit achieved (see pages 410–12). In retailing, manufacturers are framing trade marketing to supermarket chains (see pages 627–8).

No matter what organizational structure is employed, companies can strengthen relationships by:

- Providing technical support
- Sharing expertise

- Offering resource output
- Improving service levels
- Reducing customer risks

These issues are discussed on pages 112–14 of the textbook.

7. The key to sales success lies in closing the sale. Discuss.

As a general statement this is clearly wrong since it is not possible to close every sale. Many business-to-business purchases are decided without salespeople being present. In such situations, sales calls may be ended by an action agreement (see page 403) rather than a close.

Even when closing is appropriate, the statement exaggerates its importance. Before getting to the stage where closing can be practised, a salesperson must be adept at preparation, need and problem identification, presentation (and demonstration if applicable), and dealing with objections. Students should discuss the role of each of these skills and explain why each is important to sales success. (See pages 397–402.) This places closing in its proper context. However, the point should also be made that skills in the former may come to nothing if the salesperson is not willing and able to close the sale. A brief description of how this might be done is relevant here (see pages 402–3).

8. How practical is the workload approach to deciding salesforce size?

The workload approach to deciding salesforce size is described on pages 408–9. Its application relies on having reasonably accurate estimates of the number of customers the company wishes to call on, the required number of calls to each customer, and the number of calls per week that can be expected of one salesperson. Estimating the number of customers the company wishes to call on can be difficult if moving into a new area where such information is scarce, where the product being sold is difficult to define, or where new potential customers are merging at a rapid but unpredictable rate.

The required number of calls per customer may be difficult when there is little history of how many calls are needed to make a sale. Estimating the number of calls that can be expected of a salesperson per week may be error-prone when sales territories and customer density within them are highly variable, and where the length of time needed at each sales call is very changeable.

Complications also arise when prospecting forms an important part of the selling job. A separate category of customer is required together with estimates of the number of potential accounts to call on and call frequencies.

Discussions with sales managers on executive development courses suggest that they find the workload method a useful way of justifying a salesforce of a given size, or when preparing evidence to support an increase in size to present to their superiors.

Chapter 13 Study Questions

Other Promotional Mix Methods

1. **When you next visit a supermarket examine three sales promotions. What type of promotion are they? What are their likely objectives?**

This question provides the opportunity for students to relate the sales promotion issues discussed on pages 430–6 of the textbook in a real-life setting. By gaining involvement, a deeper understanding of these issues will result. If the tutor asks all of the class to carry out this exercise it is likely that most of the different types of promotion discussed in the text will be brought to class. This can provide a lively discussion through classifying them into:

- Money
- Bonus packs
- Premiums
- Free samples
- Coupons
- Prize promotions

The session can be concluded by considering what they are intending to achieve, including:

- Fast sales boost
- Encouraging trial
- Encouraging repeat purchase
- Stimulating sales of larger packs

2. **Why would it be wrong to measure the sales effect of a promotion only during the promotional period? What are the likely long-term effects of a promotion?**

The answer to this question is given in Figure 13.1 (page 430) which shows that a sales increase during the promotional period is likely to be followed by a short-run fall. This is because of the effect of customers stocking-up during the promotion. Measuring sales during the promotion would, therefore, over-estimate its effect.

The long-term effects of a promotion could be positive, neutral, or negative depending on how it has influenced consumer behaviour. A positive effect would follow a promotion that has attracted new buyers, who, liking the brand, repeat purchase. A negative effect would result from promotions (e.g. excessive discounting) that have devalued the image of the brand. Finally, a neutral effect is likely to occur where consumers have bought in large quantities because of the promotion's incentive value but revert to their usual buying patterns once it has finished.

3. **Distinguish between public relations and publicity. Is it true that publicity can be regarded as free advertising?**

Public relations is the management of communications and relationships to establish goodwill and mutual understanding between an organization and its public. Important groups include government, the general public, the media, the financial community, employees, and commerce. Activities include publicity, corporate advertising, seminars, publications, lobbying, and charitable donations.

Publicity, then, is a major form of public relations. It is the communication about a product or organization by the placing of news about it in the media without paying for the time or space directly. However, this does not mean that it is cost free. Someone has to write the news release, take part in the interview, or organize the news conference. This may be organized internally by a public relations agency. Even where this type of expenditure is absent, publicity involves the opportunity cost of employees who take it on themselves to gain publicity for their organization.

4. **There is no such thing as bad publicity. Discuss.**

Where awareness is the major goal of a publicity campaign even bad publicity which throws an unfavourable light on the person or organization may achieve this objective—hence the above statement. However, bad publicity can spoil image and ruin reputations. Hence, overall the gain in awareness can be more than offset by negative associations.

A second viewpoint asks the question: bad from whose perspective? The rock group The Who received much 'bad publicity' in the 1960s through their behaviour on stage. This was condemned in the media and by the establishment. However, it helped to achieve their cult status among the younger age group who bought their records.

5. **Compare the strengths and weaknesses of direct mail and telemarketing.**

The strengths of direct mail are:

- Specific targeting to named individuals
- Elaborate personalization is possible
- Results can be measured quantitatively
- Can be used to support the salesforce

The weaknesses are:

- Low response rates
- Initial costs of setting up a database or acquiring a list can be high
- It contributes to junk mail causing annoyance
- Mailing lists are variable in quality
- It is impersonal

The strengths of telemarketing are:

- It is personal: two-way communication occurs
- Lower cost than face-to-face selling

- Growth in telephone ownership and availability of telephone directories has made wise access to diverse populations possible
- Specific targeting to named individuals
- Results can be measured quantitatively
- Can be used to support the salesforce

Its weaknesses are:

- Lacks visual impact of personal visit
- Rejections can be high
- Cost per contact higher than direct mail or media advertising
- Labour costs can be high

Summarizing, direct mail is cheaper per contact then telemarketing but lacks the immediate interaction of a telephone call. Both suffer from low response rates, with direct mail response likely to be lower than telemarketing overall. Specific targeting can be achieved by both methods as can support of the salesforce (e.g. generating a list of warm prospects). The short term effectiveness of both methods can be measured quantitatively.

6. What are the key differences between direct marketing and media advertising?

Direct marketing is the distribution of products, information, and promotional benefits to target consumers through interactive communication in a way which allows response to be measured. It includes direct mail, telemarketing, direct response advertising, inserts, door-to-door catalogues.

Media advertising is any paid form of non-personal communication of ideas or products in the prime media, i.e. television, the press, posters, cinema, and radio.

The usual objective of direct marketing is to achieve some kind of direct response (e.g. a purchase by telephone or post, a request for sales literature or agreement to go to an event) whereas most media advertising is concerned with a less tangible response (e.g. gain awareness, or create a favourable attitude). Response to most direct marketing activity is easier to measure (e.g. coupon returns) whereas measuring the effectiveness of media advertising may require a market research agency.

There is some overlap between direct marketing and media advertising. Direct response advertising which requires a response by mail or telephone will use the prime media as the vehicle to communicate to target consumers. Often this form of media advertising will contain a coupon which interested parties can use to order a product or request further information.

Whereas media advertising attempts to target specific groups (target audiences), some direct marketing techniques are sufficiently focused to target specific individuals (direct mail, telemarketing are the prime examples). Some groups are much easier to contact through a direct marketing campaign than through media advertising because no publication or programme is specifically viewed by them. For example, a car dealer may decide to use a direct mail campaign to its customer base to promote special offers (e.g. reduced-price servicing) and new model launches. By creating specialized marketing databases of particular individuals in the target audience, direct marketing can be more cost effective than media advertising which can suffer from being less focused.

7. The major reason for event sponsorship is to indulge senior management in their favourite pastime. Discuss.

Event sponsorship involves a business relationship between a provider of funds, resources or services and an event (e.g. tennis tournament) which offers in return some rights and association that may be used for commercial advantage. Broadcast sponsorship, by contrast, involves a business relationship between the provider and a television or radio programme.

It is true that event sponsorship does provide the opportunity for a very pleasurable time for the management (not only senior) of the sponsoring company, assuming they enjoy the subject (e.g. sport or art) of the sponsorship and the attendant entertaining. However, event sponsorship can achieve five further objectives which are discussed on pages 452–3 of the textbook:

- Gain publicity
- Create entertainment opportunities
- Foster favourable brand and company associations
- Improve community relations
- Create promotional opportunities

8. Exhibitions are less effective than personal selling and more costly than direct mail so why use them?

Exhibitions bring buyers, sellers, and competitors together in a commercial setting. This means that exhibitors have to compete with sellers for the attention and interest of buyers. Buyers have the opportunity to compare closely the relative strengths and weaknesses of suppliers. They may call upon many suppliers in one day making the retention factor debatable. With a well-arranged personal selling visit there is probably more opportunity to involve the buyer in the sales presentation and to gain commitment to the product.

Exhibiting is often expensive—especially at international shows—and the question arises regarding cost per contact. Direct mail would normally be a cheaper method of reaching target customers. However, the nature of the communication is different. Exhibiting allows personal contact whereas direct mail does not. Furthermore, exhibiting brings advertising, publicity, sales promotion, product demonstration, sales staff, key managers, customers and prospects together at a live event offering the chance to impress key decision-makers with the strengths of the company, its operations and products.

The top four reasons why companies exhibit at trade shows are:

- To generate leads/enquiries
- To introduce a new product
- Because competitors are exhibiting
- To recruit dealers or distributors

Chapter 14 Study Questions

Distribution

1. What is the difference between channel decisions and physical distribution management? In what ways are they linked?

Channel decisions concern channel strategy and management. Channel strategy decisions cover:

- Channel selection
- Distribution intensity
- Channel integration

Channel management involves the implementation of strategy and addresses:

- Selection, motivation, training and evaluation
- Distribution intensity
- Channel integration

Channel management involves the implementation of strategy and addresses:

- Selection, motivation, training and evaluation of channel members
- Managing conflict between producers and channel members

The nature of strategy and management decision is covered on pages 473–85 of the text.

Physical distribution decisions concern the physical flows of materials, components and finished goods from producers to channel intermediaries and consumers. The focus is on the efficient movement of goods from producer to intermediaries and the consumer. Channel decisions, however, are related to the choice of the correct outlet to provide customers with cost-effective product availability. Both types of decision act to provide intermediaries and customers with the right products, in the right locations, at the right time, but the focus differs between channel and physical distribution decisions.

The two sets of decisions are interrelated since the choice of channel affects how and where products are moved. A poor choice of channel (e.g. too large a number of retail outlets) may raise physical distribution costs and cause prices to be uncompetitive. Also, physical distribution considerations may impinge upon the selection of channel strategy in the first place.

2. Of what value are channels of distribution? What functions do they perform?

A channel of distribution is the supply chain between producer and consumer. Supply can be direct or indirect, but the ultimate aim is to provide the customer with the right products, in the right location, in the right quantities, at the right time and at the right prices. Channel and physical distribution decisions affect the cost and service levels provided for customers. Having a wide network of distribution outlets may improve convenience of purchase but raise distribution costs. Trade-offs between costs and service levels are usually required.

The functions of channel intermediaries are:

- Reconciling the needs of producers and consumers
- Improving efficiency
- Improving accessibility
- Providing specialist services

These issues are discussed on pages 466–8 of the textbook.

3. The best way of distributing an industrial product is direct from manufacturer to customer. Discuss.

There are four main ways of distributing industrial (business-to-business) products of which direct distribution is only one option. It may make sense where the product is expensive and close liaison between producer and customer to solve technical problems is necessary. Under such circumstances the size of the order and the nature of the transaction makes direct selling and distribution economic and effective.

However, for less expensive, more frequently bought industrial products, customers may require local availability of a wide array of product types. Under such circumstances industrial distributors may be employed with selling-in being done by the producer's own salespeople or agents. Finally, agents may be employed to sell directly to customers where the spreading of selling costs is more important than exclusivity, and where customers do not demand local availability through distributors.

4. Why is channel selection an important decision? What factors influence choice?

Channel selection affects the availability of products in the marketplace and the costs of supplying them to customers. For example, packaged goods producers have to decide whether to supply customers solely through supermarkets or also through small grocery outlets. If they decide to supply to both types of intermediary they may choose different channels because of the varying size of outlet. Supermarket chains may be supplied directly (perhaps to regional distribution centres) while small grocery outlets are supplied through wholesalers.

The issues which affect channel selection are:

- Market factors
- Producer factors
- Product factors
- Competitive factors

How each of these factors affect channel selection is discussed on pages 474–5 of the textbook.

5. What is meant by the partnership approach to managing distributors? What can manufacturers do to help build partnerships?

The partnership approach to managing distributors involves marketing not to or through distributors but with distributors. Strong relationships should be built based on a recognition of their performance, and integrated planning and operations. To aid the building of a spirit of partnership, producers should consider:

- Providing assurances of a long-term business relationship with the distributor
- Frequent exchange of views
- Training distributors (see Vignette 14.3 on page 482 of the textbook)
- Arranging distributor conferences
- Joint decision-making
- Providing technical support (e.g. after-sales servicing)
- Expertise (e.g. dual selling)
- Resource support (e.g. joint advertising)
- Improving service levels (e.g. fast accurate quotes, fast delivery)
- Reducing risk (e.g. guaranteed delivery with penalty clauses, swift complaint handling)

6. Describe situations which can lead to conflict between channel members. What can be done to avoid and resolve conflict?

Conflicts between independent producers and channel members can range from minor disagreements to major disputes that lead to separation.

The situations that can cause conflict are:

- Differences in goals
- Differences in desired product lines carried by channel members
- Multiple distribution channels
- Inadequacies in performance

Each of these sources of conflict is discussed on pages 483–4 of the textbook.

Conflict avoidance and resolution is accomplished by:

- Developing a partnership approach
- Training in conflict handling
- Market partitioning
- Performance improvement
- Channel ownership
- Coercion

These issues are discussed on pages 484–5 of the textbook.

7. **Why is there usually a trade-off between customer service and physical distribution costs? What can be done to improve customer service standards in physical distribution?**

Customer service levels in physical distribution management can be raised by fast and reliable delivery including just-in-time delivery, holding high inventory levels so that customers have a wide choice and a low chance of facing stock-out problems, fast order processing and care in ensuring products arrive in the right quantities and of the right quality.

Cost savings in physical distribution management can be made by reducing inventory levels, using cheaper (but often slower) forms of transport, and shipping in bulk rather than small quantities.

Trade-offs are necessary because of the inherent conflicts in achieving these two objectives. For example, reducing inventory levels and using cheaper but slower transportation may reduce costs but lower customer service levels. (Note that if the lower inventory costs are offset by higher fast-freight charges then overall cost savings may be negligible.)

The act of physical distribution management is to achieve the correct balance between cost-efficiency and customer service. Market segmentation may be useful for identifying groups of customers who are willing to pay more for high (but costly) service levels, and those who will accept lower levels of service if that means a low price.

8. **A distributor wishes to estimate the economic order quantity for a spare part. Annual demand is 5000 units, the cost of placing an order is £5, and the cost of one spare part is £4. The per unit annual inventory cost is 50p. Calculate the economic order quantity.**

Order size depends upon the cost of holding stock and the cost of placing an order. There is a trade-off between the two costs leading to an economic order quantity (EOQ) which is the point at which total costs are lowest. The following equation can be used to calculate it:

$$EOQ = \sqrt{2\frac{DO}{IC}}$$

where

D = annual demand in units
O = cost of placing an order
I = annual inventory cost as percentage of the cost of one unit
C = cost of one unit of the product

Annual demand = 5000
Cost of placing an order = £5
Per unit annual inventory cost = 10 per cent
Cost of one unit = £5

$$EOQ = \sqrt{\frac{2 \times 5000 \times 5}{0.10 \times 5}}$$

$$= \sqrt{100{,}000}$$

$$= 316$$

The economic order quantity is therefore 316 units per order.

Chapter 15 Study Questions

Analysing Competitors and Creating a Competitive Advantage

1. **Using Porter's five-forces framework discuss why profitability in the European textile industry is lower than that in book publishing.**

Porter's five-forces model of competitive industry structure proposes that the determinants of industry attractiveness and long-run profitability are the threat of new entrants, the threat of substitutes, the bargaining power of buyers and suppliers, and the rivalry between existing competitors. Using these forces we shall examine the European textile and book publishing industries:

Threat of new entrants: many newly industrialized countries develop a textile industry since the skills and technology are relatively easy to acquire. Book publishing relies more on commissioning authors with the skills to write best sellers: it is easier to make a shirt than a book in Hong Kong that will sell in Europe. The threat of new entrants is likely to be lower for book publishing than textiles.

Bargaining power of suppliers and buyers: it is difficult to distinguish between the two industries on these bases. Suppliers of basic textile commodities (such as wool and cotton) are unlikely to have a great deal of power; authors (unless already proven winners) certainly do not. In both industries large retail outlets dominate sales to consumers. However, where retail price maintenance is practised (as it is in the UK book market) there may be less pressure on producers to trim prices.

Threat of substitutes: the key to understanding differences in profit levels does not lie in this area. It is difficult to imagine clothes not being made from textiles; television, the cinema, video cassettes, and computers are alternatives ways of communicating a story, but the different experience of reading a book makes them distant substitutes at present.

Industry competitors: it is in this area that key differences lie. The textile industry is faced with intense competition from Far Eastern companies with low cost bases. Many textile products are easy to copy (e.g. shirts, sweaters). This lowers the ability to differentiate the product. High fixed costs mean that there is a temptation to cut price to fill capacity. Book publishing, on the other hand, is not faced with such high levels of foreign competition. Differentiation is easier since each book is unique and fixed costs are lower (much editing, production, and printing work is subcontracted). Consequently competition is less likely to be based on price.

2. **For any product of your choice identify competition using the four-layer approach discussed in this chapter.**

The four layers of competition are product form competitors, product substitutes, generic competitors, and potential new entrants. Using paint as an example:

- Product form competitors make technically similar products, i.e. other paint manufacturers.
- Product substitutes are technically dissimilar products that have the same effect, e.g. polyurethane varnish manufacturers.
- Generic competitors solve the problem or eliminate it in a dissimilar way, e.g. aluminium window frame manufacturers.
- Potential new entrants are new to the industry with technically similar or dissimilar products. They may be foreign paint or polyurethane manufacturers, companies in industries that provide the distinctive competencies to make paint (e.g. other chemical companies), or companies that develop new technologies that create a substitute for paint or eliminate the need for it (e.g. rot-proof wood).

3. **Why is competitor analysis essential in today's turbulent environment? How far is it possible to predict competitor response to marketing actions?**

The degree and nature of competition has a major bearing on industry profitability. Competitors need to be monitored because their actions can ruin an otherwise profitable industry, their weaknesses can be a target for commercial exploitation and their responses can have a crucial impact on a firm's marketing initiatives.

Competitors need to be identified and their strengths and weaknesses understood, their objectives and strategies considered, and their response patterns predicted.

Response patterns can be estimated based on:

- Understanding their objectives and strategies.
- Analysing past behaviour.
- Knowing the personalities of key decision-makers.
- Considering the history and traditions of the industry.
- Acknowledging when a competitor is hemmed-in (have little or no scope to retaliate).

Some companies employ role-playing to assess competitor reactions. These points are expanded upon on pages 526–7 of the textbook.

4. **Distinguish between differentiation and cost leadership strategies. Is it possible to achieve both positions simultaneously?**

Differentiation achieves superior performance by creating added value for customers over the competition. Cost leadership creates competitive advantage by managing the lowest delivered cost. Pages 532–7 examine how the marketing mix can be designed to differentiate products from their rivals. Pages 538–40 discuss ten major cost drivers that can be utilized to achieve lowest delivered cost.

Usually, firms are faced with a choice of pursuing either a differentiation or cost leadership strategy since differentiation often raises costs. However, there are circumstances when they are compatible such as:

- Differentiation leads to market leadership, driving down costs through economies of scale and learning effects.
- A differentiator pioneers a major process innovation, creating cost leadership.
- Competitors are poor at both differentiation and cost control, leaving open a strategic window.

5. Discuss with examples ways of achieving a differential advantage.

The answer to this question is given on pages 529–37. The potential sources of a differential advantage are:

- Superior skills
- Superior resources
- Core competencies

Their location can be identified by value chain analysis. The result of implementing these sources is a differentiated marketing mix which creates superior customer value. Table 15.1 lists the elements of the marketing mix differential advantages, and how they create value for the customer. These issues are discussed with examples in the text on pages 532–7.

6. How can value chain analysis lead to superior corporate performance?

The value chain categorizes the activities of design, manufacture, marketing, distribution, and service into primary and support activities. Primary activities include in-bound physical distribution, operations, out-bound physical distribution, marketing, and service. Support activities consist of purchased inputs, technology, human resource management, and the firm's infrastructure (e.g. planning). These can be found in all of the primary activities (e.g. technology is relevant to all primary activities).

Each value-creating activity can be analysed to identify the skills and resources that may form the basis for differentiated or low-cost positions. Those activities that exceed competition are key sources of competitive advantage. This knowledge is useful in making resource allocation decisions: it would be a foolish management that denied design adequate funds when that was the key source of differentiation.

Value analysis can be extended to suppliers and customers. By looking at the linkages between a firm's value chain and those of suppliers and customers, improvements in performance may result (see page 531).

Value chain analysis can also prove useful by providing a framework for cost analysis. Assigning costs to value activities provides a basis for making cost reductions and defending cost advantages. Identifying sources of advantage also provides the opportunity to exploit them in new ways, for example by extending these strengths to new market segments (see page 532).

7. Using examples, discuss the impact of the Single European Market on competitive structure.

The answer to this question is covered in Vignette 15.1, 'The Impact of the Single European Market on Competition' (see page 520 of the textbook). Students should be encouraged to choose an industry with which they are familiar and use the Porter five-forces framework to assess likely changes.

8.   What are cost drivers? Should marketing management be concerned with them, or is their significance solely the prerogative of the accountant?

Cost drivers are the factors that determine the behaviour of costs in the value chain. The major drivers are:

- Economies of scale
- Learning
- Capacity utilization
- Linkages
- Interrelationships
- Integration
- Timing
- Policy decisions
- Location
- Institutional factors

These are discussed on pages 538–40 of the textbook.

Marketing management needs to be conscious of them as the viability of a low-price strategy may be dependent on the company being able to achieve low costs. When market conditions suggest such a strategy, marketing management may need to be able to suggest ways in which costs can be pruned to give acceptable profit margins. The cost driver framework provides a method of exploring the various options. Some of these options may be within marketing's control, such as product line pruning, service levels, channel width, using agents rather than an in-company salesforce, and attempting to exploit first-mover advantages.

Chapter 16 Study Questions

Competitive Marketing Strategy

---

1. Why do many monopolies provide poor service to their customers?

A company in a pure monopoly position faces no competitors. Hence customers have nowhere to turn if the company's service is below standard. For essential products, such as gas and electricity, the customer has little choice but to buy from the monopolist (whether in the public or private sector). Hence the supplier lacks the motivation to improve service, and may not do so for economic reasons when service improvement raises costs.

Competition means that customers have a choice: if they encounter poor service they have the option to buy elsewhere. This motivates companies to improve service: they have to try harder or lose customers. Success is related to gaining a competitive advantage, and if service is important to customers, companies will seek ways of beating rivals on that dimension.

2. Discuss the likely impact of the Single European Market on competitive behaviour.

The answer to this question is fully covered in Vignette 15.1 'The Impact of the Single European Market on Competition' (page 520) and Vignette 16.1 (page 557) 'Competitive Behaviour in the Single European Market'.

3. Compare and contrast the conditions conducive to building and holding sales/market share

A build objective is often appropriate in growth markets. All players can achieve sales growth if the market share of one or more players is falling. Hence, there is less likelihood of retaliation than in static markets. A hold objective may also be applied in a growth market if the costs of attempting to build sales and market share exceed the benefits. If the market is characterized by at least one aggressive rival, ambitious attempts to gain sales and market share by raising marketing expenditures may provoke strong retaliation. The overall result may be to lower the overall attractiveness of the industry.

In a mature or declining market a hold objective may be sensible for a market leader. In a mature market, leadership is likely to be accompanied by large positive cash flows that can be used elsewhere in the business; and holding onto market leadership in a declining market may result in inheriting a virtual monopoly as weaker competitors drop out.

Where there are exploitable corporate strengths and/or competitive weaknesses a build objective may be pursued, but their absence may suggest a hold objective.

Building may require substantial corporate resources to see off determined retaliation. Where these do not exist, holding may be more appropriate.

Experience curve effects which are dependent on cumulative output may encourage a company to seek higher sales and market share. The absence of such effects in a market may cause a firm to be content with holding.

For a complete discussion of these issues, see pages 559–60 and 568–9 of the textbook.

4. Why is a position defence risky?

A position defence involves building a fortification around existing products. It is based on the philosophy that existing products meet customer needs and all that is required is aggressive promotion and competitive price setting. The problem is that unless the products have differential advantages that cannot be copied or improved upon, a position defence provides the opportunity for competition to introduce better products (e.g. based on new technologies and/or a better understanding of customer needs) that render existing products obsolete. On pages 569–70 of the textbook appear the examples of Ever Ready, Land Rover and Range Rover who adopted a position defence to their cost.

Even when marketing assets such as brand names and reputation provide protection, a position defence can be risky. Only when a position is protected by a watertight patent can a position defence be supported in the medium to long term.

5. Why are strategic alliances popular in Europe? How do they differ from mergers?

Mergers involve the joining together of two or more companies through some form of common ownership. Strategic alliances involve collaboration typically by means of a joint venture, licensing agreements, longer-term purchasing and supply arrangements, or joint research and development programmes. Strategic alliances maintain a degree of flexibility not apparent in a merger.

Strategic alliances are popular in Europe (as elsewhere) for the mutual benefits they bring including:

- Linking of marketing assets (the product of one company with the sales and distribution clout of another), e.g. Glaxo and Hoffman-La Roche.
- Sharing research and development costs, e.g. European aircraft alliances.
- Gaining product development and production expertise, e.g. European aircraft alliances.
- Taking advantage of distinctive competencies of partners, e.g. European television manufacturers when developing high-definition televisions.
- Gaining acceptance of a technology, e.g. licensing agreements between JVC and other consumer electronics firms when marketing VHS.
- Gaining the scale necessary to compete against major international players, e.g. Renault and Volvo.
- New product development, e.g. the development of ready-to-eat breakfast products by Nestlé and General Mills.

6. A company should always attempt to harvest a product before considering divestment. Discuss.

A harvest strategy is the attempt to improve unit profit margins while accepting falling sales. By withdrawing marketing support and lowering other costs, healthy profits can be made while the product is still on the market.

Divestment is the commercial termination of a product or strategic business unit. It is often associated with loss-making products or units which drain corporate resources. They often hold low share in declining markets (although any product or unit may be a candidate for divestment if losses are heavy).

The question suggests that it is always worthwhile implementing a harvest objective (putting up prices and reducing costs) to milk any potential profit and cash flow that may be forthcoming from an under-performing product or unit before termination. Ultimately this is a matter of executive judgement. Where losses are excessive and managerial time and effort can be better deployed elsewhere immediate divestment may be preferable. Divestment may also be the best decision if a buyer for the ailing product or unit can be found. This can produce an immediate cash injection without the trouble of harvesting.

7. In defence it is always wise to respond to serious attacks immediately. Do you agree? Explain your answer.

On page 560 of the textbook the story is recounted of the attack made by Bush on Dukakis in the 1988 US Presidential election. Dukakis was positioned as 'a dangerous un-American left-winger'. Unfortunately for Dukakis this attack was not countered and the result was that a 17-point opinion poll lead turned into a similar deficit at the election.

The lesson is that strong competitor attacks should not be ignored, a point that was not lost on Bill Clinton in the 1992 Presidential election. He set up a 24-hour response capability so that when Bush attacked he could speedily respond (see page 568).

Chapter 17 Study Questions

Managing Marketing Implementation and Change

1. **Think of a situation when your life suffered from a dramatic change. Using Figure 17.3 recall your feelings over time. How closely did your experiences match the stages in the figure? How did your feelings at each stage (e.g. denial and disbelief) manifest themselves?**

The question can be used as the basis for a tutorial session in which students recount their reactions to a dramatic change. Situations could be from childhood (e.g. having to move to a different area of the country, separation of parents), from work (e.g. being made redundant), or from personal situations (e.g. death of a relative).

Through such discussion students can appreciate the validity of the transition curve (Figure 17.3). Students will not necessarily pass through every stage but most will be able to relate to the majority.

2. **Can good implementation substitute for an inappropriate strategy? Give an example of how good implementation might make the situation worse and an example of how it might improve the situation.**

Strategy concerns the issues of what should happen and why it should happen. Implementation focuses on actions: who is responsible for various actions, how the strategy should be carried out, where things will happen, and when action will take place.

Strategy can be appropriate or inappropriate and implementation can be good or bad. By combining these situations four outcomes can be predicted as shown in Figure 17.2 (page 593). An inappropriate strategy together with good implementation is one such combination.

One effect is to quicken failure. Since the strategy is wrong (e.g. setting too high a price), effective implementation (e.g. motivating the salesforce to communicate the price clearly) may hasten failure. Another example of the combination making the situation worse is deciding to increase salesperson call rates (strategy) through giving incentives based on number of customers seen (implementation). If the strategy is inappropriate (salespeople need to spend more time with each customer not less) effective implementation would worsen the situation.

However, if effective implementation takes the form of correcting a fault in strategy the outcome will be favourable. For example, if strategy suggests a price that the market will not accept, effective implementation may be reflected in a discount structure, which effectively means that the product is affordable. The reality of marketing life is that managers spend many hours supplementing, subverting, overcoming or otherwise correcting shortcomings in strategic plans.

3. What might be the objectives of market implementation and change? Distinguish between gaining compliance, acceptance and commitment.

From a strategic perspective, the key objective of marketing implementation and change is the successful execution of the marketing plan. Successful execution may require:

- Gaining support of key decision-makers and overcoming opposition.
- Gaining resources to implement the plan.
- Gaining the commitment of front-line implementers.
- Gaining the co-operation of other departments needed to implement the plan.

Support for a plan can range from the negative (opposition and resistance), to compliance, acceptance, or commitment. Compliance suggests that people act in line with the plan but lack the conviction that the plan is the best way to proceed. Their reservations mean that their behaviour lacks zeal and limits the extent to which they are prepared to go to secure its successful implementation.

Acceptance is a higher level of support that reflects people's agreement with the worth of the plan and the need to realize its goals. However, their hearts are not set on fire by the plan, reducing their level of motivation.

Commitment is the state where people not only accept the need for the plan but also pledge themselves to achieve its goals. Both their hearts and minds are won, leading to strong conviction, enthusiasm, and zest.

4. Why do some companies fail to implement the marketing concept?

The marketing concept can be expressed as the achievement of corporate goals through meeting and exceeding customer needs better than competition. A marketing-oriented company seeks ways of improving customer satisfaction in the belief that this will lead to higher profits (or the achievement of other goals for non-profit organizations).

Sometimes, however, the full implementation of the marketing concept can conflict with other valid corporate objectives (e.g. achieving economies of scale) and a trade-off between giving customers exactly what they want and other corporate needs (i.e. efficiency) is necessary. Marketers accommodate this compromise through the concept of market segmentation.

Another problem with implementing the marketing concept is the difficulty of finding out customer needs. This is particularly prevalent in nascent markets since potential customers are not familiar with the new product concept. For example, they may only be in a position to judge whether they would want to buy the product after they have seen other people using it, and confirmed its advantages through talking to them or through personal experience (e.g. leaving fax messages).

In addition to these genuine concerns are a number of personal and organizational barriers that hinder the achievement of the implementation of the marketing concept. These are fully discussed on pages 599–602 of the textbook and are:

- Marketing solutions often add costs.
- Marketing solutions often provide unquantifiable corporate benefits.

216

- Personal ambitions may conflict with customer needs.
- Rewards may conflict with marketing-oriented action.
- Managers may reduce their credibility by sanctioning actions that conflict with their pronouncements about the need to put the customer first.
- Implementing the marketing concept calls for the ability to overcome vested interests who may wish to block the introduction and growth of marketing in an organization.

5. Describe the ways in which people may resist the change that is implied in the implementation of a new marketing plan. Why should they wish to do this?

Resistance may be direct, open and conflict driven. In other instances the form of resistance may be more covert. Ten specific ways in which people may resist change implied in a marketing plan are given on page 602 of the textbook. Three common ones are:

- Arguing that the plan is too ambitious.
- Hassle and aggravation to wear the proposer down.
- Attempting to delay the decision hoping that the proposer will lose interest.

People may oppose the plan because they fear that change will have adverse affects on them personally. For example, the plan may have implications for the political structure of the organization. If the plan suggests the need for more marketing personnel it may be seen to enhance the status of the marketing director and consequently be resisted by other directors.

The plan could also imply the need for more work and longer hours at the office or a move from well-known procedures to new systems that might expose a lack of knowledge or capability.

Usually the greatest level of resistance will occur when the proposed change is implemented quickly and is a threat to the politics and culture of the organization. The least opposition will be found when change is introduced gradually (note the transition curve) and is not a threat to the existing culture and politics. Crises tend to galvanize people in organizations to the acceptance of change.

6. What is internal marketing? To what extent does it parallel external marketing strategy?

Internal marketing is the use of marketing principles to gain the support, commitment, and participation of people inside the organization for the successful implementation of marketing ideas and plans.

It closely parallels the development of external marketing strategy as it focuses on customers (those people inside the organization who we need to persuade), uses market segmentation techniques to identify various target groups, and the marketing mix to provide the framework for reaching them. A discussion of their use is provided on pages 606–8 of the textbook.

7. Describe the skills that are necessary to see a marketing plan through to successful implementation.

Internal marketing provides a framework for considering implementation strategies. Within that structure, marketing implementers need the skills of:

- Persuasion to convince people of the merits of the plan and how they will gain (or at least not lose) personally from its outcomes.
- Negotiation to prove some flexibility when bargaining with interested parties.
- Politics to understand how to use power to gain support for the plan.

The art of persuasion is based on an understanding of the situation from the internal customer's viewpoint. The benefits of the plan need to be communicated in terms which the internal customer values. Objectives should be anticipated and convincing counter arguments prepared. The psychology of the situation should be fully taken into account.

Two key aspects of negotiation are concession and personal analysis. Concessions should be viewed from the perspective of the receiver (value) not from the standpoint of the giver (costs). Proposals which are likely to be made by opponents should be considered and responses prepared.

Implementers should consider any sources of power that they hold that could be mobilized. Overt and covert power plays can be used to influence others and push through controversial proposals (see pages 609–10).

8. What tactics of persuasion are at the implementer's disposal? What are the advantages and limitations of each one?

The persuasion tactics that can be used to mobilize support and overcome resistance are:

- Articulating a shared vision.
- Communication and training.
- Eliminating misconceptions.
- Selling the benefits.
- Gaining acceptance by association.
- Leaving room for local control over details.
- Support words with action.

Each of these is described and the advantages and limitations discussed on pages 610–12 of the textbook.

9. Without the use of political manoeuvres, most attempts at marketing implementation will fail. Discuss.

Political manoeuvres involve the use of power tactics to gain support and neutralize resistance (see pages 612–13). They include:

- Building coalitions.
- Displaying the support of powerful allies.
- Sharing the rewards with opponents.
- Warning the opposition of the consequences of opposition.
- Discrediting the opposition through the use of evocative language.
- Controlling the agenda and participation in decision-making.
- Making rejection personal by threatening to resign.

These manoeuvres are most likely to be needed when marketing implementation runs counter to the culture and politics of an organization. Where there will be losers who wield some power, neutralizing their influence may necessitate their use. Implementers must also weigh up the long-term consequences of using such tactics. When relationships are likely to be irreparably damaged, the implementers must consider the importance of getting acceptance of their proposals. If they judge it to be low, the use of power tactics may not be justified.

Chapter 18 Study Questions

Marketing Organization and Control

1. **Why do some organizations lack a marketing department? Does this necessarily mean that they are not marketing oriented?**

Surveys have shown that many companies have no marketing department. There can be numerous reasons for this, including:

- Small company size means that managerial specialism can not be afforded.
- Companies are financially or production driven.
- Marketing is considered to lack substance.

The lack of a marketing department does not necessarily imply lack of marketing orientation. Other people in the organization such as the owner-manager or sales manager may carry out some or all of the tasks of a marketing department. Furthermore, marketing should be considered a company-wide activity not just the exclusive preserve of the marketing department. However, research has shown that where companies lack an integrated provision of marketing, problems of under-resourcing, weak implementation, interfunctional conflict, short-term financial focus, and low involvement in strategic decision-making occur.

2. **Discuss the options available for organizing a marketing department. How well is each form likely to serve its customers?**

The options available are:

- Functional organization
- Product-based organization
- Market-centred organization
- Matrix organization

These structures are described on pages 621–9 of the textbook.

Functional organization allows specialization of task and a clear definition of responsibilities, but as product range widens it may lack adequate attention to specific products leading to consideration being given to a product-based organization. Customers should benefit from the fact that products have dedicated staff managing them. However, brand managers are sometimes criticized for spending too much time co-ordinating in-company activities and too little time talking to customers.

To give special attention to markets, some companies adopt a market-centred approach using marketing managers who concentrate their effects on understanding and satisfying the needs of particular markets. This, in theory, should provide a high degree of customer satisfaction.

Finally, a matrix organization enjoys both a product and a market focus. Although this structure can lead to conflict in decision-making, it should in theory promote the careful analysis of both products and markets so that customers' needs are met.

In practice, the most appropriate organizational form is dependent on the size of the company, its product range, the number of diverse markets it serves and the politics of the situation. Furthermore, the structure needs to be made to work: success is heavily dependent on effective implementation.

3. What are the advantages and disadvantages of the brand management system?

The advantages are:

- Adequate attention is given to the marketing of each brand.
- Speed of response is improved.
- The system gives good training to young business people.

The disadvantages are:

- It can lead to counter-productive competition and conflict with the organization.
- New layers of management can be costly.
- Brand managers spend too much time on internal co-ordination and too little time talking to customers.

4. Discuss the effects that powerful retailers are having on ways in which consumer goods companies are organizing their marketing activities.

The growth in retailer power has meant that manufacturers are having to meet demands for lower prices by eliminating layers of management. For example, Procter and Gamble have eliminated the title of assistant brand manager. Second, companies are organizing their marketing activities around trade customer groups. For example, under a combined sales and marketing director Philips have a dedicated salesforce for multiples, independents, and mail order.

Manufacturers are also setting up category management and trade marketing teams to serve the needs of powerful retailers. The emphasis is not on selling to or through distributors but marketing with them. Vignette 18.1 'The Growth of the Category Manager' and Vignette 18.2 'Trade Marketing' analyse these developments.

5. Discuss the relative merits of centralized and decentralized management of international marketing activities.

Centralization is a response to the need for global integration, while decentralization recognizes the regional responsiveness imperative. The relative merits of the two systems are discussed on pages

630–1 of the textbook. The growth of the transnational corporation is also discussed; it is an organizational form that has resulted from the need to meet the strong simultaneous forces for both global integration and national responsiveness.

6. What is the purpose of a marketing control system and what are the major stages that make up such a system?

The purpose of a marketing control system is to review how well marketing objectives have been achieved. The two types of control systems monitor strategic and operational issues. A strategic control system answers the question 'Are we doing the right thing?' and is implemented through the marketing audit (see Chapter 2). Operational control covers day-to-day marketing activities and is more concerned with the question 'Are we doing things right?' It is conducted through customer satisfaction surveys, sales, and market share analysis, and cost and profitability analysis.

The major steps that make up a marketing control system are:

- Deciding marketing objectives.
- Setting performance standards.
- Locating responsibility.
- Evaluating performance against standard.
- Taking corrective/supportive action.

These are described on pages 632–3 of the textbook.

7. Describe the problems involved in setting up and implementing a marketing control system.

The problems associated with setting up and implementing a marketing control system are technical, political, cultural, and skill-based. There are five potential technical problems:

Objective setting: this concerns the correct choice of objectives on which to focus the control system. Priorities need to be set. Assumptions must be made regarding which decision variables (creating more awareness, affecting beliefs, widening the customer base, etc.) will have the most affect on sales and profits).

Setting performance standards: a second difficulty surrounds the question of what are realistic performance standards? How much can we realistically expect awareness to increase, beliefs to change or the customer base to widen? Setting unrealistically high performance standards can demotivate and call into question the credibility of the control system.

Locating responsibility: if an objective (e.g. increased sales) is not achieved, who is responsible, the brand manager, the sales manager, or the salesforce?

Information: a control system relies on accurate information at all stages. If information on sales, market share, market growth rates, product, and customer profitability and customer satisfaction levels is lacking, setting objectives and performance standards will be haphazard and evaluation hazardous.

Cost allocations: there can be difficulties in validly allocating certain costs to products when carrying out product profitability analysis. For example, it may be difficult to allocate sales force costs to individual products. Estimates of how much time was devoted to each product, on average, at each call may be difficult to calculate. When selling is customer needs focused (see Chapter 12) salespeople do not assign time to products making cost allocations arbitrary.

In addition to technical problems, the following political, cultural and skill-based difficulties may arise.

Politics: particularly with strategic control systems, the results of a control system may imply changes in resource allocation. For example, a marketing audit may expose the need to become more customer-oriented, raising the profile of marketing perhaps at the expense of other functional areas. Political difficulties can, therefore, arise.

Culture: the setting up of a strategic control system may be contrary to the culture of an organization which has traditionally made planning decisions incrementally (see Chapter 2). This may cause resistance to the setting up and implementation of the results of a marketing audit, for instance.

Skills: management may lack skills in performing a competitor analysis, conducting market segmentation, or commissioning a customer survey, etc. Such deficiencies may hinder the setting up of a control system and reduce the viability of its results.

8.   Customer satisfaction measurement is an expensive luxury. Discuss.

Some managers may take the view that customer satisfaction does not appear on the profit and loss accounts and, therefore, is secondary to the more urgent requirements of accurate sales, costs and profitability tracking. This is a very myopic view of the relative importance of information. The assumption underpinning the marketing concept is that corporate success is dependent on creating customer satisfaction better than the competition. Customer satisfaction is assumed to be a casual variable affecting both sales and profits.

Other critics of customer satisfaction surveys state that when customer satisfaction falls, this will show in a sales decline, rendering the need for expensive surveys unnecessary. This ignores the fact that satisfaction measurement can provide an early warning of future problems. Satisfaction may fall before sales because of customer loyalty, switching costs, and lack of competitive alternatives. Furthermore satisfaction measurement is diagnostic: it identifies the areas that demand attention before customers vote with their pockets.

Some companies, notably British Airports Authority, link financial incentives to the results of customer satisfaction surveys. Far from regarding customer satisfaction measurement as an expensive luxury they consider them an essential part of marketing control.

Chapter 19 Study Questions

Marketing Services

---

1. **The marketing of services is no different to the marketing of physical goods. Discuss.**

What is significant about services is the relative dominance of intangible attributes in the make up of the 'service product'. Most product offerings contain an element of the tangible and the intangible—e.g. a marketing research study would include a report (physical good) as well as a number of intangible elements (discussion with client, questionnaire design, etc. The distinction between most physical and service offerings is, therefore, a matter of degree.

The four key characteristics of services are intangibility, inseparability, viability, and perishability.

Intangibility: pure services cannot be seen, tasted, touched or smelled before they are bought. Rather they are deeds, performances or efforts.

Inseparability: unlike most physical goods, services have simultaneous production and consumption (e.g. a haircut, or a pop music concert).

Variability: service quality may be subject to considerable variability, making standardization more difficult than for many physical goods (e.g. two marketing courses at the same university may vary considerably in terms of quality depending on the lecturer).

Perishability: consumption cannot be stored making the matching of supply and demand important, (e.g. a room vacancy in a hotel cannot be stored for use the following week).

The marketing implications of these characteristics are discussed on pages 664–6 of the textbook. The conclusion is that the marketing of services may require solutions to problems not experienced by manufacturers of physical products (e.g. the need for a hotel reservation system).

However, the fundamental principles of marketing services and physical products are the same. Customer needs must be understood, market segments identified, and targets chosen, and a marketing mix designed to meet customer needs better than the competition.

2. **What are the barriers that can separate expected from perceived service? What must service providers do to eliminate these barriers?**

The perception of service quality actually realized may be very different from that expected by customers. Occasionally the perception levels may exceed expectations, but sadly the opposite is more usually true, leading to disappointment. The barriers which separate expected from perceived service are:

Misconceptions barrier: managers may misunderstand what customers value. They may be allocating too many resources to achieving perfection on attributes customers do not value highly. Conversely, they may be performing poorly on highly valued service dimensions.

Inadequate resources barrier: managers may understand what customers value but be unwilling to allocate the necessary resources to satisfy them, perhaps because of a focus on cost reduction.

Inadequate delivery barrier: managers may understand customer expectations and supply adequate resources but fail to live up to their promises because of failure to select, train and motivate staff.

Exaggerated promises barrier: even when the above barriers are overcome service providers need to be wary of making exaggerated claims raising expectations to such a level that even good quality service is perceived as being inadequate.

The remedies are to talk to customers directly and/or through marketing research to understand their expectations; to allocate resources to these areas which are of great concern to customers even when this means raising costs or lowering productivity somewhat; to adapt professional management techniques in selecting and training staff; to provide rewards to those people who provide outstanding service to customers; and to be careful not to raise expectations to a level which cannot be fulfilled.

3. **Discuss the role of service staff in the creation of a quality service. Can you give examples from your own experiences of good and bad service encounters?**

Because services are typically consumed at the point of production, there is a high degree of contact between service staff and customers. Staff–customer interpersonal relationships are, therefore, vital and have been called 'moments of truth'.

For service providers to treat customers well, they need to feel that they are being treated fairly and that they will be rewarded for providing a high level of customer care and concern. Maintaining motivation in the face of irate customers, poor support systems, and boredom can be daunting. Standard motivational practices such as giving recognition, providing role clarity, giving opportunities for advancement, monetary rewards, and setting achievable yet challenging targets should be considered. Also giving scope for responsibility can improve staff morale and customer satisfaction. Top service organizations are implementing the notion of empowerment, whereby staff are given authority to satisfy customers and solve their problems.

The second part of the question allows students to relate their own experiences to the ideas discussed in the chapter. The case study at the end of the chapter—Olsen Watch Repairs—gives an example of a disastrous service encounter.

4. Use Figure 19.6 to evaluate the service quality provided on your university course. First, identify all criteria that might be used to evaluate your course. Second, score each criterion from one to ten, based upon its value to you. Third, score each criterion from one to ten based on your perception of how well it is provided. Finally, analyse the results and make recommendations.

The objective of this question is to apply the framework represented by Figure 19.6 'Achieving Differentiation in Service Quality' to a real-life situation. The focus is course evaluation although you can obviously change the subject according to personal performance.

The service dimensions can fall in three areas: (i) the target area, where performance is in line with how customers value the criterion; (ii) underperformance, where performance is lower than it should be; and (iii) overkill, where the service provider excels at things of little consequence to customers.

5. Of what practical value are the theories of retail evolution?

The three theories of retail evolution are:

- The wheel of retailing
- The retail accordion
- The retail lifecycle

These are discussed on pages 684–5 of the textbook.

The wheel of retailing suggests that retailers who are considering trading up by adding on more services to become a high price–high service operator should weigh up the risks of leaving themselves vulnerable to low-cost operators.

The retail lifecycle emphasizes the fact that retailing innovations are eventually copied, meaning that the innovator needs to plan its response to emerging competition. It must also be wary of over-ambitious expansion which can prove costly when the market enters maturity or there is an economic downturn.

The retail accordion is a theory of how the width of product assortment sold by retail outlets changes over time. It is a description rather than a basis for marketing action.

It should be noted that there is nothing inevitable about any of these theories of retailing, but the wheel of retailing and the retail accordion do provide food-for-thought for marketing managers.

6. Identify and evaluate how supermarkets can differentiate themselves from competitors. Choose three supermarkets and evaluate their success at differentiation.

There are several ways of achieving differentiation:

- Wide product range
- Convenient store location
- Better service

- Lower prices
- Better store atmosphere
- Better quality products

In the UK, Sainsbury's combine a very wide assortment of quality products, including a large wine selection and connoisseur convenience foods with value for money prices. Their newer supermarkets provide massive car parking space to cater for large customer demand. Safeway typically do not provide such a wide range of choice but have been experimenting by enhancing customer service. Their staff provide a packing service at the check-outs.

Kwik Save operate from medium-sized, low-cost outlets targeting lower income groups with basic products at low prices in convenient locations. They differentiate themselves from new entrants such as Aldi and Netto by having a wider product range (although this is still much narrower than Sainsbury's or Tesco).

In the US, Stew Leonard's supermarket in Connecticut and in the Republic of Ireland the Quinn's supermarket chain differentiate themselves by creating a fun atmosphere in their stores.

7. Discuss the problems of providing high-quality service in retailing in Central and Eastern Europe.

The problems of providing high-quality service in retailing in Central and Eastern Europe are discussed in Vignette 19.1 'Services in Central and Eastern Europe' (page 669) and Vignette 19.4 'Retail Opportunities in Central and Eastern Europe (page 688). These include:

- Bureaucratic rather than customer led service
- Low awareness of service standards
- Lack of service skills
- Retail fragmentation
- Difficulty in buying suitable retail property

8. How does marketing in non-profit organizations differ from that in profit-oriented companies? Choose a non-profit organization and discuss the extent to which marketing principles can be applied.

The fundamental marketing principles of target marketing, differentiation, and developing a marketing mix (see pages 690–1 of the textbook) are common to both profit and non-profit organizations. However, there are certain features of non-profit organizations that distinguish them from most profit-oriented companies.

- The desire to educate rather than serve customers' current needs.
- The need to serve not only customers (clients) but donors (e.g. trusts, government bodies) who provide funds.
- Different and somewhat conflicting objectives.
- For public sector non-profit organizations, the intense pressure of public scrutiny since funding may be, in part, from taxes.

These issues mean that making marketing decisions purely on the basis of commercial criteria (notably profit generation) may be inappropriate. This is nowhere more evident than in the area of pricing. Prices may be set at a lower level than that necessary to maximize profits in order to encourage access among low-income groups (e.g. nursery care) or the service may be provided at no direct charge to customers, the bill being met through taxes (e.g. the National Health Service in the UK).

The second part of the question allows students to apply these general issues to a specific organization of their choice. In the UK the extent to which marketing principles can be applied to the National Health Service would be a good choice.

Chapter 20 Study Questions

International Marketing

---

1. What are the factors that drive companies to enter international markets?

There are seven factors that drive companies to enter international markets:

- Saturated domestic markets which limit opportunities to expand at home.
- Small domestic markets making internationalization a condition for survival.
- Low-growth domestic markets which provide the spur to seek expansion abroad.
- Customer drivers such as the expectation that a supplier is an international player.
- Competitive forces such as the desire not to be left behind by competitors who are expanding internationally.
- Cost factors such as gaining economies of scale or foreign direct investment in low-cost countries.
- Portfolio balance considerations which allow the problem of recession in some countries to be offset by growth in others.

2. Joint ventures are a popular method of entering markets in Europe. Choose an example (many are given in this book) and research its background (and outcomes if any).

This question can be used as the focus for a student group project. They can be encouraged to conduct a literature search to discover a recent joint venture and then to research its background and results. Alternatively, you can allocate a joint venture to each group (a number of suitable ones are given in Table 16.2 'Some Key European Strategic Alliances' on page 567 of the textbook). Students can then be asked to make 15–20 minute presentations of their findings.

3. For a company of your choice research its reasons for expanding into new foreign markets, and describe the moves that have been made.

This question can also be used as a focus for a student group project. As with question 2, the project can fruitfully end with 15–20 minute presentations of their findings. The reasons for expansion into new foreign markets can be compared with those given on pages 697–9 of the textbook and summarized in the answer to question 1.

4. Using information in this chapter and Chapter 14 on distribution, describe how you would go about selecting and motivating overseas distributors.

For some companies distribution overseas is a question of acceptance rather than selection, but for those in the position to choose, selection involves identifying candidates and developing selection criteria:

- **Identifying sources:** these might be trade sources including exhibitions, trade associations and publications, reseller enquiries, and customers of distributors.
- **Selection criteria:** these might include degree of market, product and customer knowledge, market coverage, quality and size of the salesforce, reputation, financial standing, produce and service fit, managerial competence and hunger for success.

Motivation relies upon an understanding of the needs and problems of distributors. Their needs may be met by the following motivators:

- Financial rewards
- Exclusive territory agreements
- Providing resource support (e.g. sales training, advertising and promotion support)
- Working to develop strong relationships (e.g. joint planning, frequent interchange of ideas, arranging distributor conferences)

The aim should be to develop a partnership approach to distributor management (see pages 480–1 of the textbook).

5. Why are so many companies trying to standardize their global marketing mixes? With examples, show the limitations to this approach.

Very few companies standardize the whole of the marketing mix for each of their products on a global basis. However, many such as Coca Cola, Levi Strauss and McDonald's attempt to standardize as much as possible. The maxim 'Go global when you can, stay local when you must' is a sound general rule.

Standardization seeks to take advantage of customer convergence of tastes and needs. As new markets develop (e.g. camcorders), marketers can set international standards for product features shaping customer expectations. Also as people travel internationally common experiences and lifestyles emerge. The benefit to producers is the ability to tap enormous economies of scale. Furthermore, standardization permits a greater degree of logistical flexibility whereby stocks in one country can be used to supplement those in another.

However, there are limits to the extent of standardization owing to:

- Different culture and consumption patterns
- Language differences
- Inconsistent regulations
- Varied media availability and promotional preferences
- Organizational barriers

Each of these limitations is discussed with examples, in Vignette 20.3 on page 713 of the textbook.

232

6. **What are the factors that influence the choice of foreign market entry strategy?**

The three generic factors that affect foreign market entry strategy are degree of control, level of resource commitment, and the degree of risk associated with each method. Figure 20.4 (page 711) classifies exporting, licensing, joint ventures ,and direct investment on each of these criteria.

Many specific factors are given in Table 20.1 (page 710) and include country environment, buyer behaviour, and internal (company) issues. The table summarizes research findings into the impact of each factor on foreign market entry strategy.

7. **Select a familiar advertising campaign in your country, and examine the extent to which it is likely to need adaptation for another country of your choice.**

A useful framework for discussing the issue of standardized versus adapted international advertising is the distinction between the advertising platform from the creative presentation. The advertising platform is the fundamental proposition that is being communicated. The creative presentation is the way in which that proposition is translated into verbal and visual statements.

In some instances both the advertising platform and the creative presentation need to be adapted to local tastes. This is when customers in different countries view a product differently (Dan Chow Len's comments on how US, UK and Japanese young people view Levi jeans repeated on pages 711–12 of the textbook are relevant here). In other situations, the basic advertising theme (platform) is constant but the creative presentation has to change to suit local demands. In extreme cases only the voice-over changes, as was the case of the advertising for the Gillette Sensor razor to cater for 26 languages across Europe, the USA and Japan.

By choosing their own examples students can examine the degree to which the advertising pattern and the creative presentation need to change when advertising in another country.

8. **Describe the problems of pricing in overseas markets and the skills required to price effectively in the global marketplace.**

The problems of pricing in overseas markets are:

- Calculating extra costs (such as taxes and tariffs) of supplying overseas markets.
- Defining the terms of a price quotation.
- Acquiring the necessary information on competitors and customers.
- Responding to competitor price moves.
- Allowing for the possible danger of parallel importing.
- Valuing the products received in a countertrade agreement and estimating the cost of selling-on the traded goods.

Companies require research skills to gather the necessary information and analytical skills to process that information in a way that is appropriate for making pricing decisions. They also need to be able to execute pricing tactics such as:

- Disguising price reductions.
- Creating uncertainty for the competition by abolishing price lists.
- Building switching barriers.
- Responding decisively to competitor attacks.

When parallel imports are a threat, protection may be found through lowering price differentials, offering non-transferable service/product packages, and making packaging modifications (see page 721).

Managers also need to be adept at transfer pricing (the price charged between profit centres) to take account of variations in taxation and tariff levels. However, care should be taken to ensure that transfer prices do not artificially make the price of products uncompetitive.